WITHOUT PRECEDENT

'Without Precedent' is the sixth book by Owen Zupp. His first book, 'Down to Earth', was published in 2006 by Grub Street (UK). An award-winning aviation writer, his work has been featured in magazines across the globe including Fly Past (UK), Airliner World (UK), Aviation History (US), Plane & Pilot (US), Global Aviator (South Africa) and Australian Aviation in his homeland. Owen has twice won Australasian Aviation Press Club awards and is a commercial pilot with 30 years experience.

www.owenzupp.com

WITHOUT PRECEDENT

OWEN ZUPP

First published 2016

Copyright @ Owen Zupp 2016

All rights reserved. No part of this book may be reproduced or transmitted in any form or by any means, electronic or mechanical, including photocopying, recording or by any storage and retrieval system, without prior permission in writing from the publisher. The Australian *Copyright Act 1968* (the Act) allows a maximum of one chapter or 10 percent of this book, whichever is the greater, to be photocopied by an educational institution for its educational purposes provided that the educational institution (or body that administers it) has given a remuneration notice to the Copyright Agency (Australia) under the Act.

Published by
There and Back
P.O. Box 747
Bowral NSW 2576
Australia
www.thereandback.com.au

National Library of Australia Cataloguing -in -Publication entry
Creator: Zupp, Owen, author. 1964-
Title: Without Precedent : Commando, fighter pilot and the true story of Australia's first purple heart / Owen Zupp.

ISBN: 978-0-9874954-8-8 (paperback)
ISBN: 978-0-9874954-9-5 (ebook)
ISBN: 978-0-9946038-0-7 (hardback)

Subjects: Zupp, Phillip, 1925-1991.

Australia. Royal Australian Air Force--Airmen--Biography.
Fighter pilots--Australia--Biography.
Purple Heart.

Dewey Number: 358.43092

Cover Design, Desktop Publishing and Maps Diane Bricknell

Editing Wright Stuff Editing and Proofreading

Front cover image: 77 Squadron RAAF Gloster Meteor F.8 flown by Sgt. Phillip Zupp, struck by ground fire. 6th February 1952. (Artwork by Norman Clifford)

Back Cover Images (L to R): Trooper Phillip Zupp stands guard in Japan, 1946.
Sgt Phillip Zupp returns from another sortie over Korea, 1952.

All images are from the personal collection of Phillip Zupp or the author, unless otherwise stated.

All reasonable efforts were taken to obtain permission to use copyright material reproduced in this book, but in some cases copyright could not be traced. The author welcomes information in this regard.

For Dad.

Contents

Chapter One – A Very Long Way from Home 1
Chapter Two – The First to Land 7
Chapter Three – Dare to Dream 17
Chapter Four – Into the Blue 25
Chapter Five – D-Day 33
Chapter Six – Down to Earth 43
Chapter Seven – Commando 53
Chapter Eight – Canungra 61
Chapter Nine – New Guinea 71
Chapter Ten – Mud and Blood 78
Chapter Eleven – An Uneasy Peace 87
Chapter Twelve – Hiroshima 99
Chapter Thirteen – A Restless Year 113
Chapter Fourteen – Back in Blue 123
Chapter Fifteen – Air Force Wings 137
Chapter Sixteen – A False Start 161
Chapter Seventeen – Mustang 167
Chapter Eighteen – Fighter Pilot 177
Chapter Nineteen – Jets 185
Chapter Twenty – Getting Closer 193
Chapter Twenty One – To War Again 199
Chapter Twenty-Two – A New War Begins 205
Chapter Twenty-Three – Hard Lessons 211
Chapter Twenty-Four – The Boss 217

Chapter Twenty-Five – A Day of Firsts	221
Chapter Twenty-Six – Frozen	229
Chapter Twenty-Seven – A Close Call	235
Chapter Twenty-Eight – The 1,000 Mission Month	241
Chapter Twenty-Nine – Words	249
Chapter Thirty – "There's no bloody MiGs in Korea"	257
Chapter Thirty-One – Towards 200	265
Chapter Thirty-Two – Coming Home	273
Chapter Thirty-Three – Flight Instructor	279
Chapter Thirty-Four – Peacetime	285
Chapter Thirty-Five – Fighters, Failure and Farewell	291
Chapter Thirty-Six – A Brave New World	299
Chapter Thirty-Seven – Jack of All Trades	307
Chapter Thirty-Eight – Air Ambulance	317
Chapter Thirty-Nine – The Purple Heart	323
Chapter Forty – Rising to the Surface	331
Chapter Forty-One – The Last Fight	336
Chapter Forty-Two – Without Precedent	339
Purple Heart Postscript	341
Phillip Zupp. My Dad	343
Phillip Zupp's Survivors	345
Acknowledgements	349
Bibliography	351
Index	353

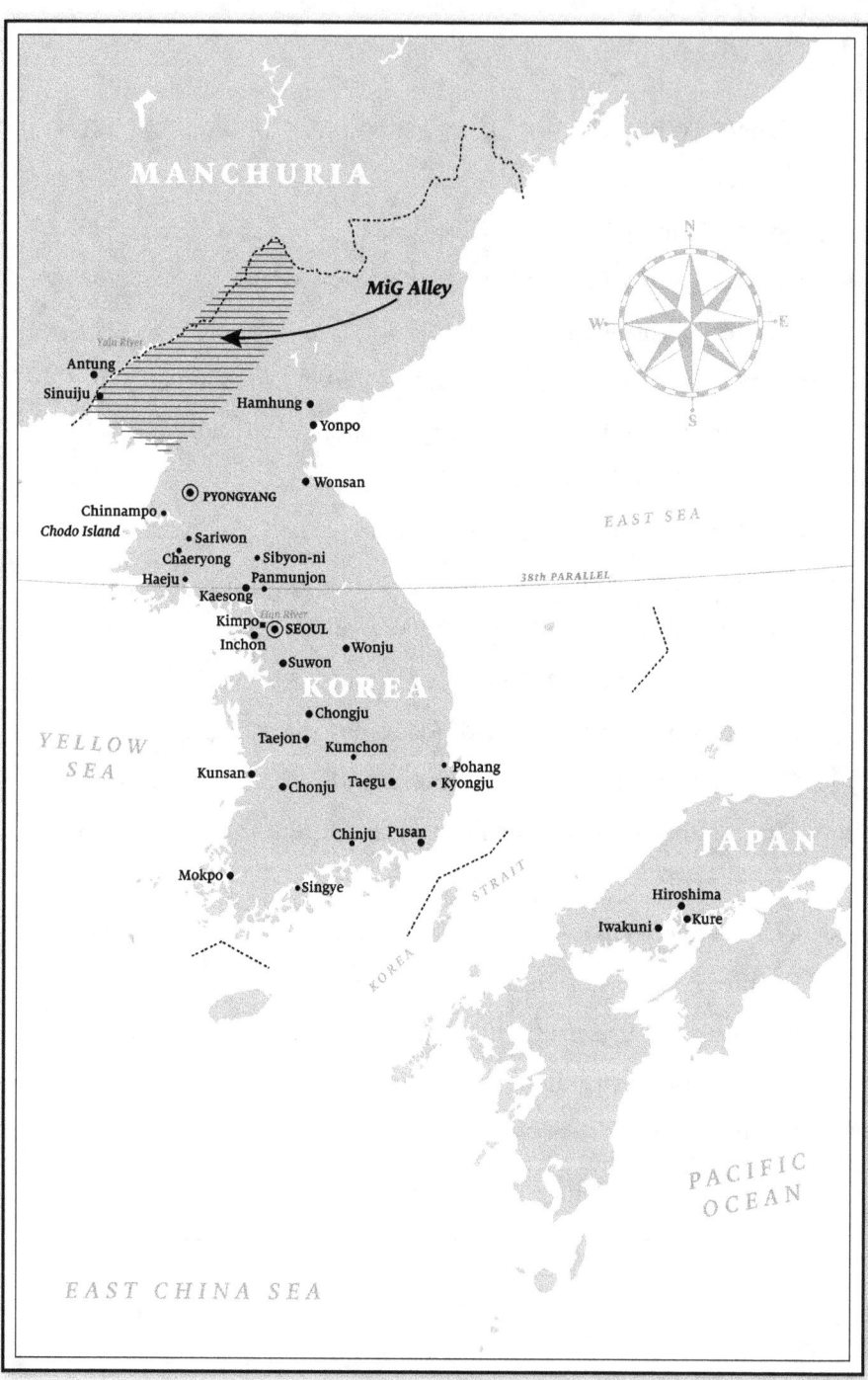

Chapter One

A Very Long Way from Home

Once referred to as the 'land of the morning calm', the modern Korean Peninsula exists on a knife's edge. Extending south from a common border with Manchuria, it is a region divided politically, philosophically and physically. The nations of North and South Korea continuously stalk each other across the narrow 'no man's land' and spar in an intricate dance of confrontations. It is an uneasy peace that exists only through ongoing diplomatic efforts interspersed with ever-sobering threats and exchanges of fire.

Yet as Phil Zupp looked down upon the Peninsula from his fighter jet in 1952, such political jousting was a world away. Korea was a country at war and his business was not diplomacy. He did not see the nation below him as politically divided; to him it was a land of dramatic terrain. The towering snow-covered mountains and deep valleys were in equally steep contrast to the pastoral undulations of the Queensland Darling Downs where he had been raised. Yet here he sat, a quiet 26 year old bloke from the Australian bush strapped into a Gloster Meteor fighter jet, low on fuel and armed to the teeth.

The cockpit of the Meteor was a nightmare by modern standards with dials, gauges and controls filling every spare inch and in no particular order. Ahead was a central control stick to steer the machine, with a throttle on the left hand wall to push it over 400 knots or take it to more than 40,000 feet in the stratosphere. Above, the clear dome, or 'bubble canopy', allowed a panoramic view of the world outside as well as a vantage point for those hostile aircraft that may penetrate the serenity.

It was a cramped workspace, but that never bothered him. He was short, only five feet, five inches, and to him the lack of space made him feel more at one with the machine. In fact, he would pull his harnesses so tight that he was almost welded to the aeroplane. And so he sat there, with snow-covered mountains below on what was planned to be a very routine mission, a 'CAP' or 'Combat Air Patrol'. It involved a pair of Meteors loitering at a safe altitude, as a deterrent to would-be attackers, while their squadron mates made the ground strikes below. The patrol was little more than a standby mission and, more than likely, they would loiter without incident before turning for home base, K14 Kimpo Airfield.

It was February 6th, 1952 and, as 'Airborne Alert Three', Sergeant Phillip Zupp had been assigned to fly alongside Flight Lieutenant Ray Taylor over Haeju, while the experienced 'Butch' Hannan led a ground attack thousands of feet below and some miles away near Sibyon-ni. As his fighter bounced lazily in loose battle formation, Phil looked across at Taylor's aircraft and checked his positioning; close enough for cover, far enough for comfort. Against the backdrop of the clear upper atmosphere, Taylor's silver jet shone and the insignia on its flank seemed to capture a brighter shade of red, white and blue. He could see his leader's head beneath the Perspex canopy, forever pivoting and scanning the sky for any hidden threat. Today there was nothing, not even the friendly contrails of the American jets.

Below, through layers of broken cloud lay the frozen jagged ranges twisting to form a maze of ravines, their edges softened by the blanket of snow. He often thought that the war-ravaged country almost looked peaceful from altitude, enveloped in its pure white shroud, until a devastated village or column of smoke indicated to the contrary. However, he appreciated that 'Butch' and the boys would not be sharing his philosophical moment at an altitude of relative safety. For the moment, only the hum of the two engines faintly permeated the serenity, gently amplified by the rush of air over the canopy at 300 knots as the pair of fighters combed the sky.

Moments earlier, 'Butch' had firmly squeezed his trigger and rained destruction upon the .50 calibre gun pits that dared point in his direction. The sense of satisfaction had been shattered shortly thereafter by his leader's call of "Ventral Tank!". Chock full of fuel and prominent on the jet's belly, the tank was vulnerable to the hail of gunfire from below. His Meteor shuddered violently and the small world of the cockpit became a kaleidoscope of blurred dials. The North Koreans had landed a knock-out punch. Streaming fuel and flame, Butch knew his aircraft was in its death throes as he turned south towards friendly territory.

It seemed far too low for the early model ejection seat, it was doubtful whether the 'chute would have time to open, so Butch clawed for more altitude. He heard Wal Rivers tell him to eject, but there was no time to reply. He retracted the bulbous gunsight away from his face and rolled the aeroplane's wings level. Straightening in his seat he reached above his head for the striped handle with both hands. Feet in the stirrups, chin on his chest, Hannan yanked down the 'blind' over his face and fired the seat. The world erupted beneath and his spine compressed under the force from below.

Blasted from the crippled aircraft, Hannan wasted no time in separating himself from the cumbersome ejection seat. As the parachute's canopy filled, Butch made out the pillar of smoke that had previously been his Meteor A77-616. It was now little more than a black hole in the white Korean landscape. Below, his seat hurtled toward the snow under the ineffective brake of its drogue chute. Hannan's fate promised to be only marginally better than the ejection seat's at such a low altitude, hardly allowing time for the 'chute to fill with the decelerating force of air. It was hard to ascertain his height against the featureless snow, but he knew it was coming up to meet him at a high rate of knots. There was little time to consider capture. There was little time to consider anything.

Brace.

Thud.

Alive.

The radio broke the serenity in an instant as the call came from the controller, the 'Dentist', that Hannan was down. Zupp saw Taylor's head pivot in his direction and the two pilot's goggles locked on each other. There was no need for words between the two as Taylor rolled the Meteor over and pointed its nose earthwards.

Taylor acknowledged the radio call as the throttles were opened wide and the diving jets accelerated under the force of thrust and gravity. Zupp closed the gap and tucked in behind his leader's wing as the speed roared through 400 knots and the Mach Meter flickered at 0.78; more than three-quarters the speed of sound. The serenity had been replaced by urgency and the rushing airflow by a roaring tide of air mass. It was one of their own and there was no time to waste.

Passing through a break in the cloud layer, the pair started raising their noses from the dive. Hannan's location was only minutes away and Sibyon-ni was beginning to loom large in the gunsight. It was a hot spot heavily fortified with permanent anti-aircraft gun emplacements thick on the ground and the surrounding hillsides. The hail of enemy fire could strike from above and below.

As they roared toward the firestorm, Taylor warned his young wingman as the array of brightly coloured tracer bullets began to spit into the air, feeling for the newly-arrived Meteors. Their eyes were downcast, scanning for any sign of Hannan, amid the chaos. Nothing. Not even his aircraft.

The 'Dentist' steered the pair towards new co-ordinates for the search, unknowingly leading them towards more ground fire. The Meteors swept by, their cannon fire tearing a trench through the enemy gunners' pits, sending dirt, snow and men into the air. But still the search for Hannan was fruitless.

Taylor and Zupp then intercepted the remaining three Meteors of Hannan's flight overhead where they had seen the aircraft, but not the pilot, hit the ground. Taylor began to orbit overhead as Zupp broke away in an attempt to meet and guide incoming aircraft under the callsign 'Midas'. With 20mm flak bursts erupting in every direction, there was little chance of sighting the other searchers.

He turned back towards the crash site and raced his lone Meteor low along the road, past the ground fire for a second time. Where was Butch? Then, something. A fleeting glimpse of something red in his peripheral vision. Zupp strained against his shoulder harness, twisting his torso, to look back. Could it be a scarlet 'marker scarf' like the one wrapped around his own neck?

He wrenched the Meteor around, vapour streaming from its wingtips. Through his angular Mark V goggles, Zupp's eyes struggled to recapture the red object by the roadside. His eyes darted from side to side as his Meteor whistled in at tree-top height. Nothing. Turning his head to enhance his field of view, he sensed movement ahead to his right. He unfroze his gyro and his trigger finger curled at the ready. No distress signal from Butch, but a barrel jutting up from the snow and it was pointing in his direction. Zupp's brain sent the signal to co-ordinate his eyes, hands and feet in the direction of the target. That signal did not arrive in time.

"ROOAAR!!!" The sound of air blasting into his face overwhelmed the sound of the projectile hitting. Zupp's world turned from controlled aggression to chaos in an instant. Below him the Meteor bucked and heaved, its wingtip almost ploughing a trench in the snow. One gloved hand tightened on the stick and hauled the column back into his guts while the other slammed the throttles forward to the limit of their travel. The disorientation was overwhelming as he aimed the jet away from the white ground toward the white sky, his vision misty as the buckled goggles sat twisted across his face and his oxygen mask now sat askew his mouth.

A whirlwind seemed to be enveloping his cockpit. Heaving in lungfuls of frigid air, the taste of blood filled his mouth. The G-forces of the pull up were kicking in and he tensed his stomach muscles to keep the blood from rushing to his feet. Even so, his world began to turn grey, slipping away as he was on the verge of losing consciousness….

He was a very long way from home.

Phillip Zupp. Aged 10 Months.

Chapter Two

The First to Land

Prussia was an old German kingdom that had seen more than its share of war and turmoil over the centuries. From the Teutonic Knights in the Middle Ages to the Napoleonic Wars, it was a land of ever-changing borders and alliances. West Prussia in the mid-19th Century occupied much of the land that today constitutes modern Poland with a narrower neck of land extending west towards Berlin. To the north is the port city of Gdansk, located on the Baltic Sea. It's a cold land where the average daily temperature is around nine degrees Celsius and there are lots of sub-zero days that keep the median so low.

Despite the harsh environment, farmers of the 1800s eked out a living from the frozen soil, often under a tenancy-type arrangement with a 'land lord' in the truest sense of the term. For Johann 'Carl' Wilhelm Zupp the future did not hold any great promise and as the father of seven children, he undoubtedly wanted better for them in the years ahead. Despite 25 years of loyal service as a farmer and cabinet-maker on the Von Hissmann estate, the fact remained that 'Carl' and his family would always be in the service of a 'land-lord' as long as they stayed in the Deutsch Krone province of Eastern Europe. No one can be sure what ultimately motivated the 54 year old 'Carl'; whether it was an encouraging letter home from other German emigrants who had made the voyage to Australia, or just amazing tales by a fireside. Perhaps he had signed up for the Queensland-sponsored immigrant scheme to attract Germans to the northern state as, prior to the 1860s, most of those settling in Australia had made their homes in the cooler climes to the south in the states of Victoria and South Australia. Under the Queensland scheme, the fare for the family's voyage was paid and they would subsequently be employed in compulsory service for a nominated period after which time they were free to purchase their own land.

Given the Zupps' low financial standing in Prussian society, the latter is highly likely but, for whichever reason, the Prussian father decided to uproot his family from all they had known in search of a better life in an unknown land on the other side of the world. Von Hissmann was sad to see his loyal employee leave, but wrote a glowing testimonial that 'Carl' could take as a letter of introduction to the new world. It re-affirmed that he was sad to see 'Carl' leave after years of service and emphasised that "He was always diligent, strict, honest and never drunk".

A voyage across the globe can be a daunting prospect in the 21st Century. It was almost unfathomable in the 19th. Before the voyage could even begin, the family traveled more than 500 kilometres on barges through the extensive networks of canals and channels that led from their Prussian home to the point of departure, Hamburg. Mortality rates on the ships were often high and accommodation for the majority was little more than hammocks slung between darkened decks with minimal ventilation. The prospect of such a voyage with his wife, Henrietta, and five of their children, ranging in age from five to 24, could not have been taken lightly. However, 'Carl' had obviously assessed that the potential return justified the risks. Two other sons journeyed to Australia in the years that followed.

Their vessel for the voyage was a ship named *Peter Godeffroy*. It left Hamburg in April 1865 and sailed for 121 days before it reached the distant shores of Australia. On board were 238 immigrant passengers. Fifty-nine died at sea. With a rate of attrition verging on 25 per cent, the Zupp family was fortunate not to lose at least one of their number, or perhaps it was that they were bred from sturdy stock. Regardless, the ship's arrival on August 10th did not escape the attention of the people of Queensland and their Government who subsequently ordered a parliamentary enquiry into the sizeable loss of life. Ultimately, after a degree of newspaper coverage, the villain of the hour was determined to be the spread of measles and not any degree of negligence by the crew or ship's surgeon.

For some of the 179 survivors, their first days in Australia were spent in the Brisbane Immigration Depot where they were quarantined and assessed before being allowed to enter the general population. In so many ways it was a world away from West Prussia. In contrast, the Australian state of Queensland was a relative wilderness. Vast in size, the state boasted floods the size of Germany, droughts that lasted a decade and heat that shattered the mercury above forty

The First to Land

Phillip on horseback with his older brother Fred.

degrees Celsius. In a country of extremes, the north-eastern state held its own at all ends of the spectrum yet it was here that the Zupp family chose to disembark while their vessel continued its voyage south to the cooler lush world of South Australia and the Barossa Valley's vineyards.

One can only wonder the confusion that confronted them as they took in their first glimpses of the new world. Surrounded by foreign sights, sounds, smells and language, their excitement must have been tempered with a degree of disorientation. Aside from a couple of wooden trunks inscribed with their name, the Lutheran Bible and a letter of reference from a kind employer, they were starting from scratch. Furthermore, their journey was still not complete as their new home was the Darling Downs, 80 miles inland of the state's capital, Brisbane, and a climb of more than 2,000 feet above sea level to the top of the Great Dividing Range. Today it is a steep incline for a motor vehicle to conquer with the benefit of sealed roads, but in 1865 bullock teams and horses trudged a winding path among the towering gum trees to reach the crest of the ridge. Once there, the view back east towards the coast would have been spectacular and unlike anything they had ever seen. They had arrived.

'Carl' successfully established the family as farmers on the Darling Downs and in the years that followed other members of his family made the long voyage. While the Franco-Prussian war raged at home, he set about tilling the Downs' black soil and breeding up a stock of cattle. German families dominated the region, establishing a new land, but still holding on to many ways and beliefs from the 'Old Country'. They spoke German, held strong to their Lutheran beliefs and congregated for communal events such as 'sausage making'. Some even continued to build their roofs with a steep pitch to allow the snow to run off. But the snow never came. The families inter-mingled and inter-married. The eldest child, Karl Wilhelm, had made the journey with his parents in 1865 and married a Prussian girl in 1871, a year after her arrival on the Downs. The younger Karl and his new bride, Henriette Nuske, wasted no time in building upon the family name and, a little over a year later, the first of their eleven children was born. However, it would be three daughters and five years before their first son was born and he was given what was becoming the family name of Wilhelm.

Wilhelm August Zupp was born at Spring Creek just out of Toowoomba and would grow into the farming life established by his grandfather. However, 'Bill' always seemed to have more of an aptitude for horses than crops and an ever-inquiring mind into how things worked. He became skilled with tools and leather-working but remained primarily a farmer which many suspected was neither his forte nor his interest. He was relatively old for the times when, at the age of 35, he married Louisa Frederick, ten years his junior, in 1914. At the time, the world was at war in Europe and the very real possibility existed that Zupps were fighting Zupps on the battlefields of France. However, their roots were now well established in their new homeland and to this backdrop their sons and brothers signed up to fight. John Zupp would lose a leg while Louisa's brother, James, would die at the Battle of Hamel.

'Bill' and Louisa's home was near the crest of a hill at Glenvale, nearby to the lands of his brothers and sisters. Appropriately named 'Hilltop', the sound timber home possessed a bull-nosed verandah and fancy green and yellow glass along the sides of the front door that boasted an ornate lock. It sat atop solid hardwood posts, for ventilation, taken from trees on the property while the walls inside were 'tongue and grooved' from flawless timber 'Bill' had chosen personally.

Fruit trees grew in the yard and crops in the adjoining fields while a few head of cattle completed the rural picture. Into this setting was born five children in the ten years from 1914 to 1925. Two of these died in their infancy and were rarely mentioned for the rest of the lives to the siblings that survived. Except perhaps in the bitter drunken mumblings of 'Bill' late of an evening when his language drifted between German and English. Those that survived were a daughter, Alice, and two sons, Frederick and Phillip. Of the three, Phillip was the youngest and in many ways the runt of the litter. A small quiet boy with a lazy right eye and prone to bouts of asthma, he grew up under the increasingly fierce temperament of his father which was often fuelled by too much alcohol and desperate times. He was a hard man who ruled with an iron fist and a leather belt and any frivolity was not well received. He would point out people playing sport and reinforce to his sons that this was an absolute waste of time and not to be encouraged. Nor did 'Bill' suffer fools. After having a neighbour's cattle stray onto his property a third time, he dispensed with the effort of moving them on again and simply branded them with his own iron. This was much to the ire of their owner and the local police. However, his point was effectively made. In contrast, Phillip's personality was more akin to his mother's quiet, determined manner that was, in many ways, equally fierce but held entirely within.

At an age when he first began to gain an awareness of his surroundings, the world was sliding into the Great Depression and drought ravaged the landscape. Times were tough for those trying to eke a living out of the land and young Phillip was caught in the midst of the turmoil. His world and his escape revolved around his older brother Fred, their cousins, Stan and Charlie Zupp, and the Campbell boys. In what was almost a 'Tom Sawyer' style existence of bare-footed freedom mixed with hard work, being the youngest came with certain drawbacks and frequently placed him directly in the line of fire. Known to them all as 'Brig', Phillip was always called upon to prove himself worthy of a place at the big boys' table. He would have to stand barefoot on the bull ants' nest the longest, as their ferocious mandibles savaged his feet, or climb the highest tree and the thinnest branch to raid a nest of its eggs. In fact, he soon gained a reputation for nerves of steel at daunting heights and the call of "Up it 'Brig'!" was made whenever a towering tree was encountered on their numerous long expeditions to Gowrie Mountain and beyond. As it turned out, he 'upped' it once too often when he climbed Auntie Winnie's Persimmon tree to relieve its bowing limbs of their fruit. As their Auntie came down from the house towards her beloved tree, the others scampered away leaving a silent Phillip frozen in the foliage hoping to escape detection. His efforts were in vain as his Auntie knew exactly which nephew would be the one in the tree and after he was ordered down he received a few rapid strokes on the behind with a thin fallen branch for his efforts.

Even so, on occasions his cousins did their best to leave the little 'Brig' behind. These occasions usually involved the carriage of firearms and, until Phillip was at least eight, Louisa forbid him to go along unsupervised with the other boys. Her fears were heightened by the recent death of a boy shot by his brother who was climbing through a fence with a rifle. To escape, various tactics were employed of which Fred was the prime exponent. One involved leading Phillip into the middle of a wheat field where the husks towered above his head before abandoning the disorientated child. Another had a proud young Phillip demonstrate the flying capability of his home-made kite, tethered high into the sky at the limit of its chord. The other boys would then dash off before Phillip could reel the kite back in. Even so, he always took it in his stride, although that's not to say he didn't possess a temper. From an early age he was fascinated with aeroplanes and machinery. He would toil over models and kites that would be built to perfection. If things did not go exactly to plan, the quiet little boy could explode and dash the offending device against the nearest wall.

Eventually the boy became old enough to tag along on the shooting adventures, but his escapades were far from limited to firearms. Despite being ordered to the contrary, Phillip and Fred secretly entered a rodeo competition when it came to town and the outcome was not favourable. Although being far from a fire-breathing bull, the young bovine still took objection to having a human across its back and threw young Phillip down into the dirt without too much effort. He landed heavily, taking the brunt of the force with his left forearm which became severely swollen and ached for weeks afterwards. Hiding the injured limb from his father through the judicious use of long sleeves, he recognised that the pain was worth enduring when he compared it to the flogging he would receive for disobedience. It would be years later that a military radiographer would detect that the arm had actually been broken in that fall.

Nevertheless, the boyhood freedom was set to the backdrop of the Great Depression. Phillip's father was drinking more than he should for a man in tough times and the youngster would often be sent to retrieve him from one of the local hotels. On other occasions the, 'Old Don', with a cart in tow, would bring 'Bill' home on a well-worn route for the trusty old horse. Man and beast would clip-clop past the family farms with the drunken patriarch mumbling to himself in broken German. If he knew his father was coming, Phillip would hide by the roadside with a slingshot on hand, determined to smash the bottle of cheap plonk he knew his father would have concealed beneath the cart.

For Queensland, the hardship of the Depression was compounded by a devastating drought that struck the land simultaneously in the 1930s and left farmlands barely viable. In the paddocks, despite intense labour, the crops were more viable if they were sowed back into the earth. For Phillip, the drought and Depression were synonyms and he would be a grown man before he ever knew there was a difference. To him, the town-folk spoke of the Depression and he saw cattle dying or being skinned for the value of their hide rather than their milk. The drought would outlast the collapsed financial markets so they would drive their cattle for miles in search of feed and the grass on the verge of the stock routes.

These outback roads were both affectionately and desperately known as the 'long paddock'. From the time he was able to ride, Phillip would accompany Fred and their father on these miserable pilgrimages. They would eat what they could catch, with Crested Pigeons being a favourite choice, and camp beneath the stars with their cattle nearby. Occasionally they were fortunate to camp near a body of water where both man and beast could rehydrate after a long day on the dusty road. One evening Fred and Phillip watched as their father drank a bottle of cheap wine and progressively slid into his mumbling German tirade. Simultaneously, their 'Old Bill' began to physically slide down the embankment towards the creek, much to the merriment of the two boys.

Slowly the brothers recognised that their father was not reacting as he slipped below the water's edge to the level of his belt. Soon the water was moving up his torso towards his face and their mirth rapidly transformed into concern as they raced to their father and attempted to heave him from the water. But 'Old Bill' was a big man, and Phillip and Fred were mere boys of nine and eleven, making the task monumental. As their feet slipped on the muddy waterline, their father continued to slide down until finally they were able to secure a rope beneath his armpits and lash it to a tree in the manner they used for errant bullocks that had fallen down a bank. Slowly they established a foothold and gradually moved their father back up to safety. Filthy and exhausted, they sat and looked at their father snoring and blissfully unaware of their efforts.

Food was neither plentiful for the cattle nor 'Bill' and his two boys. The youngsters became very adept at trapping birds and foraging for the day's meal in the dry paddocks that surrounded them. The sight of a kangaroo one morning spiked both Phillip's interest and his appetite. As Fred and his father readied the horses and prepared to move the cattle on, Phillip nabbed the rifle and stealthily made his way towards the unsuspecting kangaroo. The dry grass crackled under his weight and the animal turned its head towards the sound. Lying flat, his elbows dug into the ground, Phillip pulled the rifle butt against his shoulder and released the safety catch as he lined the blade sights up on the centre of the roo's body. His breathing slowed and his heart along with it. His finger eased the trigger back to the first point of resistance. All was steady, all was calm.

Crack!

His small boyish finger set the bullet on its way, spiraling down the barrel and across the paddock. The kangaroo never flinched initially, but then folded on one leg and fell to the ground with a single hole through the centre of its chest. Phillip reset the safety catch and started to breathe again. 'Old Bill' and Fred turned toward the gunshot only to see Phillip rising from his concealed place in the grass and walking away, rifle in hand. The rifle seemed almost as large as the small boy and the dead kangaroo he proudly showed them certainly was. After initially chastising the youngster for spooking the horses and cattle, 'Bill' congratulated his son on bagging their next meal.

His father's approval was a happy moment when the harsh experiences of childhood were forming a less positive outlook on rural life that would stay with him forever. He was angered by his father's drinking in such harsh times. He was sickened by the endless line of dying cattle and wearied by the fruitless labour that went into growing crops for market. He knew that he did not want a life on the land surrounded by all the difficulties he had seen bear down upon his family. However, nor did he know what life he could pursue as his options were limited by his locality and education. Like all boys, he had dreams but they seemed too fantastical to even entertain. For him, flight represented freedom and a means to escape the bonds of the world he knew, but he never realistically considered becoming a pilot. Perhaps he could become an aircraft mechanic but even this was far-fetched. He continued to dream and persevere, although things would become a good deal worse before they ever started to get better.

Phillip (second from right) as an Air Training Corps cadet in 1942.

Chapter Three

Dare to Dream

Every aspect of flight fascinated Phillip. From an early age he trapped finches and parrots and watched their behaviour before releasing them back into the skies. He was only a young boy when Bert Hinkler and Charles Kingsford Smith set the aviation world alight and had a profound effect on the youngster. A fellow Queenslander, and also of German descent, Bert Hinkler in particular captured Phillip's imagination with his solo exploits across the globe. Hinkler was a quiet character who often shunned the limelight and let his flying do the talking. In a time when heroes like Bradman and Phar Lap distracted Australians from their woes, Phillip Zupp clung to Hinkler.

Years later Phillip would reflect that one of his earliest memories was as a very small child lying on his back as a formation of military biplanes roared slowly overhead. Their shapes and sounds were etched into his memory from that day but it would be many years later that he would learn that the aircraft were a group of old Airco DH.9A light bombers setting out to search for two pioneer aviators lost in the outback. Along with their aircraft, the 'Kookaburra', the lost pilots had been in search of the great Charles Kingsford Smith when they were forced down in the Tanami Desert. Unfortunately, those brave aviators, Keith Anderson and Henry Hitchcock, perished before help could arrive.

Beyond the passage of the occasional aircraft overhead, the family had a tenuous link with the fledgling aviation industry in the form of John Zupp. He had returned from the war minus a leg and was known to back himself into the corner of the local bar and challenge two-legged patrons to a fight. Even without his leg, he was a big man and there were no takers to the challenge. In daylight hours, John had been entrusted with maintaining the local Wilsontown Airfield and Louisa would take her youngest child to peer at the aeroplanes through the fence. It was a real treat but he was frequently unsatisfied by the view from the fence. When Phillip was only four, Louisa was forced to hang onto his britches for grim death as he attempted to dart under the fence towards a spinning propeller. It was a manoeuvre mother and son repeated the day his brother Fred left home for the first time to start school. It was obvious that her youngest child was smitten by aviation but, in the drought-ridden existence they led, she could not perceive any means to assist him on this path other than occasional visits to the aerodrome.

When he wasn't doing his utmost proving his toughness to his peers or displaying his prowess as a crack rifle shot, Phillip was a quiet, studious pupil in an education system that was meagre to say the least. Glenvale State School was founded in 1882, not long after the first Zupps arrived on the Darling Downs. It sat a fair distance from the family home but was too close to warrant the effort in rounding up and saddling a horse for the journey. The distance could be reduced significantly by cutting across the various farms, one of which notably owned a tenacious bull. Phillip was logically sent in first as bait to distract the bull away to provide safe passage for his brother and cousins. On numerous occasions he only just made it beyond the fence before the snorting, charging beast came within striking distance. The school consisted of a single wooden classroom and was administered by one teacher, Mr. Maurice Maloney. From young Phillip's perspective, 'Old Maurice' was little more than a disinterested Irishman who smelt of grog. He handed out the books to read, and dealt out discipline, but imparted very little else to his young students. Whether Maurice was one of the many 'shell-shocked' veterans of World War One who were 'parked' in the education system, Phillip never knew, but he could see that his educational opportunities were very limited.

Even so, the quiet young lad was starting to show potential. He had a knack for drawing and his simple works won awards in the local newspaper while his woodworking skills won first prize at the Wilsontown Show. At school he had a thirst for knowledge and sought out every book available. He would spend hours poring over the atlas, imagining the world beyond Gowrie Mountain, and tracing his finger along the routes of the famous aviators who had crossed the oceans. In 1937, and again in 1938, the School Committee found Phillip deserving of an award and presented him with a treasured book on each occasion.

By now Phillip was the ripe old age of thirteen and taking on an increasingly significant role on the farm. The situation was becoming desperate at home and there was no longer any certainty that the family could hold on to the prime property at Glenvale. When 1939 dawned, it brought with it a series of upheavals that would turn life upside down. Firstly, the family's fears became reality when they lost the farm and were forced to move to little more than a shanty on 150 acres at nearby Middle Ridge. Whereas Glenvale had constituted prime pastoral land, Middle Ridge was on the edge of the escarpment. Its land was steeply sloping and pockmarked with rocky outcrops that made any form of farming extremely difficult. Today those slopes offer stunning views for prime real estate, but in the 1930s they were little more than the dregs of rural development.

The humiliation of the loss culminated on the evening that the family loaded their cart and moved their belongings from Glenvale to Middle Ridge. Phillip suggested a discreet route, via the back streets of Toowoomba, but his proud Germanic father insisted they travel along the town's main street. Phillip would reflect in later years that for him the journey to Middle Ridge that evening was one of absolute disgrace and he felt the eyes of neighbours and friends but never raised his head. The Zupps were well established on the Downs, but here was one of the founding families driven from their land. The shame was unbearable and it was a scar he never lost.

Their new dwelling was little more than a slab hut with a dirt floor. It was miles from the state school at Glenvale and, with the family's worsening financial problems, the option of Phillip continuing his education disappeared. So, despite his application and promise, any chance of a formal education and the opportunities it may bring were dashed in an instant. In fact, possibly more than any other factor, the deprivation of an education would throw up obstacles for the rest of his life. Leaving school abruptly before his fourteenth birthday, Phillip never even had the opportunity to sit the 'Scholarship Examination' which was generally regarded as the exam marking the completion of primary education. In effect, he had no educational requirements whatsoever and this would not only shape his own life but the subsequent emphasis on the lives of his children with respect to education and formal qualifications. Phillip would later relate that this lost opportunity made him feel like the dumb farm kid; a 'hick'.

It was a tag he loathed but, within, knew was unjustified. However, without any pieces of paper to justify his potential, he found his way into the workforce at the 'Southern Cross' foundry in Toowoomba where they made windmills. Young, shy and naïve, he was soon the victim of practical jokes by the older workers and was endlessly sent to find items that didn't exist. Withdrawing further into his shell, when his time wasn't being wasted on his workmates' pranks, there was hard work to be done among the furnaces and smelters. Because of his diminutive dimensions, he was tasked with climbing inside the furnaces at regular intervals to scrape down the walls. There was residual heat and no ventilation within the metal vaults as he labored away, scratching, chipping and scraping. With work conditions that were not far removed from Dickensian England, there were few signs of hope and Phillip simmered with frustration at the lack of opportunity and the ongoing bullying by his peers.

Amid the chaos of his situation, the world fell into its own chaos when World War Two was declared. Those who had seen the first conflict feared for their sons and dreaded what such news meant for the country and Empire. For Phillip, the news of the war filtered down slowly and literally seemed a world away. He had heard the old folk speak of the Great War in sombre tones, but was more interested whether this conflict would breed a new generation of knights of the air and the same chivalrous deeds that had filled his childhood stories. The likes of 'Smithy' and Hinkler had first gained their wings while in the service of their country at a time of war and they had ultimately become pioneering heroes of the sky.

But for Phillip it all seemed so very far away. There was, however, one exception, while he was too young to fly or fight, the war had brought with it the emergence of the Air Training Corps. The ATC was a youth organisation that was the air force's equivalent of the army cadets and formed part of the air force 'reserve' from mid-1941. The intention was to provide a ready supply of youth to the permanent air force who had already been educated in the theoretical and practical aspects of service life and aviation. Despite its promise, the ATC called for a minimum age of sixteen, and that was still some time away, but for Phillip it was the first inkling that his dream of flight might just be possible. He continued to work hard under trying conditions, faithfully bringing his pay home to his family and working hard on the land at the day's end. He did, however, manage to save the princely sum

Dare to Dream

of six shillings to buy a copy of 'Every Boy's Book of Fighting Planes'. This spoke excitedly of a new British monoplane fighter, the Spitfire, although its top speed was 'Top Secret'.

Finally, he was old enough to join the Air Training Corps with his father's permission. This consent was critical as enrolment in the cadet body also called for an "honourable undertaking" to enlist with the Royal Australian Air Force when he came of age. Phillip completed the form in his best handwriting before seeking his father's endorsement and his sister Alice's service as a witness. His application was not a guarantee of selection as competition for a position with No. 58 Squadron Toowoomba was fierce, particularly considering the high conversion rate of cadets to the coveted position of RAAF aircrew. However, the quiet lad's luck changed when he was accepted into the squadron and his pride on receiving his uniform was a highlight in his young life.

The ATC now offered a glimmer of hope to an otherwise depressing outlook. There was a sense of belonging and pride that he had not previously experienced in his young life. Aside from the RAAF orientated topics, such as marching and enhancing their knowledge of the air force, serious study was required to complete the syllabus of training set out for the young cadets. Arithmetic, algebra, trigonometry and geometry were just some of the mathematically based subjects while science, Morse code and aircraft recognition covered other areas of knowledge. There were speed and accuracy tests, mental computations and physical fitness challenges to complete as well.

Given his minimal education, Phillip was called upon to rise to the challenge just to survive among such a diverse range of subjects. However, tenacity was never a problem for the youngster and he applied himself in every spare moment to the task of studying his training manuals. He gorged himself on the content and would not let a topic go until he fully understood it and could answer any question put to him. He was still very reticent in nature and with marginal written language skills, yet when asked to explain some aspect of the training he was surprisingly competent. His peers saw an uncanny knack in Phillip that allowed him to break down complex concepts and explain them in relatively simple terms. When the 'hick' kid spoke, he actually made a great deal of sense. He just didn't speak very often.

His efforts brought results and, after initially simply passing his first stage of proficiency, over the next two years he went on to pass the second and third advanced stages with distinction. The academic challenge of the ATC syllabus was far higher than the basic schooling level he had been asked to complete but he had risen to the challenge. It was not through brilliance but through dogged application and an absolute refusal to give up or slacken off. Slowly but surely a level of self-belief was stirring in the otherwise under-confident kid and the possibility of joining the ranks of aircrew were now a definite possibility.

At home his mother had provided encouragement but there was little more support available and absolutely no guidance forthcoming from his family. He was aiming for a target beyond their range and there was no comprehension of the dreams he held close. If his father considered sport to be frivolous, then his youngest child's aspirations to fly bordered on fantasy. Fences, ploughs and a beer was all 'Bill' needed and it was left for his son to find his way in the new world.

From such a heritage, Phillip had learnt to fight for every yard and to ignore disappointment at every turn. He believed that the words of others ultimately didn't matter and that only your own actions could possibly define you. As a man, he had no time for people making excuses, shifting blame or failing to be accountable. Sliding into relative poverty, surviving drought and the Great Depression, labouring in filth when other children were playing games, all contributed to the tough mindset he was to maintain throughout his life.

Yet as his days with the Air Training Corps drew to a close and 1944 dawned, he did not see any great philosophy in his actions, merely a means to survive. It was a mechanism that had served him well as he grew from a boy to a man under trying circumstances on all fronts. As he entered his teenage years, Phillip quite understandably saw very little future for himself and yet, through the lifeline thrown to him by a youth organisation, he had entered manhood with achievable goals and an inherent sense of tenacity and determination. He still possessed a temper, and his words often failed to portray thoughts, but he had learnt to work with the tools he had at his disposal.

The world was still at war and he was now old enough to play his part. The global devastation was his chance to move beyond the farm and set his own course. God willing, that would entail an opportunity to take to the skies. What he could not possibly foresee was the dramatic road that lay ahead. The previous decade had seen him scrape for every breath of hope without ever venturing more than a handful of miles from the farm life that he was so very scared of.

By contrast, the decade ahead would see him cross oceans, make headlines and fly so high he could see the curvature of the earth. In his wildest dreams on the warmest Toowoomba nights, he could not have perceived the events that lay ahead and yet he had unwittingly armed himself with the tools and traits he would need to survive through the best of times and the worst of times. He was a country boy about to be thrust into the heart of the world's turmoil. The dumb 'hick' had grown up and was going to war.

1944. The young navigator in training at Mount Gambier.

Chapter Four

Into the Blue

Late in 1943, Phillip's tenure with the Air Training Corps was coming to a close. He was rapidly approaching his eighteenth birthday and the time was looming for him to honour his oath and seek to serve his country with the Royal Australian Air Force. Far from being an obligation, this was a dream come true, although a position in the ranks of aircrew was still some distance away from being a certainty.

In his favour, he had proven himself a worthy candidate during his two years of service with the Air Training Corps and, fortunately, the RAAF recognised his ATC passes with distinction as meeting the academic standard for consideration as aircrew. This was in spite of the absence of any formal educational qualification through the school system. Furthermore, in July of 1943 he had undertaken preliminary aptitude testing for aircrew and been assessed as suitable, with a particular leaning towards numerical calculation and mechanical matters. On completing his application, an anomaly came to light for the first time; he had been misspelling his name his entire life. He had never previously sighted his birth certificate but, on examination, he saw that 'Phillip' was spelt with two L's not one as he had been told since childhood. His mother's intent was for the spelling to be 'Philip', but when his father went to register his birth he erroneously spelt 'Phillip'. Consequently, all of his awards, certificates and correspondence up to this time reflect a different spelling to the one he used for the rest of his life.

With the administrative oversight in order, Phillip submitted his application for aircrew training and made his way to the recruiting centre in Brisbane where he was poked and prodded, quizzed and questioned, over the next two days. The first day, the candidates' health and fitness was scrutinised in detail. By general standards Phillip was a small lad at five feet, four inches and weighing only 130 pounds. His rugged upbringing had left him with no shortage of distinguishing scars to list on the doctor's clipboard, although a significant wound to his right calf was indicated by a four-inch scar. It was the result of accidently putting an axe into his leg as a young boy and, just as he had done when he'd broken his arm at the rodeo, he concealed the wound from his father. This was done by packing the wound with flour and walking without a limp to the best of his ability.

The medical examination was to prove a long day and was the first time he had ventured to the city. Stern-faced men shuffled the group along the hallways with cropped, crisp instructions while between tests the common room was filled with the nervous young men all dreaming of flying and fearing failure. As they waited, they chatted in hushed tones about the possible dreaded tests they would be asked to perform to prove their physical worthiness for aircrew training. The shy boy from Toowoomba tended to sit apart from the group, a little unsure of his right to be there, but no less determined to succeed. He could overhear the others airing their concerns and trepidation and it helped put him at ease, although the degree of scrutiny his body was subjected to embarrassed him a little. There were tests of co-ordination and reflexes and blood was drawn from his veins to screen for all manner of antigens and antibodies. He was forced to exhale into a U-shaped tube of mercury for a minute to demonstrate adequate lung capacity; an exercise that he feared given his bouts of asthma at a younger age.

Next he was exposed to an X-Ray machine for a series of see-through images; a concept which absolutely fascinated him. It was from these x-rays that evidence of his fractured forearm first surfaced as well as a number of broken ribs. When quizzed about the origins of the breaks, Phillip was at a loss despite his suspicions. When further probed about the doctor's original diagnosis at the time of the injuries, the youngster innocently informed the panel that he had never seen a doctor, much to their chagrin.

The next day dawned and saw the recruiting officers focus on the mental ability and aptitude of the would-be aviators. While he attacked the new round of testing with vigour and a level of knowledge stemming from a great deal of study, he lived in terror of the face-to-face interviews. Inevitably, though, he was called to front a panel of officers all seemingly void of any warmth. He initially sat awkwardly in his chair before forcing his back straight and forcing himself even harder to look them straight in the eye. When they asked him why he wanted to be a pilot, he struggled to find the words. He had the passion, but none of the skills required to express in words the burning desire that filled every waking breath and every night's dream. He could feel his face turning red with embarrassment as he made his best effort to convey some sort of enthusiasm to the panel. The next line of questioning revolved heavily around sports as this was seen as a sound indicator of co-ordination and teamwork. Phillip had written on his form that he had played cricket and football at school, but in all honesty he knew that was stretching the truth. His father had not condoned the perceived frivolity of sport so the hard-working youngster had hardly ever picked up a ball. His embarrassment was now bordering on panic as it was obvious to the panel that he was getting out of his depth. Regardless of his inner turmoil Phillip maintained his posture and continued to look the officers in the eye without flinching, even though he couldn't control the redness in his cheeks.

The panel then seemingly went for the kill and asked the youngster to complete a few mental calculations but he snapped back the correct answers without hesitation. Next, they tapped out a word in Morse code with a pencil on the table and once again Phillip supplied the correct answer without pausing. He had regained a slight footing, but it was when he was asked to explain an aspect of the theory of flight that he transformed entirely. A wave of confidence surged through him as he set about explaining how a wing stalls. He was no longer lost for words and articulated the concept of the airflow separating from the wings surface with the confidence of a flight instructor and the conciseness of a technical manual. In the absence of pen and paper he used his hands to portray the wing, the air and the relative angles in between them. The panel seemed to be caught off guard, but pleased with his closing argument. He was dismissed and the jury would now deliberate on the verdict.

Despite his recovery, he was sure that his dream had just slipped away. He cursed his own ineptness and lack of schooling as his angst welled up inside. This had been his one shot at the title and he'd blown it in devastating form. He could only think of a life land-locked on the farm as the world slid past him now that any chance of escape had been dashed. It was one of the lowest moments in his young life.

And yet, somehow, at the end of the process, he was deemed to be suitable for aircrew training. A pilot position had eluded him, but, amazingly, not on the grounds of his interview performance. Medically, he had been placed in category A3B which stated that he was suitable as a "combatant passenger" such as a navigator or air-gunner. Perhaps he wasn't seen as pilot material because of the newly discovered fractures, or because he was lacking in the tall lean stature and Hollywood looks that defined the recruiting posters of the day. Regardless of the reason, he was accepted for training as aircrew in the role of Navigator-Wireless Operator and his dream was coming true.

He was overjoyed at being accepted into the RAAF in an airborne role and made his way to Brisbane once more in January 1944 to take his oath, sign the forms and enter the service. His identity photo was that of a dour young man. His hair cut in a haphazard manner and without a trace of a smile threatening from his furrowed brow. With his serial number of AC440626 stamped across the bottom edge, the photo was more reminiscent of a gangster's mug-shot, than the face of a youngster setting out on life's great adventure. Even in this moment of joy, Phillip seemed to bury any emotion beneath his steely exterior.

Nevertheless, when he arrived at his first training posting at Kingaroy, Queensland, he was brimming with enthusiasm. The rural township of Kingaroy is about a two and a half hour drive north from the Queensland capital of Brisbane and one hundred miles in the same direction from Phillip's hometown. While it is known today for its ability to produce high quality peanuts, in 1944 it was home to a thriving air force base that included a mix of training units and operational fighter squadrons resting and re-equipping before heading north to New Guinea once again. Its four grass runways criss-crossed the bulk of the land, while the remainder played host to a variety of huts, offices and Bellman hangars. The air was filled with the crackling of machine guns and the smell of cordite as the armourers fired the fighters' guns into the pit designed for calibrating the gunsights. The excitement of No. 50 Aircrew Course was palpable as they passed through the gates for the first time.

The commanding officer of No. 3 Initial Training School (ITS) was an airman of note in his own right. John Rutherford Gordon had landed on the Gallipoli beaches as an Army sergeant in 1915 and received his officer's commission while serving on the Turkish peninsula. Suffering from typhoid he was invalided back to Australia before transferring to the newly formed Australian Flying Corps (AFC) where he undertook flying training, but failed to complete the course on medical grounds. Not to be beaten, he returned to England where he served with the Royal Flying Corps (RFC) as an observer, downing fifteen enemy aircraft with his lone machine gun and being awarded the Military Cross in the process. In 1918 he finally gained his pilot's wings and saw action as a fighter pilot prior to the end of the First World War. When the second conflict erupted in 1939 he joined the RAAF and rose to the rank of wing commander.

At Kingaroy, Wing Commander Gordon M.C. was the boss and it was here that his charges would be introduced to service life and primed for specialised aircrew training at a later date. Together the new recruits were in the fledgling stage of a greater program known as the Empire Air Training Scheme. Gordon had been a part of the EATS from its inception, taking the first group of Australians across to Canada to undertake their training. This massive scheme was tasked with providing the huge number of aircrew required to fight the air war. Employed across the nations of the Commonwealth including Canada and South Africa, Australia would ultimately train nearly 30,000 aircrew members by the end of the war in 1945. Despite the numbers, selection for the program was competitive and the trainees proudly wore a white band across the front of their small navy blue caps to signify their status as aircrew under training.

Along with Phillip were two other Queenslanders, Eric Geldard and Mike Heffernan, while an older recruit, John Collins, hailed from South Australia. Collins had already served with the Army since 1941 but was now seeking to change the direction of his life by 'defecting' to the Air Force blue. At this time the four rookies were virtual strangers and fate would deal them a remarkable hand within a year. However, for the moment they were simply content to line up and receive their initial issue of uniform and be shown the way to their new homes. A mass of equipment - boots, overalls, bedding, towels and toiletries - poked out the top, and strained the seams, of their blue cylindrical canvas kit-bags. There were forms to complete and a series of needles harpooned into their flesh. Soberingly, they were called to complete a Will and issued with two named discs, or 'Dog Tags', to hang around their necks. These tags would be used to identify their bodies should they be killed and served to remind the excited boys of the ultimate sacrifice their new vocation may call for. Sparse wooden barracks greeted them with rows of stretchers interspersed by small personal lockers. The heat of the Queensland summer seeped through the walls and the young men's boots created a racket as they clip-clopped their way to their bunks. Consisting of straw-filled mattresses and drab grey blankets, their bedding was humble but sufficient and would be called upon to be in perfect order when inspected by their superiors. Everything had a very minimal, military feel to it. And Phillip loved it.

From the outset he was at home with what the Air Force had to offer. He thrived under the ordered, disciplined way of life and found it almost unbelievable that he was being clothed, fed and paid six shillings a day to study and learn. Barracks life was his first experience of any formal community living, but there was a spirit of excitement and camaraderie among the young airmen. He was treated as a peer and not bullied or harassed for sport as he had been in civilian life. He soon became known as 'Zuppie' and it was a term of endearment that would follow him through the rest of his adult life. Still shy in many ways, he ventured beyond his defences with his mischievous sense of humour that proved to be popular with the other trainees.

Everything they did, they did together. They ate, slept, studied and sweated as a group under the watchful eye and barking voices of those entrusted with their education. They moved around the base in ordered groups, stepping in time with eyes locked ahead. On the parade ground they were drilled to the point of fatigue as they were moulded into a cohesive, disciplined unit while the screaming form of Warrant Officer Bliss willingly accepted the role as a common enemy. Their past identities were left at the door in many ways as graziers' sons stood shoulder to shoulder with urban bankers' offspring. Phillip was not alone in his level of education as the Great Depression had taken its toll on many families, although the vast majority had at least attained their intermediate certificate. From all walks of life and corners of the island continent, the scene was repeated across Australia as its young men answered the call to arms.

Many had some insight into the military way through their indoctrination with the Air Training Corps. The organisation had also offered a sound grounding in the range of subjects that had to be studied, including the new world of the theory of flight, or aerodynamics. The volume of information was daunting, and the critical stream of facts and figures seemed unending to their young minds, and yet there was never a word of complaint as they set about studying in every waking moment, determined to excel. For Phillip, such dedication paid dividends and his marks were consistently above average. He continued to display a degree of self-belief that his past life had not permitted, prompting his commanding officer to assess him as "wholesomely self confident and decisive". He recognised that his aircrew category of A3B prevented him from having a shot at pilot training, but he hinged his hopes on becoming an Observer-Navigator and continued to record marks of 98% in mathematics to assist his cause.

The assignment of a specialist field could make or break the young trainees and yet history has shown that, regardless of any disappointment, they were able to accept their designated role. And while most young boys dreamed of a slot on the pilot's course, the reality was that the numbers were stacked against them. For while a fighter houses its lone pilot in the cramped cockpit, transport, maritime and bomber aircraft have extensive crews combining to operate and protect their complex machines. Observers, bomb-aimers, radio operators, air-gunners and navigators made up the bulk of the crew and played critically vital roles while the pilot so often received the recognition.

Yet there was even more to the assignment of a specialist role. Firstly, it would determine the pay rate that filled the wallet. Secondly, it could have a direct impact upon the individual's chances of seeing out the war's end. As an air-gunner there was a real likelihood of seeing action over Europe in Bomber Command where more than 55,000 men, over 40%, would be killed before the cessation of hostilities. Such statistics were sobering, but death was a new companion to the youthful airmen that was not limited to the theatres of war. Many young men would die training under the Empire Air Training Scheme during World War Two before they ever saw the enemy. To survive, some brushed death off with bravado or a belief that fate would always call upon the other guy. Unfortunately, this was not always true as the silent rows of graves at Kingaroy testified.

Death was not a preoccupation that Phillip invested any time in and he was of the school that believed that it would not be him that would fall. His focus was solely dedicated to passing the course with the highest possible marks, well aware that better educated chaps most probably had his measure. The awareness bordered on an inferiority complex and it was something that would haunt him for the rest of his life. And yet, when the names were called after nearly three months of initial training, his name was called into the ranks of the navigator trainees. He watched with envy as the handful of pilot candidates packed their kit-bags to ship out to one of the Elementary Flying Training Schools, but was still satisfied with his posting to the world of charts and compasses.

He had never before ventured out of his home state of Queensland, but now he readied himself for a journey to the distant land of South Australia. With his entire life packed into a canvas bag that could be slung over his shoulder, he set out for the next stage of his journey knowing he would soon be taking to the air for the first time. It was a comforting thought as he left all that he knew behind and rode the rails in a cramped carriage southward to Mount Gambier. For a boy who had dreamed of flying his entire life, the dream was now only days away. As he nodded in and out of sleep to the train's rhythmic rattle, he pictured what it would be like to wheel about the sky, clipping clouds and looking down upon the earth from such a height. To fly miles above the drought-ridden land of his youth and a world away from the barriers that had been laid down in his path. Phillip had always seen flight as a means of escape. Now it was to be his home.

Chapter Five

D-Day

If the heat had seeped through the walls of the barracks at Kingaroy, then they leaked water at Mount Gambier. The young Queenslander had never seen such rain or felt such miserable cold as he disembarked and made his way to the Air Observer's School (A.O.S.). The South Australian air base sat on the southern shores of Australia, perched midway between Adelaide and Melbourne, and was subjected to the low-pressure systems and cold fronts that came sweeping across the Great Australian Bight from the Southern Ocean, making it the wettest place in the state. While its summers may be warm, winter was only days away as Phillip sheltered under the eaves of a weatherboard hut, shivering in his thick wool Air Force greatcoat with the collar turned up.

Despite the inclement greeting, there was an air of anticipation among the shivering men as they were soon to take to the skies and learn the art of navigation. Forty fresh faces made up A.O.S. School Course 17 that first day, although their numbers would be nearly halved by the end of the course through circumstances beyond their control. As they queued alphabetically to receive their bedding and blankets, Phillip stood at the rear with a fellow trainee, Reg Young. Reg had already served a stint in the Army, but had been lured to the RAAF by the chance to fly. He joked with Phillip that it was the first time in two years that he hadn't been at the end of the line, while Phillip retorted that with Zupp as his last name he guessed he'd be waiting a long time to have someone behind him. The two chatted until they were finally issued with their gear and sent on their way to their new lodgings.

The rows of beds and lockers were reminiscent of Kingaroy but colder. Many things were similar to the initial training including the marching, the food and being the lowest in the pecking order. However, there were new manuals to be studied and new equipment to become familiar with. These were specialised tools

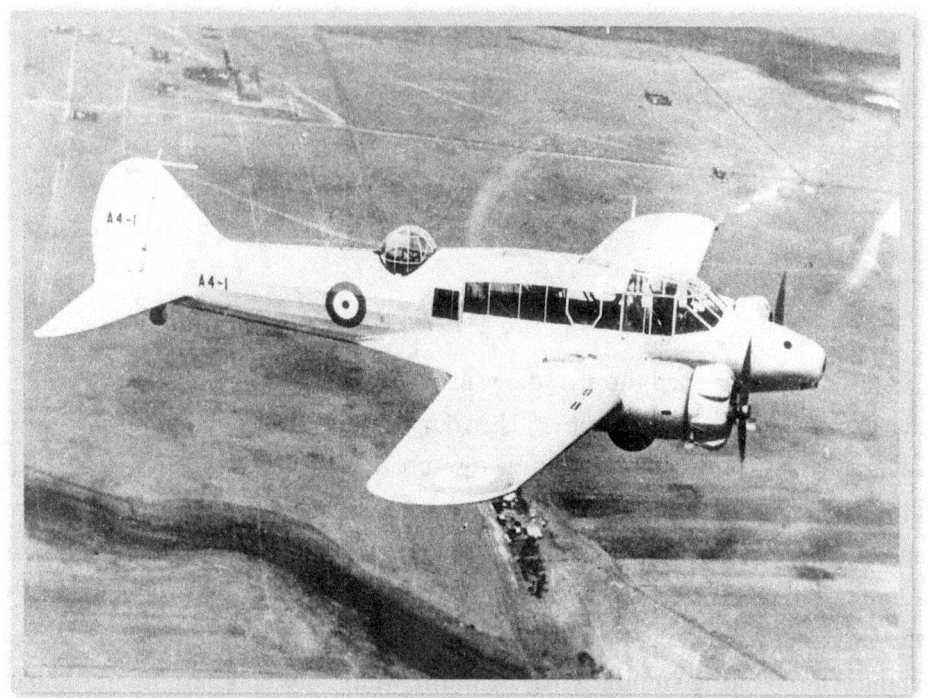
Phillip first tasted flight in the Avro Anson. (Source: RAAF PR via Stewart Wilson)

of trade such as sextants, compasses, charts and navigation computers. The latter were, in effect, a circular slide rule. It seemed all very technical to the boy from the bush, but his real excitement was saved for the lineup of aircraft that sat beyond the parade ground and the rows of buildings. Sitting on the edge of the airfield, wingtip to wingtip, were more than twenty Avro Ansons.

By 1944, the Avro Anson could not be classed as a sleek beauty. In fact, it would be a stretch to even politely call her a 'lady of the skies'. Developed from a civilian airliner, the Anson was designed to carry two crew and ten passengers and was powered by a radial engine on each wing. It sat nose high on the ground, resting upon a small wheel beneath the tail that further defined it as a tailwheel aeroplane. Its mainwheels were state of the art at the time of inception as they retracted into the wings, although the earliest models called for the pilot to wind an awkward crank handle 140 times to achieve this. While a top speed of 160 knots was quoted, its realistic cruising speed was in the realm of 135 knots and a 'state of the art' Perspex dorsal turret housed the gunner and his single Vickers machine gun

The first military Anson had flown in 1935 before war was on the horizon and it had been rather overtaken by technological progress even before the war had started. Initially destined to fly with the Royal Air Force's Coastal Command in Britain, the Anson saw action and even possibly sank a German submarine, or U-Boat. Already obsolete, the type came into its own as a trainer for crews as they progressed to flying larger and heavier aeroplanes. Its success in this role led to more than 11,000 being built with the last one rolling out of the factory in 1952. As such, the twenty or so that sat on the Mount Gambier flight-line represented a mere speck on the Anson's family tree.

Work was underway sealing new runways as the trainees settled into their first classes. The subject matter was broad covering 'dead reckoning' to meteorology and everything in between. Maps and charts were studied while the inner workings and operation of the Direction Finder were demystified. Then there was Morse Code, light signals, electrical theory, aircraft recognition, pyrotechnics, radio operation and aerial photography. The topics seemed to go on and on when all Phillip desperately wanted to do was get into an aeroplane and take to the skies.

These were the days before satellite navigation and GPS. Radar was still in its infancy and navigators were a critical member of any crew. The majority of these young men were destined to guide the lumbering bombers on their devastating missions over Europe. Generally, the operations were by night and frequently in weather far worse than any Australian lad had witnessed. They would ultimately be responsible for finding the bomber's targets in lands they'd only read about and then, low on fuel and with dense cloud lurking over the English Channel, they would be called upon to guide their aircraft and crew back to safety.

Like the larger bombers, the Anson was equipped with wireless radios, a direction finding receiver linked to a loop aerial on the aircraft's upper surface, and a trailing aerial that was manually wound into the airflow during flight. There was even a bubble sextant that was closely related to the brass sextants that had guided vessels for centuries through their sightings of the sun and stars. Even with this mix of old and seemingly modern aids, navigation still called for a high degree of 'dead reckoning' and accurate flying by the pilot. It centred on the premise that if you started from a known point and then flew for a certain time, at a certain speed and steered a steady course, your eventual position could be calculated. However, nature was not quite so defined.

The varying wind could blow an aircraft off course or mean that it travelled faster or slower over the ground if it was flying with the wind or against it. The navigator had to factor such variables into all of his calculations to provide the pilot with a course to steer and an estimated time to be over the next turning point or the target. An error could lead to the failure of the operation or, worse, the loss of the aircraft. Yet here were these boys studying and preparing to take their new-found knowledge into dark and angry skies on the other side of the world.

Fortunately for the trainees, their training grounds of South Australia and western Victoria were a little friendlier. There was no anti-aircraft fire or marauding fighters to deal with and even the terrain, generally flat and with no shortage of railway lines and straight roads, was conducive to teaching navigators their new skills. Even so, the young 'Navs' were called to perform all of these calculations in a timely fashion in the cramped, noisy workspace that was the Avro Anson.

As Phillip donned his flying gear for the first time, there was a real sense of excitement. He now wore a flying suit with gauntlet-like gloves and a life jacket and parachute which all combined to bulk up his short, slight frame. As he walked towards the Anson for his first flight, the aircrew experience seemed very real for the first time. With the tools of the trade tucked under his arm, he stepped up through the door behind the Anson's right wing and entered his new office. The classroom and parade ground now seemed far removed from the task at hand.

Inside the Anson was rustic, like old scaffolding with fabric stretched over it. There seemed to be metal tubing everywhere and no shortage of places to hit your head. The flanks of the aeroplane hosted a long row of generous windows on either side which with the metal framework combining to give the impression of a greenhouse. Overhead, the roof played host to the loop aerial, while to the rear it was home to the gun turret (a window to the stars for taking sextant sightings). Inside, a bank of radio receivers and a small bench made up the navigator's work station.

As the pilot started the engines, a cacophony of noise, smoke and vibration enveloped the Anson. It shuddered and shook before the engines warmed up and slipped into harmony. Bumping across the ground to the runway, Phillip looked across the airfield through the greenhouse windows and checked his harness one more time. His Bakelite headphones were pulled down tight across his blue uniform forage cap, although in time he would hopefully receive a leather flying helmet that would incorporate his headphones for communication.

The Anson came to a halt and revved up its engines again as the pilot completed his final checks before take-off. With little warning, and even less delay, the aircraft swung its tail around and the engines roared. The bumping across the ground became more violent and the whole aeroplane shook as the world whipped past outside the windows. One of his books went to slip on the floor but Phillip grabbed it before it could embarrassingly evade him. He had dreamt of the romance of flight but this was like being on the inside of a drum that fell off the back of a truck. Then the tail rose and a lightness came over the aircraft. The mainwheels left the ground and they were airborne.

This was it; flight. Even the roaring engines seemed to fade into a bearable background drone as the world fell away from the wheels. The hangars and huts were rapidly receding from view as he now moved through the air faster than he had ever travelled before. Ahead in the cabin, another trainee was busily cranking the wheels up, using a handle at the rear of the cockpit, and seemed to be repeatedly skinning his knuckles in the process. But from where Phillip sat, the world was well at peace and the boyhood dream had come true.

This was little more than a familiarisation flight and the pressure of the navigator's role was not yet applied to the youngsters. They were free to watch the clouds slide by at an incredible speed and look down upon the farming properties whose paddocks appeared stitched together like a massive rural quilt. It was everything he had imagined and more as he sat there silently with a smile creeping across his face. He looked ahead once more to see the pilot looking back at him, also with a smile on his face as if he knew exactly what the young trainee was feeling. Phillip smiled back and for a moment felt a pang of disappointment at not making the grade as a pilot, but it was only for a moment. He realised the blue sky outside was his new home and neither the sky nor the clouds discriminated between pilot and navigator.

The wonder of that first flight was only tempered by the fact that it had to end. Slowly the aircraft descended back towards Mount Gambier and the quilt grew back into paddocks, trees and the like. The pilot lowered the flaps and then extended the wheels in preparation for landing. All too soon the rumbling and bumping returned before the aircraft parked and once more fell silent.

Phillip took a deep breath and snapped back to attention, carefully listening to instructions on how to disembark and where he would be next required. His feet were tingling as they touched the ground and he wasn't sure if it was due to the excitement or simply having been shaken for the previous hour. Either way, he was still elated as he made his way to the mess hall for lunch where the conversation centred on that first flight with questions coming rapidly from those still awaiting their turn. Always shy, he tended to be on the outer of such conversations although he listened with great interest and shared in the palpable excitement.

The classroom theory and study continued, but soon he was back in the Anson for his first full-blooded training flight. The winds were blowing strongly and the sky was not quite as blue as they taxied out for the second time. He had been assigned the task of winding up the wheels after take-off on this occasion and he silently hoped he didn't make a mess of it. They accelerated down the runway and soon the familiar bumping of the take-off roll was replaced by the relative smoothness of flight, although the aircraft continued to lunge and lurch as it was buffeted by the winds.

Phillip began winding the crank handle vigorously and the wheels began to lift slowly into their bays. Fifty, sixty, seventy turns and the wheels were still not retracted so he kept winding away, routinely catching the back of his hand on nearby metal fittings. Finally, the wheels were up and he made his way to his seat, glancing at the blood on the back of his cranking hand. Strapping in, the aircraft jolted, rocked and rolled as he attempted to organise his charts for the forthcoming lesson. There was no time to take in the scenery outside as he readied his equipment. He hadn't even started and the pressure was on. At first he felt a little tired, and then light in the head, so he paused for a moment and looked outside. The tail of the Anson wallowed through the turbulence and Phillip began to feel increasingly unwell as sweat began to pour from his forehead and his mouth went dry. He tried to concentrate but this was becoming more difficult by the minute and then his stomach began to churn.

Dread rose within and he feared that this was the airsickness that others had mentioned. The more he considered it, the worse he felt and now he was feeling a ball welling up in his throat. He reluctantly looked for one of the sick bags, determined to win this battle with his body. His instructor said something to him that he didn't quite grasp but he felt better for an instant.

The nausea rose from his guts, accelerated up his oesophagus and burst forth from his mouth. He tried in vain to hold the next surge in but his gulping only prolonged the inevitable as he heaved into the bag. He sensed the instructor was smiling, but this was no fun for him. The embarrassment was outweighing even the sickening taste that filled his mouth and running nose. Bring on the enemy. He just wanted to die.

Phillip recovered enough to gain some value from the flight but dreaded the consequences for a navigator that got airsick. He feared that he may be 'scrubbed' and kicked off aircrew training, destined for a life in a ground job. His case became worse as he continued to fall ill on subsequent sorties despite all the effort he could muster to keep his stomach in check. He continued to perform in the classroom but, every time that he went aloft, he vomited no matter what he tried to do to combat the feeling. He was rapidly becoming fatigued, as he couldn't sleep for worry about the next flight, but he was determined not to give up.

An instructor suggested that he might be dehydrated, so young Phillip made sure that he drank enough water leading up to each flight. Initially, it seemed to make no difference until, finally, for reasons unknown, he returned from a flight with his stomach contents still where they should be. It had been a close thing, but he had managed to allay the periodic surges inside and survive the flight. His confidence returned and, now uninhibited, he was able to execute his sound performance in the classroom while he was in the air.

Amid their constant training, word filtered down about the Normandy landings on June 6th; D-Day. The Allied forces had successfully returned to Europe and had now set about driving the enemy back to Berlin. By all accounts the invasion had gone well and the Allies now virtually possessed air superiority over the continent as the Luftwaffe's stocks of fuel, men and machines began to dwindle. For the trainees, they began to wonder if the 'Big Show' was going to be over before they ever had the chance to fight. This was particularly in Phillip's mind as he began to achieve a level of consistency in his course.

Airsickness was an unexpected hurdle that he had not foreseen and it was a close thing for him to survive. As the first three months of Air Observer School drew to a close, he keenly anticipated the next phase of training at the Bombing and Gunnery School. Ever since a young age, he had been a keen marksman and he looked forward to applying this old skill in his new world. There was also a sense of belonging, having successfully endured the same trials as his classmates. He could never express such a sentiment, but still it was there for the first time for the young boy from the Queensland bush.

Then, without warning on August 5th, everything changed. The commanding officer called the trainees together to address a signal that had been issued by the Chief of Air Staff. As instructors and trainees assembled in the gymnasium, they wondered what had necessitated their immediate attention. They did not have to wait long.

Wing Commander Wittschiebe informed the gathering that there was to be a reduction in aircrew training and there was consequently a call for volunteers. Recruits were asked to either re-muster within the RAAF as ground crew or apply for a transfer to the Army in order to reduce the number of trainees. A sinking feeling fell upon the young trainees and Phillip Zupp was no exception. He realised that if there weren't enough volunteers, they would start to cull trainees and that could end up with a posting to a 'dead end' somewhere on the ground.

The tone was mixed among the young men in blue as they returned to their lodgings to start the inevitable conversation of who would go and who would stay. Phillip was concerned that his bouts of airsickness may count against him and thought he may be on the list to be cut from the course. Furthermore, it was inferred that even those who continued to train as navigators may never leave Australian shores and were even less likely to ever see combat. Neither option was particularly attractive to Phillip who had thought that he had finally broken the shackles of his previous life and was now charting a course in a totally different direction.

He began to consider the third option of transferring to the Army. If he was destined for a ground position, then he'd rather be in a fighting force and he knew that they were still shipping men to New Guinea. He was aware that his fellow trainee Reg Young had served in the Army before transferring to the RAAF and discussed the option of changing teams. Reg looked at him with astonishment and politely suggested that he "wasn't right in the head". He reminded Phillip that life in the Army would consist of sleeping on the ground, living on rations and the very real likelihood of getting shot at overseas. Reg couldn't fathom changing services at this late stage and reminded Phillip that he may not be one of the number to be removed from the course.

It was a strong case that his mate had put forward and he carefully considered the facts as they lay before him. To him, it seemed straightforward and in due course he presented his decision his superiors. He had elected to transfer to the Army and would reluctantly hand back the navy blue uniform that he was so very proud of. His dream of flight had stalled but he could not leave his fate to be decided by others. In a matter of days the wheels were in motion and the boy who had dreamed of service in the skies was set to don khaki and webbing and learn to fight on the ground.

A page from Phillip's Army pay-book shows him on enlistment.

Chapter Six

Down to Earth

There was no hiding his disappointment, but Phillip was never one to dwell. He had received his fair share of kicks in the guts already in his young life and knew there was no point in whining. He packed up his kit and made his way to the railway station for another long haul across the countryside. For a lad who'd hardly ventured beyond the Darling Downs in his first seventeen years, he had now seen a lot of Australia in the past six months.

This time the train was rattling him north to Queensland. As he stared out the window he wondered if he was ever going to break free from his home state. The time in South Australia and the hours spent wheeling around the clouds had been among the happiest in his short life. He had felt he was making progress and putting some distance between him and the life that was being chiselled out for him only a few years earlier. Now as the train pressed on and the climate became progressively warmer, it was like returning home without having really accomplished anything. He had been so very close to a life in the skies, and a chance to play his part in the conflict abroad, but now he was on an earthbound train with a sore backside and still six hours to go.

When he finally reached Queensland his first stop was at RAAF Station Sandgate, the home of No. 3 Embarkation Depot. It was here that he had originally hoped to return to be equipped and cleared for operational deployment overseas but instead he was lining up to hand in his deep blue uniform. Queues and forms seemed to be everywhere in the military and the process of being discharged from the RAAF felt particularly slow and painful. Yet, as soon as the Air Force no longer owned him, he was trucked a matter of miles away to Redbank to join a whole new set of lines and fill in a different set of forms.

This time, the air in the room was different and the predominant colour was khaki. Hob-nailed boots scraped the floor as instructions were barked from stern looking men in stern looking uniforms. With eight months of military service under his belt, the barking was nothing particularly new, but it was particularly obvious that these chaps were not here to suffer fools.

If it had been tedious to be discharged from the RAAF, his enlistment into the Army was at break-neck speed. There were forms, questions and medical examinations, but all were done with due haste. He chuckled to himself as the doctor signed him off as 'Class A1' medically, remembering that the Air Force had precluded him from pilot training on medical grounds of an unknown nature. By the end of the day he had sworn his oath, been kitted out with his khaki clothing and given his orders to 'march out' for initial training in four days time. Cowra, in western New South Wales, was the destination and it was another good train ride away.

For the moment, he had three days' leave and made his way home to Toowoomba. He had been almost triumphant when he left Toowoomba before resplendent in his aircrew uniform. Now he was back again in a different set of circumstances. However, he was in no way embarrassed by his return wearing khaki. To tell the truth, he already felt the Army may be a better fit for the country kid with a rough bush upbringing. Only time would tell.

His mother was outside tending to a tree when he arrived home at Middle Ridge. With his kitbag over his shoulder, his new boots crunched their way towards the house. His mother smiled with the limited emotion that she ever expressed and called out to Fred who was also home on leave from the Navy. The two brothers had been inseparable as boys, but hadn't seen each other in over a year since Fred took to the sea aboard a minesweeper. The three made their way into the house as their father made his way up from the paddock below.

Phillip sensed that the relationship between his mother and father was not the best and knew that Louisa had moved out of the family home for a period. She was unaware that her youngest had any idea of the friction in the household and was not about to burden him with the saga. Nevertheless, as 'Bill' came through the back door, Phillip looked at his father with a low-lying anger that he kept suppressed with his other emotions. For Louisa's part, she maintained an even temper, happy just to have her boys home again and to have one more photo taken with them before they had to leave and make their way back to the war.

Without fuss, Phillip was on another train, this time heading south for his initial training. As the miles ticked by he was made aware that Cowra had been the scene of a violent prison breakout only weeks earlier as the quiet rural township was not only home to an Army training facility, but also Number 12, Prisoner of War Compound where thousands of prisoners from Japan, Italy and Germany were interred. The occupants were a mixture of Japanese soldiers captured during the war in the Pacific, while the Italians came from their failed campaign in North Africa. Those of German descent had mainly been taken prisoner at sea.

The prison camp sprawled over 75 acres of picturesque undulating farmland but, within its barbed wire fences, four defined areas divided the prisoners by nationality and rank. Six towers looked down upon the prison and by night searchlights swept its grounds and the surrounding roads. The majority of the prisoners were Italians and within their culture there was no stigma attached to being taken into captivity by the enemy. However, for the Japanese, failing to die in the field and falling into enemy hands was a source of deeply rooted humiliation and shame. Many provided their captors with false names so their disgrace would not be known of at home.

Their disgrace overflowed in the early hours of August 5th when a bugle broke the silence and one thousand Japanese prisoners emerged from their huts. The attempt to break out en-masse was planned with three groups making for the wire in three different directions while a fourth endeavoured to link up with their officers in a separate compound. To screams of "Banzai!", the sea of prisoners stormed the perimeter with sharpened butter knives and baseball bats for weapons and catcher's mitts and blankets as protection against the wire.

On the fence-line, Australian soldiers Private Benjamin Hardy and Private Ralph Jones manned their No.2 Vickers machine gun as the wave of screaming Japanese charged them. They fired into the prisoners with a slowing effect but ultimately the weight of numbers overwhelmed the two isolated men. In his final moments, Private Jones removed and concealed a critical component of the Vickers gun and undoubtedly saved a number of lives in the process. Both Jones and Hardy were killed but their machine gun was now useless to the Japanese.

As hundreds of prisoners poured over the wire and made their way into the open country, those within the camp began setting the huts alight. Among the chaos, other Australian gunners were starting to lay down effective fire, pinning a number of would-be escapees until control of the camp was finally regained. Those Japanese who had made it to freedom were rounded up the next day by local police and soldiers, including those stationed at the training camp Phillip was steaming toward. Some miles away from the camp, Lieutenant Harry Doncaster was ambushed and killed by a group of prisoners but otherwise there was little resistance to being recaptured. Those who could not face the thought of further incarceration had committed suicide to avoid disgrace for a second time. In all, more than 230 Japanese died that night with another hundred wounded.

In the wake of the breakout there was a heightened level of intensity around the training camp as Phillip entered the gates for the first time. Like 70,000 other new recruits over the course of World War Two, Phillip would make the Recruit Training Centre his home while he learnt the basic skills of soldiering. As he gazed up at Mount Fulton behind the camp, he could make out the forms of men moving in numbers and gashes in the green hill that were serving as makeshift trenches.

With his brown canvas kit bag slung over his shoulder, heads were counted and names marked off yet another roll. It was a little warmer than Mount Gambier, and it wasn't raining, but there was an immediate sense that this was to be a tougher indoctrination that he had experienced so far. The camp itself consisted of rows of huts upon piers arranged fairly close together and in an orderly fashion. There were rows of tents pitched just beyond the huts while a substantial parade ground bordered another edge.

One of the first orders of business was to arrange accommodation. Life was rather sparse inside the huts. The walls were unlined and made from corrugated iron with large pivoting framed windows to permit some level of ventilation. There were no bunks but each recruit was allocated a space about five feet wide with a small shelf fixed to the wall above for the limited number of personal effects he had squeezed into his kit bag. Below the shelves were hooks for hanging coats and rails for towels but, other than that, there were just bare wooden floors. It was a far cry from the relative comfort of the Air Force lodgings, but it mattered little for a boy who had grown up sleeping by the roadside upwind of his grazing cattle.

An older non-commissioned officer with three chevrons on his sleeve barked something at the fresh-faced recruits that steered them towards the door like sheep under the gaze of a cattle dog. With their mess tins and cups in hand they moved out of the hut and lined up in single file for dinner as the sun started to sit low on the horizon. After eating their ration they moved along to be issued with more equipment and this time the items had the genuine feel of war. There was the .303 Lee Enfield rifle; the basic tool of trade. There was a bayonet and scabbard and a British style round helmet or 'tin hat'.

Again they lined up in single file at yet another building and Phillip took the time to silently survey the men around him. They were of all shapes and sizes, some were fair and almost pasty, while others were well built and bronzed. Phillip felt that he fit somewhere in between although he was less than average in height. As he looked at the faces of the other recruits, two caught his eye in particular. Almost in disbelief, he recognised them as Eric Geldard and Mike Heffernan who had also been on the recruit course with the Air Force at Kingaroy. Geldard and Heffernan had both gone to Wireless-Air Gunner training at Maryborough when Phillip had made his way to Mount Gambier for Navigator training. Like him, they had been told they were 'surplus to demand' and were offered the choice of a 'ground job' or joining the Army.

The three exchanged stories as they queued for their issue of bedding which consisted of grey woolen blankets and a hessian sack that would be filled with straw to serve as a mattress or palliasse. Their kitbag would suffice as a pillow. By this stage Phillip was weary of lining up and signing for gear. It had been a long day and he just wanted to lie down and catch his breath. When his issue of bedding was finally completed he was then steered towards another line of men waiting to fill their palliasse with straw. The recruits were now being hurried up and yelled at to get their bags filled and move on. By now Phillip had enough of waiting and without any sense of disobedience he bid Eric and Mike "G'day" and slowly walked back to his hut, threw down the empty hessian bag in his allocated five feet of space and lay down. With his head on his kit bag and a grey blanket over his back he rolled over and went to sleep. Neither the clatter of hob-nailed boots entering the hut nor the bugle announcing the end of the day stirred the youngster. Nor did he notice that he had already drawn the attention of his superiors.

Phillip was already awake when the sergeant burst into the end of the hut yelling at the sleeping recruits to get their day underway. As he stomped down the centre of the building he encouraged them to get up and get ready as roll call was in half an hour and they had to be dressed and ready to go at that time. As the 'old man' exited at the far end of the hut Phillip leapt into life, tidying his bed roll in the customary manner before shaving and throwing on his uniform. After roll call came breakfast and then session after session of training with minimal breaks for eating and none for rest or recreation. Although, in one spare moment, he managed to have his palliasse filled with straw. Such was the pattern of a recruit's life. Being barked at, hurrying everywhere and never stopping from daylight to dark was a new soldier's lot in life. When they failed to meet the standard, as they inherently did at some point, they would be screamed at, chewed out and forced to undergo some penalty that frequently called for a further test of their endurance and temperament.

For Phillip, Eric and Mike, it wasn't a game, but they knew how it worked. Being yelled at didn't intimidate them in the slightest as they had seen the same indoctrination during their Air Force recruitment. Furthermore, for Phillip, if 'Old Bill' only yelled at him as a boy, that was a good day, for more often than not a strap was involved during his childhood misadventures. These chaps could scream until they were blue in the face as far as he was concerned. He would simply acknowledge them and then carry on giving his utmost. Ultimately, this was all the Army was asking of him. To his superiors he came across as a very quiet, determined chap who seemed unflappable. There was a rough, unfinished quality about him but, as Army recruits go, he was already being watched with a keen eye. For, in addition to equipping the recruits with new skills, they were being assessed for which branch of the service they would be best suited and subsequently trained. Phillip was displaying all the right traits of an infantryman, if not something more.

From his term in the RAAF, Phillip was already well versed with military life, badges of rank and how to march around a parade ground, but it was the real skills of soldiering that grabbed his interest. Significant time was spent learning about the workings, care and use of the Lee Enfield .303 rifle and Phillip enjoyed every minute. Not all of the recruits had the rural upbringing and exposure to firearms that he had experienced, so everything from how to load the rifle and how to line up a target in the blade sights was drilled into the keen new soldiers. On the range Phillip's comfort with rifles came to the fore and he excelled, demolishing bulls-eye after bulls-eye with closely grouped shots. In the same manner that he had shot the kangaroo as a boy, his breathing was always steady and his aim rock solid, unfettered by thought or emotion. He also demonstrated a particular care for his weapon, 'pulling the barrel through' with his cleaning kit and wiping it down at regular intervals. He recognised that it was a tool of trade that needed both attention and respect.

And yet, while comfortable in the presence of firearms, the seriousness of the training and its potential for tragedy was reinforced very early on in Phillip's time at Cowra. Three trainees and their instructor had been killed at Howell's Creek when a live firing exercise had gone wrong and the mortar bomb the team were using detonated prematurely. They had all been killed in a bloody instant and now they were to be buried in Cowra with full military honours with the young recruits standing by in an act of respect. Phillip's mind was cast back to the lines of crosses at Kingaroy and of the young airmen who had perished without ever seeing a shot fired. Now there were four more white crosses at Cowra to add to the long list of those killed while training for war.

Along with rifles, bayonets and mortars, there were lessons in unarmed combat and obstacle courses to conquer, clambering over walls and climbing ropes. In the midst of one field exercise, the westerly winds began to stir while Phillip and his cohorts were making their way across a long, dusty paddock. At first the odd cloud of dust was apparent, but soon the wind became increasingly stronger and seemingly gale-force. Gusting up to fifty miles an hour, the trainee soldiers began to lose visibility and struggled to move forward any distance. Their instructors were barking commands but these too were swept up and away by the fierce winds.

Phillip lay prone on the ground, tightening the chin-strap on his slouch hat and lowering its brim to guard his face from the stinging storm. Conscious of the dust filling every exposed orifice, he covered his mouth and nose with a handkerchief and, with equal care, sheltered his rifle; an act that was seen and noted by a nearby instructor. As soon as the first wave of the dust storm subsided, the young troopers were on the move again, making their way back to their lodgings.

On entering the hut, it was immediately obvious that everything there had received a recent coating of Cowra dust. As bedding was shaken out and personal belongings were wiped down, an instructor quizzed Phillip on how his gear had fared and complemented him on protecting his weapon during the dust storm. Phillip acknowledged the complement and said that only his wallet was on the shelf at the time, so no damage was done. As much as he was impressed by the care of his rifle, the non-commissioned officer was aghast that Phillip left his valuables on the shelf and informed him that he was lucky that they hadn't been stolen.

Phillip was taken aback. As rough as his upbringing had been, it was one of open honesty and unlocked doors. He had never imagined there was any risk of theft in the Army and was shocked by the instructor's inference. The older man smiled, patted him on the shoulder and walked away, bemused by the country boy's innocence as he trained to go to war.

As November of 1944 rolled on, their general infantry training continued and Phillip had his first introduction to automatic weapons in the form of the Bren Gun. The Bren was a light machine gun capable of firing 500 rounds per minute and effective up to six hundred yards when it was fired from a prone position with the muzzle resting on a bipod to steady the aim. However, the Australian's had taken to aggressively firing the Bren from the hip as they advanced rather than laying down. Phillip took an immediate liking to the Bren and its firepower and impressed his trainers with his ease of operation despite his short stature.

With the summer, the weather at Cowra grew steadily hotter and the sweat steadily more profuse. Loaded up with packs and weaponry, they were no longer the rawest of recruits and the level of expectation increased along with the temperature. The war in the Pacific was still bloody and any number of those training at Cowra could find themselves face to face with the Japanese. The pressure was becoming more evident on some of the recruits and the reality of the situation was further emphasised when they were addressed by their Commander-in-Chief, General Sir Thomas Blamey. As the young soldiers gathered on the banks of the Lachlan River, General Blamey warned them of what lay ahead and the importance of the role they were yet to play. The words were both sobering and inspiring.

Throughout the training, Phillip surpassed every physical and mental challenge he was set without a single word of complaint. They were long, taxing days that drained the energy yet Phillip grew in both stature and confidence as he was now among the leaders of the pack for the first time in his life. He was no longer the little country boy struggling to hold his own among peers who had received a better start. The best training ground for the Army seemed to be the 'school of hard knocks' where Phillip had graduated with honours. He felt comfortably at home in khaki.

By the end of the recruit course and initial infantry training, he had proven his worth and was seemingly destined for the infantry. As the allocations officer sat across the desk from Phillip, he was weighing up written reports on one hand and the face of the young soldier in front of him. He was obviously impressed with what he saw and voiced what both men knew; that the infantry was Phillip's calling. But there was something more. The officer placed the file on the desk and stared Phillip straight in the eye before asking him if he would be prepared to commit to a more demanding role. Commando.

There was only ever going to be one answer.

The 'Rising Sun' of the Australian Commonwealth Military Forces.

Chapter Seven

Commando

It was late 1944 and the weather in Cowra was dry, hot and dusty as Phillip packed his kit bag and made his way by truck a mere sixty miles up the road to Bathurst where it was equally dry, hot and dusty. His fellow RAAF 'refugees', Eric Geldard and Mike Heffernan, had also been selected for Commando training and joined him as they were 'marched out' of their old home and into the back of the standard army issue truck. Just before leaving Cowra, a parcel had arrived from home and Phillip knew that by its shape and size it was one of his mother's fruitcakes. While it now sat patiently at the top of his kit bag, he couldn't wait to sit down and eat something that didn't come rationed in a mess tin and dished out with a ladle.

After a few hours of rocking, bumping and swaying, the truck lurched to a halt at the front gate of the Bathurst camp. His new home, complete with dust, heat and flies, looked a lot like Cowra. Originally built to accommodate an armoured division, Bathurst was now home to the advanced infantry training battalions where the serious business of combat soldiering would be instilled in every one who passed through these gates. Like Cowra, there were rows upon rows of the unlined corrugated iron huts, with pivoting windows and wooden floors, with yet another 'Tent City' just beyond the permanent buildings. However, unlike Cowra, there were no raw recruits to be found here.

Phillip and the others clambered from the back of the truck and immediately attended another roll call, as if to check if someone had fallen out along the way he thought. He was then pointed towards one of the huts, while the others were in turn steered towards the other buildings. Alone and loaded up with his full issue of gear, the small lad from Toowoomba lumbered up the steps of the hut with a resounding thump coming from his hob-nailed boots.

It was late afternoon as the door creaked open and he could see that the building was almost bare and obviously awaiting the arrival of its new occupants. In the far corner sat one other soldier with his back against the wall and his gear on the floor beside him. The other digger looked up, half-smiled and nodded in Phillip's direction in a form of greeting. Phillip clomped across the floor where the other chap rose to his feet and introduced himself as Bill Elliott, a native of Tasmania, the 'Apple Isle'. Bill was tall and broad-shouldered with a thick head of dark brown hair. He could easily have stepped out of a recruiting poster whereas Phillip provided a total contrast.

The two exchanged basic pleasantries and Bill explained that he had been at Bathurst for some time training as a machine-gunner when he had been transferred to the Advanced Infantry Battalion to become a Commando. He had only been given a moment's notice of the transfer and was left waiting hungrily in the hut having missed eating earlier. Phillip immediately pulled the fruitcake from the top of his kit bag, tearing the wrapping off as he went. Bill eyed the cake keenly as Phillip unsheathed his bayonet and cut the homemade treat into two chunks. The two young soldiers then sat back down on the floor and consumed the entire cake as they chatted, joked and spoke about the days to come. Little did they know that this 'breaking of bread', miles from home, was the beginning of a friendship that would endure for the rest of their lives.

The day then set on their impromptu meal and gradually the hut filled with the familiar forms of men, equipment and palliasses. The conversation exuded an excited tone as these men realised they were being groomed for an elite branch of the Army. They also realised that not all of them would be there at the end of the training. When lights out was sounded, the excitement subsided to the low steady breathing of young soldiers at rest. The rest would not last for long.

Whereas Cowra had provided basic military training for those first entering the Army, Bathurst was where they would learn the advanced skills of a frontline infantryman. It was here that the training was stepped up a level and would introduce Phillip to new weapons such as the Owen sub-machine gun and the hand grenade. It was the first time he had been trained in the use of the hand grenade or, as they often called it, the Mills Bomb. "Mills Bomb" referred to the specific type of hand grenade in use by the Australians; specifically, the No.36M.

Commando

The Mills Bomb was typical of a grenade in appearance with its segmented surface resembling a pineapple to assist in both gripping the grenade and its fragmentation upon detonation. A lever ran down one side and was held in place by a ringed pin and, when that was removed, a closed hand. Throwing the grenade released the lever, bringing down a central striker, and setting the detonation in motion following a four second lapse as the fuse burned down. The grenades were not light, weighing the best part of a kilogram. They could be thrown accurately to about twenty yards and then it was time for the thrower to take cover as the fragments could travel much further.

Training started with simply learning the correct way to throw the grenade using disarmed examples in open paddocks before progressing to live examples. Much greater care was taken when live grenades were used, with trainees being given one-on-one tuition while his mates sheltered in a brick bunker. At some distance away, another instructor was positioned in an observation post to assess the outcome. A number of the trainees were a little nervous the first time, knowing they had an explosive device in their hand with only a four second fuse, and dreaded the thought of dropping the weighty weapon.

Phillip had no such reservations and while he had never graced the sporting fields to perfect his arm throwing a cricket ball, he was very adept at hurling grenades. His distance and accuracy impressed the instructor as his small frame suggested that this was an exercise he would struggle with. In fact, he greatly enjoyed the experience and keenly waited for his turn to toss another grenade and feel the reverberations and hear the explosion as it detonated. It was fun and reminded him of throwing rocks at trees on Gowrie Mountain when he was a boy although he knew, at a deeper level, that ultimately it would not be gum trees on the receiving end of his grenades.

When found to be proficient at tossing the grenades, Phillip was shown another means of launching the lethal projectile using his rifle. This was achieved by clamping a cup-like discharger on the end of the barrel and screwing a disc to the base of the grenade. The disc allowed for a snug fit when the pin was pulled and the grenade placed in the cup. A special blank cartridge would be inserted into the breech and, when the trigger was pulled, pressure from the blast would race up the barrel and launch the grenade, releasing the lever and triggering the fuse as it left the cup. It was fired with the safe end of the rifle jammed into the dirt and could send the grenade up to 200 yards. Once again, Phillip thought that this was all good fun.

Christmas Day offered a rare reprieve and a special meal for the trainee soldiers. Unfortunately, the day was one of oppressive heat and a plague of flies that seemed interested in both the cuisine and every orifice of the dining soldiers. If the mercury was nudging forty degrees Celsius, then it was a good deal warmer in the hall. Even so, it was a day for camaraderie and some old-fashioned cheer and no pestilent insect was going to spoil an Aussie Christmas.

Phillip was in his element. The heat, long hours, minimal food and rough conditions suited him down to the ground and he thrived on the challenge. It was a structured existence where he was assigned tasks and simply did what he was told; no great deal of thought needed and no particular philosophy required. In his limited downtime he had no interest in having a beer from the canteen and preferred to sit back and read from the AP129 Pilots' Flying Manual that he acquired during his short stay in the Air Force. The well-worn manual was a treasured item that lived in his kit bag despite the sheer lack of room available. The AP129 was a tenuous link to a dream he still held onto, although the reality of his situation meant it was a distant dream. Even so, he thumbed through the pages every chance he had, absorbing the facts and figures of flight.

From his thoughts of the skies, he would return to earth with an explosive thud. Beyond the hand grenades he would spend hours training on the Bren light machine gun he had first fired at Cowra. Now he would get to know the weapon even more intimately, stripping it down, cleaning it thoroughly, before re-assembling it and firing it once again. He knew every part of the Bren off by heart and could pull it apart blindfolded. Best of all, he loved firing it from the hip.

Bill Elliott was also right at home with the Bren having already spent a good deal of time training on the heavier Vickers machine gun. The two young soldiers shadowed each other as they progressed through the various stages of training and inherently wound up side by side whenever they were called to take part in field exercises that simulated warfare. On one occasion Phillip and Bill scrambled into a slit trench dug into the ground as a tank advanced on them in a simulated frontal assault.

Amid the thundering sound of the advancing tanks, Phillip decided to sneak a look over the edge of the trench only to come face-to-face with the wide track of the tank seemingly inches away. He slid back down into the slit trench as the lumbering beast passed over the top of them, showering the two soldiers in dirt and noise. The very earth shook and reverberated through their chests as they were held in its shadow. The tank turned and made a second pass with its machine guns ablaze and coloured tracers flitting across the sky. A moment later, the threat had passed and they moved up, out and onwards from their hole in the ground.

Phillip's mates from his Air Force days were shaping up as well as the days at Bathurst ticked along. Along with Eric Geldard and Mike Heffernan, the reality of advanced jungle training was approaching fast. For while the basic principles of soldiering could be taught at Cowra and Bathurst, their rural New South Wales pastures were far removed from the ultimate destination; the jungles of New Guinea. It was a land of narrow tracks and rising ridgelines where the enemy was expertly concealed in the dark depths of matted foliage. Downpours would pound on the slouch hat and mud would well up from beneath the boots. Wounds would fester in the tropical heat and malaria would visit in the form of mosquitoes sneaking through the nets in the middle of the night.

Every soldier bound for New Guinea would undertake jungle training before shipping out from Australia. However, for those designated to train as Commandos, that training would be longer and more intense. As the weeks passed at Bathurst, Phillip, Bill, Eric and Mike knew that the real test was yet to come and their time training in the skills of jungle fighting would ultimately determine whether they would make the grade.

The level of camaraderie was growing with every passing week and their time at Bathurst was drawing to a close. When Mike Heffernan was partly hobbled by a badly infected toenail, his first thought was not one of pain but of being left behind when his mates set off for jungle training. He concealed the injury from the instructors but it grew steadily worse. His mate Eric Geldard performed some minor surgery with a razor and a pocket-knife, but the relief was only temporary. Mike then had the idea to strike the offending toenail to shed it, much like losing a thumbnail when you hit it with a hammer.

He immediately stripped off his boot and sock, lit a cigarette and asked Eric to smash the offending nail with his rifle butt. Eric couldn't do it. Too little force and it wouldn't work, too much and he could break Mike's toe and neither outcome would solve the dilemma. He would still end up moving back a course while his mates shipped out. In the end, Mike found a more viable solution with trained medical assistance. One night on leave in Bathurst he tracked down a civilian doctor who he convinced to pull the nail clean off without a word to anyone. With the minor surgery completed, Mike put his boot back on and returned to camp and resumed his training without complaint. Fate can deal an interesting hand and, given what lay ahead for Mike Heffernan, perhaps submitting to the toenail would have been a more favourable outcome. But he wasn't to know.

When May 1945 arrived, their time at Bathurst had come to an end and it was time to move on to the next phase of training that would ready them for New Guinea. When the orders came through, Phillip, Mike and Eric were all given a short leave to go home. Such news was generally well received, but Phillip realised that Bill had not been granted leave and was going directly into the next intense stage of Commando training without him. It was disappointing for Phillip as he remained the same quiet lad from Toowoomba and becoming mates like he had with Bill was not an easy process. Nevertheless, orders were orders and they each had their own road to tread.

It was time to once again pack their limited belongings into their brown canvas kit bags and move on. Phillip carefully packed his Pilots' Flying Manual among his other mandatory issued equipment. As he readied himself for a short break, Bill was preparing for a totally different few weeks. Where he was going, Phillip would soon follow and, despite being within Australian shores, it was a destination that some referred to as 'Hell Camp'.

The Army knew both the realities of jungle warfare and the cost of ill-prepared soldiers only too well. To ready them for this alien world, they had devised a training base that would replicate the harshness of their future theatre of operations in every possible way. Every soldier destined for the Pacific war since the end of 1942 had passed through its gates and very few had fond memories of the experience. It lay to the north, in Queensland, among dense rainforest and steep ranges. It was terrain designed to take a man's physical will to the absolute limit while the combat conditions would tax his mental state like never before.

Aboriginal people had inhabited the region for centuries and from their language came its name. It was an inconspicuous name that belied the challenge that lay ahead. One simple word of three syllables.

Canungra.

Phillip (far right) with fellow trainee commandos at Canungra. Ron Wells is behind the tent pole.

Chapter Eight

Canungra

There was no denying that a couple of weeks' break in Toowoomba provided a pleasant change from the barking NCOs and long days of Army training. Most of all, Phillip appreciated his mother's cooking served up on a plate and seated at a table. He would help his father in the paddocks, or fix a shed somewhere to keep occupied, but it all seemed a little mundane compared to tossing grenades and firing Bren guns from the hip. More than anything he lamented the fact that Bill was already at Canungra and training for the real thing.

During his leave in Toowoomba, the war in New Guinea came a step closer when Phillip heard about his cousin Ivan being shot. Ivan hailed from up the road at Boonah and was the son of his father's brother. He was a few years older than Phillip, but they had played together as boys when their families got together. The details were very sketchy but apparently Ivan's unit had been attacked and he had been shot through the chest as he manned his Bren gun. He had survived and there was even talk of a medal for his heroism.

Phillip was proud of his cousin, and relieved to hear of his survival, but Ivan's chance to see action also frustrated him to a degree. The newspapers continued to announce that the war in New Guinea was virtually over and the Americans were now chasing the Japanese from island to island, all the way back to Tokyo, albeit with horrendous losses. Just as the downturn in the war in Europe had put paid to his aircrew ambitions at Mount Gambier, it seemed like the shooting in New Guinea may stop before he ever joined the fray. He reflected that his entire military career may span two branches of the armed services, and involve years of training, but fail to ever see active service. The thought irritated him and, when combined with the daily labour of the farm, it had him just about bursting out of his skin to resume his training.

His mother couldn't understand his urgency, although it did remind her of her brother James before his departure on the 'great adventure' in World War One. Now he lay in a French cemetery beneath a headstone that bore the same rising sun that now adorned her son's slouch hat and jacket collar. James was older when he enlisted, 34, and happily married. He could have easily stayed at home and tended the farm but he too had that urgency; that need to play a part. Louisa could neither understand their motives nor express her reservations in either case. James was dead, John Zupp had lost his leg in France and now Ivan had been shot. It seemed to be something that men simply must do and she would be as stoic and supportive as required despite what her heart may feel.

Phillip was her youngest and a kindred spirit. He shared her love of reading and possessed an enquiring mind that had always called him far beyond the Darling Downs. He had been fragile as a small child, wheezing and struggling for breath when the nights grew moist and cold, but he survived when little Reggie and Edna had not. He was her youngest and her brightest hope in what had been a tough life on the land. At the tender age of nineteen, he was still just a boy to her despite what he had seen and accomplished in his short life. Now he was not only marching to war, but he could not wait to be there and it weighed heavily upon her.

Phillip was never attuned to such matters of the heart and, even if he was, he never entertained the possibility that he would be the one who would catch a bullet. He simply wanted to head for Canungra and counted down the days until the train would once again set him free from the farm. When that day came he simply kissed his mother on the cheek, shook his father's hand, threw his kit bag over his shoulder and walked out the door without hesitation. It was a fair distance to the railway station but trudging miles was now his vocation and he was contentedly on his way again.

It was a good thing he was content to walk for miles, for there was a good deal of distance to cover at Canungra. Even when Phillip stepped off the train from Brisbane and joined his fellow soldiers at the railway station, the instructors informed them that the trucks was only for their gear and that they'd be marching to the camp.

Compared to the rolling paddocks and black soil of the Darling Downs, Canungra was another world. Located south-west of Brisbane in the rugged

Macpherson Ranges, the terrain possessed sheer climbs and drops through dense rainforest. It had become the Jungle Warfare Centre a couple of years before, but still the area had not been adequately mapped. It was prone to torrential downpours that only made the way ahead more difficult and was home to all forms of pestilent insects and quite literally more snakes than you could poke a stick at. It was a dark, dank environment that smelt of rotting vegetation and a variety of other stenches. All in all, it was well suited to prepare Australian soldiers for warfare in the jungles of New Guinea.

The Jungle Warfare Centre had different units to train the basic foot soldier, officers and, in the case of Phillip, Commandos. This section was known as the Independent Company Training Centre (ICTC). At the beginning of World War Two, the Australian Army did not possess any 'Special Forces' units, as they are known today, so by 1941 they had set about doing so in earnest. Rather than being known as Commandos at this stage, they were Independent Companies and received specialist training tailored to their task. Patrolling in small numbers, sabotage and demolitions were just some of skills employed by these companies that operated 'independent' of the normal regimental structure. In the ensuing years, the companies were re-structured and became Cavalry Commando Squadrons; the units that Phillip and his contemporaries were bound for.

However, there was still some way to go before they could rightfully wear the black beret of the Cavalry Commandos. As they formed up at Canungra, Eric Geldard, Mike Heffernan and John Collins were there as were a number of faces that Phillip didn't know. Gradually introductions took place and the group grew with the likes of Ron Wells, Les Turner and Ian Wharton adding to their number. Les and Ian had both enlisted back in 1942 but this was their first taste of Commando training. Once again, Phillip was one of the smallest in the entire unit, although, in the time since he first enlisted, he had developed physically and now boasted a pair of square-set shoulders and a far more muscular frame. Army life agreed with him.

This group of lads would form the core of Phillip's circle over the coming weeks but, for the moment, the first task was to form groups to share a tent. Les Turner was older than the rest at 34 years of age; the same age as Phillip's Uncle James when he set off for France in World War One. It was a rather broad gap in years, but he and Phillip seemed to hit it off from the outset as the two stowed their gear in their new home.

There was little time for rest and this was a pattern that would become the norm throughout the course. Their eight weeks of training would be intensive to say the least, starting at five in the morning each day and extending deep into the night, six days per week. Part of this intensity stemmed from the amount of content that had to be taught in a short time but, more to the point, it was aimed at introducing the incredible physical and mental fatigue that is indicative of combat operations.

The instructors at Canungra were veterans of active service who had a genuine appreciation of what their students were in for. From the first briefings they set about creating a mind-set and dispelling any myths that might be in the young soldiers' untrained minds. These lessons were taught in the civility of permanent buildings and were the only time the trainees would see a floor, table or chair. Like any good classroom, the walls of the buildings were lined with educational displays and the nature of these was indicative of the school's purpose.

There were charts of New Guinea supplemented with pins, flags and photographs to further detail the current situation to the north. There were full-sized dummies of Japanese soldiers, complete with Asian facial features, kitted out in their full military issue. There were photographs of the enemy's artillery and armoured vehicles, the contents of their packs, more charts, flags and the occasional propaganda poster. There was a deep emphasis on knowing the enemy for the war against the Japanese was also a war against a vastly different culture and philosophy.

From the outset, the training instilled a deep sense of suspicion and mistrust of the Japanese. These men didn't look like, or fight like, the enemies in the European conflict and they were very prepared to fight to the death. Even when they had apparently surrendered beneath a white flag, they were known to detonate a grenade killing themselves and their captors in one final, defiant act. Bodies of their dead would be booby-trapped and live soldiers would play dead before opening fire when the enemy approached. They were not to be trusted and they did not fight fair.

There were also reports of Japanese cannibalism emerging from the Pacific war that reviled every Allied soldier to his core. Along with their proximity to Australia, these acts of barbarity made it easy to hate the enemy. The instructors were also keen to dispel any myth that the 'fight to the death' mentality made them exceptional soldiers. They were men, just flesh and blood, like any enemy. They were cunning and expert in the art of ambush, but they were just men and would fall to a bullet or a bayonet like any other.

The tales of Japanese brutality and suicide struck a chord with Phillip but, like his mother, he always buried his opinions deeply within. He never weighed in on a philosophical debate. For him there was no point. He was a soldier and this was his job, it was not a place for moral debate or self-examination, it was war and people kill people in wartime. He sat attentively and absorbed every scrap of information that his instructors imparted, often tagged with the line, "this may save your life!" He pored over the charts of New Guinea on the wall as now his childhood fascination with the atlas was supported by the knowledge gained during his navigator training. To him, the topography of the country looked brutal and he could only imagine what it was like to gain a footing, let alone fight on the steep muddy slopes, at places like Kokoda. He thought of his cousin, Ivan, and wondered where he was right now and how he was faring.

It was not long before Phillip was confronted with his own challenging topography. Soldiers had died while training at Canungra and others had 'downed tools' and given up, too exhausted and mentally shattered to continue. The philosophy was to reproduce the jungle combat situation as closely as possible and this included the exposure to the live firing of weapons in their general direction. The entire camp and assault course was pockmarked with concealed fox-holes from which instructors would fire rifles and machine guns over the heads of their new recruits. As the rookies crawled beneath the barbed wire in full kit, the instructors were there again firing live rounds from a Bren gun over their backs.

When they went to cross over rivers on narrow logs, snipers would drop shots near them in an attempt to shake their nerve and send them plunging into the water. Whether on land or in the water, mortars could be dropped close by at any time, while in places pre-set charges were remotely triggered only feet away from Phillip and his mates. Everything they did was accompanied by the rattle of live fire and explosions with plumes of water or clumps of dirt spraying in their face.

The goal was to de-sensitise the soldiers to the noise of combat, allowing them to shut out its confusing effects and focus on the task at hand.

The terrain around Canungra was ideally suited to the task, offering up rainforest conditions and steep slopes, but also valleys. These valleys were ideal for simulating patrols where the main body could move through the valley, shadowed by platoons on either elevation, providing protection. Phillip would march for twenty miles and swear that all of it was uphill, while the sheer density of the foliage offered its own challenges. Stinking of the rotting vegetation in the moist world below the jungle canopy, the thriving, tangled vines provided a green wall that could take hours to hack through for a gain of only a couple of miles.

Out of the bush and back in camp the lessons and drills continued. Bush-craft and survival skills, digging foxholes, bayoneting dummies, throwing grenades and stripping down a variety of weapons blindfolded. Blindfolds were also used in a drill that saw a lone soldier with a weapon, deprived of sight, standing within a circle of troops. The surrounding troops would randomly make a noise such as snapping a twig, scuff their feet or even cough while the 'digger in the middle' had to swing around and point to where he best judged that the noise had originated. It was the very opposite of the other noise de-sensitisation training.

Ever since Cowra, bayonet practice had been on the schedule but at Canungra the intensity stepped up with more frequent training. There were marked trees that had to be bayoneted on the assault course as well as chaff bags arranged on poles to represent the human form. The key was not merely to skewer the dummies, but to ensure that the bayonet was twisted on entry; this gave a greater chance of an immediate kill.

The days were long, starting with a sprint to the creek to wash off and get ready for the day. Food was rationed sparsely and 'Bully Beef' and 'Dog Biscuits' became the norm. There never seemed to be enough food for the amount of exertion. Being hungry and tired was the normal mode of operation at Canungra. However, none of the Commando trainees seemed to complain and for Phillip it all seemed fair enough. While others were losing weight, he continued to bulk up and was quickly becoming the fittest that he'd ever been.

Phillip wondered if he would see Bill at Canungra, but they never seemed to cross paths. In fact, he didn't really interact with anyone but his own group of

CANUNGRA

trainees. Having been selected for this specialist role, the training was harder and more intense than the average infantry chap received. They were made to move more quickly and often overtook infantry sections along the way as they climbed the steep tracks of Canungra. A key requirement of their new job was to be highly mobile and to operate independently in small groups. Their course lasted two months, weeks longer than the standard course and their pack marches covered more ground.

The assault course possessed 'pop-up' targets made of iron that had to be shot or bayoneted. There were trees to climb and ladders to scale as well as substantial flying foxes that spanned great distances and heights. One particular exercise involved crossing a river between two cables with full equipment. The trainees would hold the upper cables with their hands and move their feet along the lower cables while live firing rang in their ears and the water beckoned below.

When Phillip's turn came he prepared to set out on the wires but could hardly reach the upper cable. He stretched full length and slowly curled his fingers around the cable before using all his strength to pull it closer. Slowly and methodically, he heaved on the cable every time he changed hands as he made his way across the river, straining with every step but refusing to give in or fall. Ron Wells was next in line and watched him grit his teeth and make his way across before turning to the other Commando trainees and saying, "That Zuppie's a tough little bugger." From that day on his nickname stuck.

Phillip took everything in his stride, his only shortcoming being tasks that directly involved water; he was a very poor swimmer. He had fooled around in some creeks and dams as a boy but never formerly learnt to swim. Unfortunately, Canungra had a fair share of water-based challenges. There were crossings to the backdrop of exploding mortars and there were crossings in the nude to preserve valuable clothing and equipment. Phillip conquered them all. However, there was one demon that involved leaping into the deep Coomera River. The twenty-foot jump was made from a tower in full kit, including pack, helmet and rifle. There were tales told in hushed tones of soldiers that never surfaced having leapt into this dark, bottomless water mass. It reminded him of tales of Boomites and Bunyips that lived at the bottom of dams and rivers.

When his turn came Phillip walked to the edge without hesitation even though his heart was beating out of his chest. He paused and looked down into the dark water below, sucked in a chest-full of air and jumped. The fall was okay, and even the impact with the water was acceptable, but the burbling nothingness that filled his ears as he became submerged was eerie. He opened his eyes and saw nothing. He wondered if he was even the right way up until he saw bubbles racing towards the light of day above him. He kicked his legs, weighed down by his cumbersome boots and endeavoured to use his arms in an effective manner.

All too slowly, but surely, the surface grew nearer until he was free once again to breathe in the fresh air. Now all he had to do was make it to land, which he did using the most ungracious dog paddle ever seen, much to the amusement of Les Turner and the lads. Phillip didn't care, he'd made it and not a single Bunyip had dragged him to the bottom.

As he briefly returned to the tent lines that afternoon, there was a group of Commandos, resplendent in their black berets, packed up and ready to depart Canungra. He was mid-way through wishing he was leaving with them when he recognised the tall figure of Bill Elliott among their number. The two mates shook hands and exchanged Canungra tales. Bill gave him a 'heads up' on what to expect in the final weeks and Phillip asked where Bill was headed. As usual, the newly trained Commando had no idea at this stage. It was a meeting in passing and Phillip now wished even more that he was leaving and wondered if Bill would be seeing action soon. For Phillip, the final challenge was still to be conquered, but he knew that his turn would come.

Their training would culminate in a week-long exercise in the wilds of the surrounding terrain. They would be operating independently for a week, living off rations, sleeping little and making do the best they could. Navigation was difficult in this unmapped area, although the Jungle Warfare Centre had a series of fire beacons atop various hills that would smoke by day and blaze by night to help guide the trainees. It was a tough exercise that tied in all of the challenges Canungra had thrown at them but, with the training they had been given, they were well prepared. In the few spare moments he had, Phillip pondered where he would be going next. His money was on New Guinea but these matters were never discussed in advance.

One dark night blended into another until the course was at its end. He had trekked hundreds of miles, crossed rivers, fought physical and mental fatigue at the deepest level, and now he was finished. As he arrived back at the tent lines he was tired and hungry, but extremely satisfied. The past couple of months at Canungra had been the toughest he'd known, but he had succeeded and, with that, many of the demons of the shy country boy had been banished. If the military had offered him self-respect when he enlisted, the Jungle Warfare Centre had now stamped it on his papers.

He knew the biggest challenge still lay ahead as he thumbed the Rising Sun on the black beret that showed the world that he was now a Commando. He then tossed it with his other gear, lay back on his bedding and turned over in his mind what the future may hold.

He needn't have pondered too long. In a week he would finally be on his way to war.

Phillip with his mother and brother, Fred, prior to embarking for New Guinea.

Chapter Nine

New Guinea

Phillip spent his leave at home in Toowoomba before making his way back to Canungra one last time. There was still no word on what the next posting would be, although their new instructions offered up a substantial clue. From Canungra, the next stop was readying for embarkation overseas at the 5th Australian Reinforcement Depot at Logan Village about twenty miles away. As the hum went through the gathered men, the infantry soldiers were instructed to board the nearby trucks while, once again, the Commandos only loaded their heavier equipment on board. Again, they were to march to their destination, still carrying their light gear, rifles and the Bren.

On July 12th 1945 the newest Commandos of the 2/6th Cavalry Commando Regiment made their way to Newstead Wharf and boarded the troop-ship HMAS *Duntroon*. Zupp, Geldard, Heffernan, Collins, Wells, Turner and Wharton all made their way up the gang-plank and onto the converted armed merchant cruiser. Built in 1935, *Duntroon* had originally been a civilian vessel but now plied her way across the ocean delivering her vital cargo of Australian soldiers.

A bitter irony struck Phillip and his mates as they waited to depart and sail to war, for all around them 'wharfies' sat smoking and playing cards. They were having a stop-work 'meeting' over one issue or another and had brought the docks to a grinding halt with greater efficiency than a Japanese bombing raid. Here were the young soldiers preparing to leave their homeland, and possibly die in the service of their country, only to be delayed by an industrial issue.

When *Duntroon* finally steamed out of Brisbane, it was only the second time that Phillip had seen the ocean in his nineteen years. The first was as a boy, before times had become hard, when the family ventured from the Downs to the coast for a short break. He and Fred had rides atop camels along the beach and tasted the rare delicacy known as ice cream while his sister Alice snapped photographs with her Box Brownie. The day had also left a stinging memory of sunburn with Phillip.

Now he was a young man and not merely splashing in the ocean's edges, he was on his way to a foreign land. A number of the young soldiers continued to wave to loved ones until the last glimpse of the city had faded from view. Then they remained a little longer to ponder the days ahead and contemplate whether they had walked upon Australian shores for the last time. No one was there to farewell Phillip but he didn't care. He went below decks, found himself a hammock, stowed his gear and waited for news of their destination.

Australia was well behind them when the news was announced that they were bound for New Guinea and the current campaign on the northern coast between Aitape and Wewak. The 6th Division, their division, had relieved the Americans in the region about a year before and had gradually worked its way up along the coast, pursuing and flushing out the remaining Japanese. The 2/6th Cavalry Commandos had played a major role in patrolling and moving out ahead of the main Allied forces as they slowly, but steadily, reclaimed the territory.

On receiving the news, Phillip dug out a small atlas from his kit bag and ran his finger along the New Guinea coast. He recalled the topography from the charts at Canungra and knew that, while Aitape and Wewak lay at sea level on the coast, not many miles needed to be covered inland before the terrain rose steeply and became the thick jungle they had trained for. The war was now only days away.

The *Duntroon* was a slow vessel and seemed to pitch and roll even on the smoothest of seas. The railings that were once occupied by waving soldiers were now handholds for those same brave men as they emptied their guts over the side of the ship. So far Phillip had kept his nausea down in his belly, which surprised him given his bouts of airsickness at Mount Gambier, and, as the days passed, the rest of the soldiers found their sea legs too.

By day, the decks were covered with men keen to take in the sun and breathe in the fresh air. Space was at a premium and life at close quarters was the norm. By night, the swinging hammocks would be filled with young men tossing and turning, some because they were uncomfortable, others in anticipation of the days ahead. Some passed the time by reading while others played cards for fortunes

New Guinea

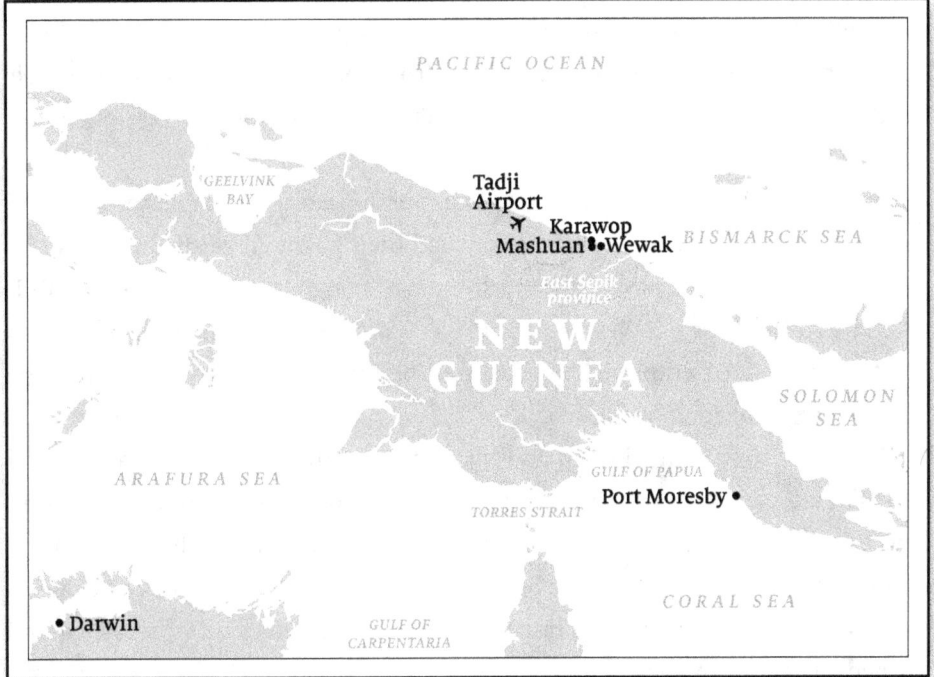

they did not possess. Phillip took to standing by the ship's railing and absorbing the sights and sounds.

The sheer enormity of the ocean struck him greatly. The horizon was so distant that it was beyond the eye's ability to focus. Of a morning, as the first rays of light breached the line where the world met the sky, an array of colours would slowly transform the blackness into day. All the while, the ship's engines throbbed and the water churned against her sides. Occasionally they would have visitors, dolphins that skimmed the surface and fish that completely breached the waves and seemed to fly. For a boy from the bush, these were amazing sights of an almost alien world.

Slowly, the *Duntroon* parted company with Australia, tracked around the eastern tip of New Guinea and set about sailing up the country's northern coast towards Wewak. Inevitably, the conversation among the troops would return to the topic of the war and what they could expect. At Canungra they had been told to travel light and only carry what was absolutely necessary. Their issue of a steel helmet seemed to be at odds with that philosophy and this was a sentiment echoed by their immediate superiors. A helmet was fine in open warfare as protection from falling debris stirred up by artillery but, in the jungle, it was simply too heavy and too hot. So Phillip and the other boys from the 2/6th took to throwing their helmets overboard as they neared Wewak. From here on it was to be slouch hats or black berets.

The coastline grew closer and activity on the ship started to increase. A general hum came about the soldiers as they packed their gear and readied to leave the *Duntroon* after a week at sea. Finally, the vessel's engine tone changed before it slowed to a halt just off Wewak near Cape Wom. With the men marshaled on the deck, they stood crammed together waiting their turn to disembark on to the landing barge pulled up alongside.

When the time came, Phillip and his mates scrambled down the nets in full kit with rifles slung over their shoulders. Once in the landing barge they moved forward to allow others on and stood shoulder to shoulder behind the raised ramp that formed the bow of the barge. With no forward view, the short ride to the beach was accompanied by instructions being barked as water smashed and sloshed against the barge.

As the barge slowed to a stop, the rifles came down from their shoulders and into their hands. Phillip was unsure what to expect. While the area was in Australian hands, the sight of newly arrived soldiers spilling out from the front of a landing barge would surely make a tempting target. Whatever the outcome, he was ready and knew that his war was about to begin.

On that July morning, the ramp opened with a rattle and a thump, tethered by two huge chains. As soon as it hit the water the NCOs and officers began to call their men forward and down the ramp where they entered the shallows, just before the beach, but hardly got their feet wet. The coarse sand of the beach crunched beneath their boots and Phillip was immediately taken aback by the devastation. Huge palm trees had been blown off at the base and entire areas of foliage flattened by some form of bombardment; probably naval. Wrecked motor vehicles lay motionless and the ground was littered with abandoned military equipment. They kept moving forward towards the waiting trucks as he attempted to take in every sight, sound and smell.

Once loaded the thirty new Commandos were driven north-west along the coastline. Everywhere they looked seemed to lay more Japanese equipment;

wrecked and abandoned. Phillip thought that, with so much gear just wasting away, surely they must be beaten by now and wondered if there was really any fighting left to do. The truck finally came to a halt at Cape Karawop and they took the first look at their new home. This was where the 2/10th Cavalry Commando Squadron was stationed and, for Phillip, Ron Wells, Les Turner, Ian Wharton and most of the other reinforcements, it was the end of the voyage. Eric Geldard and Mike Heffernan were destined for the 2/9th Squadron, further up the coast at Dagua Airstrip. Once a thriving Japanese base, Dagua was now overgrown and littered with more than a hundred wrecked aircraft and rusting engines.

He bid farewell to Eric and Mike who he had known ever since his first entry into the Air Force eighteen months earlier. They had been to Kingaroy, Cowra, Bathurst and Canungra together but now it was time to part ways. He shook their hands, confident at seeing them again at some point. After all, they were going to be just up the road.

As they drove off Phillip realised that a connection had developed amongst this small band of Commandos that he had only ever felt before with his brother and cousins scouting around Gowrie Mountain. These men weren't family, but they had sweated, strained, endured and laughed together to form a mutual bond that he couldn't really put his finger on. They were men that he was prepared to fight beside and, if need be, die beside. By any other name, this was Australian mateship and it was new to the small lad who had been harshly bullied at the Toowoomba foundry. Yes, these were his mates. He liked the sound of that.

Now here he stood with Ron, Les and Ian as they were assigned a 'Troop' and lodgings. Phillip hoped that as the names were called he'd remain with the other lads, but fate intervened and it wasn't to be. As Les and Ian made their way to join 'B' Troop, Phillip was assigned to 'C' Troop. His disappointment was short-lived when he realised that a smiling Bill Elliott was the culprit behind the allocation and even had a space lined up in his tent. The two shook hands and made their way to Phillip's new digs, busily chatting as they made their way through the tent lines.

The camp was situated on a small cape with the water to their backs and the New Guinea jungle beyond the 300 yards of fence-line. A small knobbly hill stood nearby overlooking the rows of tents where the commandos lived when they were not on patrol or engaging the enemy. Sitting on their stretchers, Bill and Phillip caught up on what had happened since they were last together before Canungra and shared a few tales from their training there. Phillip was curious as to whether the war was just about done and whether there was anything still going on. Bill soberly assured him that there was and that he'd seen enough already. This month had already seen Bill Gray permanently blinded by a hand grenade and Ray Jones had lost a leg to a booby trap at Koanumbo. Lieutenant John Ryan had been wounded and Cahill killed in an ambush in the same area. The 2/10th had been in the thick of it.

Phillip was relieved on one hand to think that he might see action and yet he realised from Bill's tone that this was still a deadly serious business despite the inference that they were simply mopping up the last remnants of General Adachi's 18th Army. For the 2/6th Cavalry Commando Regiment, the Aitape-Wewak campaign had been a significant affair that had commenced late in 1944. They had sent out the preliminary, probing patrols in advance of the 6th Division's drive east towards Wewak.

The motto of the 6th Division was 'Through Mud and Blood to the Green Fields Beyond' and, while it dated back to World War One, it was equally appropriate in the current situation. It was a difficult campaign characterised by stretched supply lines and hideous terrain. Progress had been slow as one arm of the advance progressed along the coast while the other moved east via an inland route, along the Torricelli mountain range, aimed at driving out the Japanese and cutting off any access to food in the process. The shortage of food had become a major problem for the enemy and disturbing reports of cannibalism were beginning to circulate among the Australians.

One by one, the Australians assumed control of But, Maprik and finally Wewak in May 1945. By the time Phillip arrived in Karawop, General Adachi's 18th Army had withered from its original strength of 140,000 men in 1942 to less than 20,000 and was holed up in the mountains south of Wewak, riddled with malaria and malnutrition. There was, however, still a great deal of fight left in them.

The 2/6th Commandos had actively patrolled the area throughout the campaign and continued to do so. Clashes were inevitably on a small scale, but no less lethal to those soldiers involved as the Japanese remained expert in the art of concealment and ambush. Even at Karawop, the enemy continued to come down from the hills and probe the camp's perimeter.

Only days after Phillip's arrival, a 'sentry boy' patrol, consisting of local natives familiar with the area, reported they had located the enemy at Mashuan, around three miles south of Karawop and a mile beyond Suik. The sentry boys had not been able to identify the strength of the force in the village, only their presence, so the 2/10th decided to send a patrol the next day. Their objective was to determine the strength of the force and ideally destroy them, recovering any documents or maps that may be in their possession.

'B' Troop was to participate in the patrol led by two officers, Lieutenants Lawler and Redmond. The newly arrived Lawler would be the patrol leader while the experienced Redmond would be there to offer guidance and assess the unit's performance. However, the bulk of the patrol was made up of the newly arrived reinforcements including Les Turner and Ian Wharton. All in all, the two-day patrol was seen as a means to offer exposure to the new Commandos and they were scheduled to leave Karawop early the next morning.

When news of the patrol filtered down the next day, Phillip was disappointed that he was not going. He wondered whether Bill's bid to have him placed in 'C' Troop had cost him a place on the patrol and a chance to see action. As the morning sun began to draw sweat through their khaki, the 22 Commandos moved beyond the camp's perimeter and started out on the main track south towards Suik. Phillip sent Les and Ian on their way with an envious wave and half-hearted smile. They nodded back at their mate before he turned and walked back towards the tent line. The war had started in earnest for them, he thought, when would his time come?

Chapter Ten

Mud and Blood

Les and Ian were on their way, each armed with an Owen sub-machine gun capable of emptying its 32 round magazine in the blink of an eye. They continued along the main track out of Karawop and began the arduous climb into the mountain range. By midday the patrol had located an abandoned Japanese position and shortly after paused for lunch. Moving on to Suik, they checked the village for any indication of enemy activity before establishing a defensive perimeter on the high ground and settling in for the night.

As they moved further south the next morning, it would later become apparent that their patrol was not going unnoticed. The jungle had eyes and not all of them were friendly. By ten o'clock on the morning of July 23rd, they had reached the approaches to Mashuan. The village was located on a narrow spur of rising land with the track running along the crest past a number of huts. From the first hut to those at the far end of the village was only about two hundred yards and at that point human habitation gave way to long kunai grass.

At first, all that was to be found were vacated Japanese sentry posts at the entrance to Mashuan. However, the patrol's sentry boys reported that there were also a further two sentry posts at the extreme end of the village on either flank. The decision was made to attack using fire and movement, an old military tactic that has one unit laying down suppressive fire while another moves forward. It was decided that the scout group, with Lance Sergeant Jack Simpson, Les Turner and Ian Wharton, would advance to one side of the track, while the support group, with Lieutenant Redmond and Trooper Jeffers, would lay suppressive fire from the other.

As they readied to advance, the young Commandos may well have believed that the greatest potential threat was posed by the sentry posts that lay ahead of them. In fact, as if anticipating the Australians' arrival, the Japanese had moved up to forty men with light machine guns into concealed positions within the kunai grass at the far end of the village. They now sat silently waiting for the unsuspecting Commandos.

None of the Australians had moved more than ten yards when the Japanese opened fire, cutting down Les Turner and Ian Wharton immediately. They fell together, one atop the other, as the machine gun fire carved into the support group on the other side of the track. Redmond and Jeffers were now brought down and their medical orderly, Corporal Mahoney, shot through an arm and his throat himself, crawled to aid Jeffers. Similarly, Simpson broke cover from behind a mound of dirt to aid Turner and Wharton, but was initially repelled by gunfire striking him in the shoulder and neck.

The firefight was intense with the Australians pinned down by superior, concealed firepower. Corporal Mahoney now lay in the open at the mercy of his critical injuries and the enemy until the covering fire from the unit's Bren gun permitted Trooper Denzel to emerge and retrieve the wounded medical orderly. It was an amazing act of bravery for the native of Woodstock, New South Wales, as this was his first time under enemy fire.

The battle continued, with the Australians managing to claim some of the Japanese who were not hidden in the kunai, but it became apparent to the patrol leader that continuing the fight was futile. Lieutenant Lawler ordered the withdrawal and the Australians fell back, recovering their dead and wounded to the edge of the village. They paused and took stock. Redmond, Jeffers, Turner and Wharton were dead. Simpson and Mahoney were both wounded, and were being attended to by Denzel, but needed to be evacuated. Lawler estimated that they had accounted for eight of the enemy. It was now time to head back to Karawop, although this time they did not follow the established track from Suik.

The remnants of the patrol entered the camp at four o'clock that afternoon. 'B' Troop had paid a heavy price and Lieutenant Lawler set about reporting the events of the past two days and offering suggested artillery positions from which Mashuan could be bombarded. Phillip had seen the patrol arrive at Karawop and immediately noticed the wounded and then the absence of his mates, Les Turner and Ian Wharton. It was a little while before the details of the fight began to filter through the camp, but he knew early on that Les and Ian were dead.

At first it was difficult to grasp as he had only seen them the morning before as they set out on what was meant to be a routine patrol. However, after only a matter of days it was now obvious to Phillip that the word 'routine' was incongruous with any aspect of warfare. When he had seen the abandoned equipment and demolished palm trees at Wewak, he knew that he had arrived in a war zone, but only now had the absolute, finite reality of the stakes hit home.

He was not taken aback by the realisation. In fact, now he wanted even more desperately to play his part and square the ledger to some degree for the loss of his mates. As he lay in his tent that night he processed the loss, but felt no particular grief. It was as if that element of human emotion had not ever been bestowed upon him. He felt deeply for his mates and their families, but knew there was no room to have his logic blurred by the events at Mashuan and he could best serve Les and Ian by continuing on. His thoughts in order, he rolled over and went to sleep.

The next day saw another patrol of twenty depart Karawop to escort an artillery contingent to Suik from where Lieutenant Lawler had suggested Mashuan could be fired upon. This time the patrol did not follow the established path out of Karawop, but followed a network of creeks cross-country to position at Suik and conduct their barrage. Unfortunately, the patrol lost wireless communications early in the day, but the barrage of Mashuan was later reported as "successful" and with "excellent coverage". The patrol also reported that they were unable to find any trace of the ill-fated patrol's track to Mashuan due to the torrential rain that had fallen overnight. Without any sentry boys who were familiar with the area, it was decided to re-trace their steps and return to Karawop, their job done.

Over the next two days another patrol was organised to return to Mashuan to make a reconnaissance of the area with a view to identifying and burying the Australian soldiers killed on July 23rd. This time the patrol was to leave nothing to chance. It was to leave on the morning of the 27th and be comprised of more than fifty men under the command of Lieutenant James McDonald. Those men would come from 'C' Troop and Phillip, along with Ron Wells and Bill Elliott, would be among their number.

The recce started out early Friday morning and also stayed clear of the main track and prying eyes. They cut directly through the jungle following a previously laid signal wire to a 'Kanaka pad' and then tracked due south to Mashuan. It was rugged jungle with minimal clearance ahead and virtually no visibility to either side. As the line of men made their way through the matted vines and mud, Phillip thought of the similarities, and the differences, to Canungra.

While the terrain and foliage possessed a fairly common nature, the constant live firing by the instructors had sought to de-sensitise a soldier to the element of surprise. However, what Canungra had failed to capture was the silence of the jungle broken only by the rustling of the moving soldiers and the occasional squawk of a bird Phillip could not identify. Then there was the water. Water drip, drip, dripping from the canopy above onto the leaves and ground around him. The sound of trickling water weaving between rocks, squelching beneath his boots in the mud, or sloshing in the water bottle on his hip. It was an array of sounds that would normally fail to attract his attention.

The lead scout was ten paces ahead of the second scout who, in turn, was another ten paces ahead of the next group of men who were at least three good paces apart. Armed with a mixture of rifles, Brens and Owen guns, they had reasonable firepower, but many also had minimal experience. Phillip was conscious of maintaining his spacing, not to group up and offer an easy target, but he didn't want to get separated either. He'd heard that's what had happened to Cahill a few weeks before and he'd been killed. He watched every footstep, conscious not to trip and fall. The weight of his pack seemed insignificant, as he'd hauled heavier at the Jungle Warfare Centre, but now it was the intent of his gear. He had his rifle, extra ammunition and three grenades hung from his belt and, given the events of the 23rd, there was every chance he would be called upon to use them in anger.

The dark green wall that was the jungle was just so dense that he found it hard to comprehend. You could step on the enemy and you wouldn't know it until it was too late and yet his dug-outs and booby-traps were potentially everywhere just waiting to turn the wet darkness into a cacophony of flames and pain. Phillip sucked in a breath, hacking some foliage and watching the webbing straps of the man ahead step after bloody step. It was hard work, but he was young, fit and well trained. But what about some of those blokes in the infantry who'd gone straight from their fancy schools to a technical college in Sydney? Those who'd slept in beds, between four walls and beneath permanent ceilings every day of their life until they joined up. The volunteers and the militia-men, the 'chocolate soldiers', who'd found themselves caught up in the horror of Kokoda with their backs to the wall and the enemy in their face. Mud and Blood, he thought, it should be the motto for any man that fights in the jungle.

Life had prepared Phillip for this world. Long days, sleeping by the track and eating whatever you could scrounge had been a way of life. It hadn't seemed tough at the time. It was simply the way it was. Now it was proving to have been the best form of education for this life in the jungle. Here, in this alien world, the runt of the litter and the butt of the foundry's pranksters was holding his own in an environment where many might falter.

The line of Commandos paused momentarily and squatted to bite through one of their 'dog biscuits' and take a swig from their drink bottles. It was a simple act that seemed to challenge the sky above for, from the moment they stopped, the heavens opened up with a mid-morning downpour. Within minutes, cascading rivulets appeared from nowhere and flooded their boots while drops that seemed as large as golf balls pounded down from above making the jungle even wetter and even darker. Phillip squatted, hunching over his weapon in a vain attempt to keep the critical mechanisms dry in a gun that was designed for far more exposure to the elements. Then, as quickly as it had started, the rain stopped and humidity took its place. Wet gear, wet boots, wet track, wet jungle. Drip, drip, drip. On they moved.

After a few hours, the sounds of the jungle were interrupted and the squawking bird set to flight as the artillery position opened up and sporadically fired on Mashuan for thirty minutes. The canopy of leaves above seemed to shed a few more drops as the sound wave bounced across the treetops. A short time later they opened fire again and Phillip thought that if they hadn't softened up the Japanese the first time, this second inundation should do the job. If not, it would serve as a good warning that they were on their way.

Around midday they had reached Mashuan and held their position some distance off. Two sentry boys made their way forward and scouted the village for any indication of the enemy but returned some time later convinced that the Japanese had moved on. Very cautiously the patrol advanced into the village and set about securing their position so they could attend to their dead mates. It appeared that the Japanese had been gone for some time as there was no evidence of particularly recent habitation, although the question that remained was just how far distant were they now.

Three dead Japanese were found close to where the firefight had started, but it was the bodies of the Australians that really mattered to the men of 'C' Troop. Ron Wells came upon the bodies of Les Turner and Ian Wharton first, with Phillip close behind. At that point the reality of the war hit them both with a vengeance. They had trained side by side with these men, shared a tent with these men, travelled by ship to New Guinea with these men. Now they were dead and horrific violence had befallen their mates' bodies. The desperation of the Japanese and the absolute brutality of war in its most primal form confronted the two young soldiers and it was something that neither man would speak of again for half a century.

There was still a great deal of tension in the air and the very real possibility that the Japanese were concealed only feet away, waiting to open fire just as they had a few days before. Ron and Phillip set about digging graves for their mates near the entrance to the village with one digging, and the other standing guard with weapon at the ready. Ron particularly sensed that they were being watched and felt sure that someone was a mere stone's throw away as the tension continued to well up inside him. That tension too would remain with him long after that day at Mashuan. After a couple of hours, the four Australians and three Japanese had been laid to rest by the men of 'C' Troop and it was time to return to Karawop.

It was dark by the time they entered the camp and the Commandos had been going for fourteen hours. They were tired and hungry as they retired to their tent lines after what had been a very long day physically and mentally. They all knew that the war must be drawing to a close soon, but today had cemented in their consciousness that it was definitely not over. There was still an active enemy. He was starving and he was under-equipped, but he was tenacious and very prepared to stand and fight. Phillip knew they were out there, but today had not been the day.

Following their return from Mashuan, offensive patrols seemed to cease for the 2/10th. Even so, the Japanese continued to probe the perimeter of the unit's encampment, primarily by night. It was an uneasy pause in operations with the end of hostilities seemingly just around the corner, but with an enemy that were not aware of such developments and even less inclined to give up the fight. Some of the soldiers exhibited signs of mental duress with two being removed from duty while a third became extremely anxious and determined to set out alone on patrol and confront the Japanese. His armed attempt to recruit one of his officers to accompany him ended badly and he was stripped of the loaded weapon before being sedated and evacuated out the unit. Still the Japanese probed their defences.

One such evening Phillip reclined on his stretcher in his trousers and singlet, resting with his hands behind his head. Without warning there was a crack and a slap of the canvas beside him and slowly the realisation of a stinging sensation across his abdomen. He raised himself to a half-sitting position and looked at his stomach only to see that a narrow slice had been taken out of his singlet and a long thin graze was beginning to redden with a small oozing of blood. He reached down to check that there was no further damage than a deep scratch and all was in order. He lay back down and laughed and laughed. His first enemy action had been a stray round that had literally caught him napping and, fortunately, he'd been sucking rather than blowing, he thought.

In the wee hours of August 6th, a sentry fired on two Japanese who were probing the perimeter near 'A' Troop. They h ad s ucceeded i n p ositioning themselves beneath a cliff that prevented the Australians firing upon them, although they did attempt to root out the culprits using grenades. After two hours, the cloud cover moved across the moon and plunging the cliff into darkness. The Japanese took the opportunity to make good their escape. The subsequent Australian clearing patrol found an abandoned 'Blast Bomb' constructed of sticks of dynamite and a mortar fuse as well as evidence of one of the enemy being wounded. The improvised device had the potential to cause significant damage but had fortunately not been delivered.

As these events unfolded at Karawop, an American B-29 Superfortress named 'Enola Gay' was taking off from the Pacific island of Tinian. Under the command of Colonel Paul Tibbets, the 'Enola Gay' was carrying the atomic bomb, code-named 'Little Boy' and destined for Japan. The Superfortress secretly swept across the northern tip of Saipan and over Iwo Jima with mainland Japan now only three hours away.

While this historic flight was unfolding, the decision was made at Karawop to delay 'C' Troop's flamethrower exercise until the next day. Phillip was disappointed at the news, but instead prepared to watch the 2/10th take on the Regional Headquarters that afternoon in a softball match. As he was waiting at Karawop, the 'Enola Gay' arrived overhead Hiroshima at 30,000 feet and released 'Little Boy'. The bomb detonated 2,000 feet above a T-shaped bridge in Hiroshima's central district with a force equivalent to 12,500 tons of dynamite at over 7,000 degrees Fahrenheit. As the massive mushroom cloud rose into the upper atmosphere it was visible up to 400 miles away, while the land below was flattened with devastating force.

By the time the B-29's wheels had touched down at Tinian Island, the 2/10th had asserted their authority over Regional Headquarters in the softball by nine runs to four. It was a small, obscure victory, but little did those participating in the match realise that the date had just been etched in history and an end to the war in the Pacific had just drawn a good deal closer.

News of the atomic bombs over Hiroshima and, subsequently, Nagasaki did not reach the Australian troops with any great haste. Rumours that "the Yanks had dropped a big one" circulated, but official reports were far harder to come by. When the rumours were substantiated, it caught most of the Australians by surprise and Phillip, without knowledge of nuclear physics, found it difficult to grasp how one single bomb could create such widespread, comprehensive damage. Nevertheless, the bombs dealt the death blow to Japan, killing thousands upon thousands of their citizens and introducing the spectre of a "rain of ruin from the air" as President Truman described it. As the world stood in awe of the sheer brutality and power of the dawn of the atomic age, Phillip was without any deep philosophical perspective regarding the horror of Hiroshima and Nagasaki. He was simply a soldier.

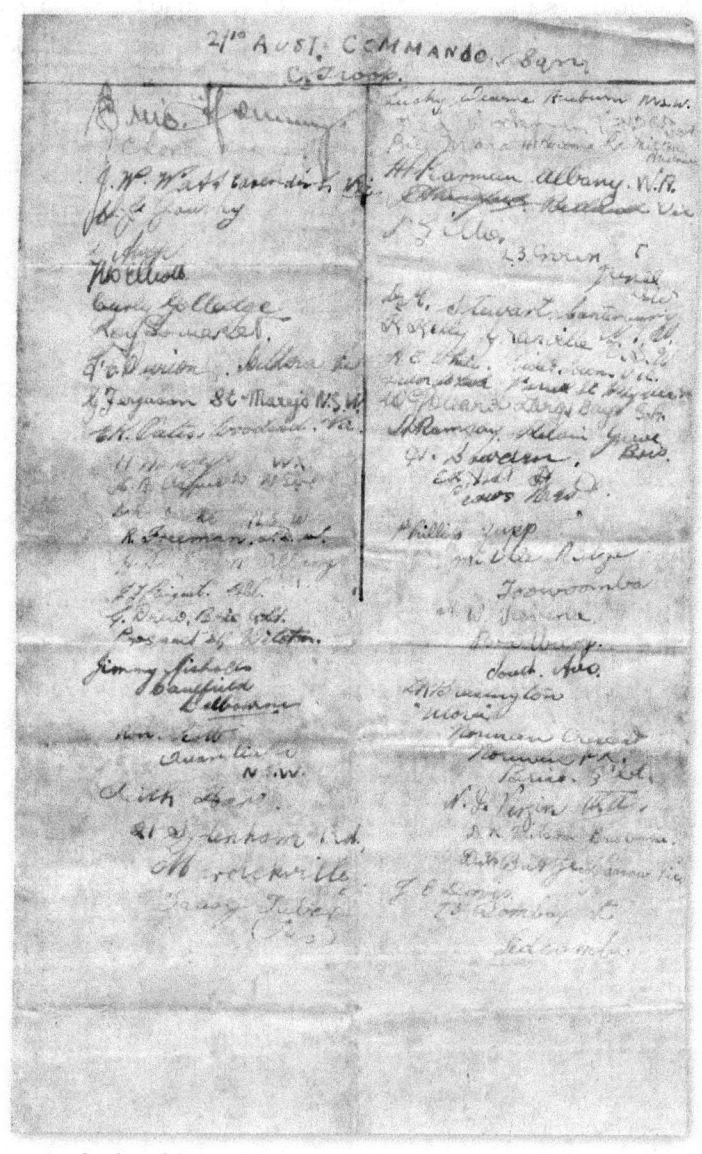

On the day of the surrender, Ron Wells had the members of the 2/10 Cavalry Commando squadron sign this piece of fabric. Phillip has signed midway on the right-hand side.

Chapter Eleven

An Uneasy Peace

While the atomic bomb had for all practical purposes put the outcome of the war beyond doubt, news was slow to travel to Karawop and even slower penetrating into the mountains beyond where the last contingents of General Adachi's army remained. For all the power and might displayed by the Allies from the skies over Japan, any news of an unconditional surrender was still not forthcoming. So life for Phillip and the 2/10th continued much as it had for the past couple of weeks with no patrols, but the occasional night raid by a small number of brazen Japanese troops refusing to give up.

The cape-based camp at Karawop was defended by a perimeter of around 500 yards running from water's edge to water's edge with the triangular point of land behind it. Along the fence-line were nine sentry posts that were manned by night and two outposts further out on higher ground that were occupied around the clock. From the wire hung tins with bullets in them, designed to jingle and jangle as an early warning system should the perimeter be breached. Even so, the Japanese would still come down from the hills by night and poke at the Australian defences leading to brief, sporadic exchanges of fire.

By day, there was less tension and the men participated in softball matches and swimming carnivals with the occasional evening movie. Their spirits rose at Karawop on August 11th when the Overseas News hinted at an early unconditional surrender by Japan. For Phillip the war seemed to be ending very quickly. Void of patrols, it was a waiting game punctuated by a couple of hours each night on sentry duty. That night, the Japanese were particularly active.

One evening he heard the exchange of gunfire a few hundred yards away and seemingly from one of the outposts ahead of the camp's perimeter. Within the hour there was commotion once again but this time it was much closer to his tent lines. He threw his legs off his stretcher and grabbed his rifle, scampering across to the perimeter at the water's edge where he knew the Japs had tried to penetrate previously. Amid the firing of the Australians, the night turned momentarily into day as a Verey pistol fired a flare high into the air. In those seconds of illumination, Phillip spotted a couple of Japanese scampering away and immediately dropped to the ground to fire.

Lying flat, his elbows dug into the ground, Phillip pulled the rifle butt against his shoulder and released the safety catch as he lined the blade sight up on the centre of the man's body. At that moment his breathing slowed and his heart along with it. The sound of the gunfire around him seemed to fade into irrelevance. His finger eased the trigger back to the first point of resistance. All was steady, all was calm. All in an instant.

Crack!

Like the kangaroo all those years ago, the man in his sights never flinched initially, but then folded on one leg and began to stagger. The flare's light was fading fast.

Reload.

Crack!

Now, once again, it was too dark to see. The enemy continued to test the defences throughout the night until daybreak finally pushed them back deep into the jungle. The next day a clearing patrol found evidence of enemy casualties out near the attack on the outpost, but little was to be seen near where Phillip felled his Jap. In his heart and until the day he died, the shooting that night provided little solace or any real sense of satisfaction.

For Phillip, it was one small blow against the enemy that had taken Les and Ian. He knew that, in the grand scheme, it meant little, but it meant something to him and the absence of a body was frustrating. It seemed that in all of these actions where the Japanese pushed at the camp's perimeter and shots were fired, drag marks and blood would be found, but never any bodies. This was never how he'd imagined the war to be and now it was close to an end.

The next day the 6th Division was officially instructed that no more active patrolling would be carried out; not that any had been taking place at Karawop anyway. So it continued, softball and flamethrower practice by day and sentry duty

An Uneasy Peace

by night with the enemy occasionally surfacing in small numbers. There was DDT spraying to combat malaria and ongoing issues with mis-firing hand grenades were being addressed. However, for Phillip, the war seemed to be in limbo.

Then, on Wednesday, August 15th, the official word came down the wire. The war was over! Japan had agreed to an unconditional surrender. The camp erupted at the good news. While Phillip had only been in New Guinea for a matter of weeks, this was the end of a long road for some members of the 6th Division who had been at war for years. The Sixth had seen action at Bardia, Tobruk, Greece, Crete and Syria before returning to Australia only to be turned around to fight in the jungles of New Guinea. Yes, for them it had been a very long war.

Guns were fired and cheers were sent spiraling into the air. An old Japanese 75mm Field Artillery Gun was called back into service to fire a few rounds too. The weapon had seen better days, however, and was ultimately fired by holding a metal file against the shell's percussion cap and smacking it with a hammer. Softball was played in the afternoon while others laid back and thought what it all meant. In the evening, Padre Bramich held a Thanksgiving Service for all to attend.

However, telling the Japanese that the war was over was yet another matter as they remained in the jungle, isolated and out of communication. Well aware of this, General Blamey's 'Order of the Day' on August 15th reminded the Australians that "no order has been received to cease fire" and "the enemy will be killed wherever he is found unless bearing the white flag of surrender." They were sobering words but a poignant reminder that, until the Japanese knew the war was over, they were still in the business of engaging the Australians. It was a very restless and potentially dangerous peace.

In the small dark hours of one morning, Phillip and Bill Elliott were on guard in a slit trench, silently reviewing the day's events. It was a hot, clear evening and the two young soldiers sat there in unlaced boots and no socks, attempting to stay cool as the sweat ran down their backs. The sounds of the jungle were isolated, as Bill looked out with his grenades at the ready while Phillip manned the Bren gun. Then there was an uncharacteristic rustle from beyond the perimeter and in an instant they were under attack with shots emerging from the dense jungle ahead. The unmistakable cracking of small arms fire was pouring out of the jungle as the bullets skimmed and thudded around the two young Aussies.

Bill began to throw the grenades as Phillip brought the Bren to life firing measured bursts towards where the jungle was erupting. Seconds later, Phillip yelled in agony but continued to fire the Bren. Between the curses, he continued to send bullets spiraling towards the enemy in rapid succession while Bill readied to change the Bren's magazine. As he slammed the new batch of ammunition into the weapon, he paused for a moment to check that his mate was alright, sure that he'd been hit by enemy fire. Then Phillip yelled again, "I'm okay, I've just got a boot full of bloody hot shells!". In this case Phillip had been 'wounded' by his own Bren gun ejecting its steaming used shells onto his bare leg. When the danger had passed, the two sat back in the slit trench and laughed until they were nearly in tears. It was the last action Phillip would see in New Guinea, although an unforeseen war lay in his future.

That conflict was years away as the 2/10th began preparing for the surrender of the Japanese in the area. Food was still scarce, even for the Australians, so catching a five-foot shark provided the entire squadron with a welcome meal of fried fish. As the Commandos participated in an athletics carnival at Karawop, their mates at the 2/9th were still at work, responding to reports of Japanese activity in the area.

Phillip's mate from Canungra, Eric Geldard, was in the hospital at Cape Wom having been on the receiving end of a bullet from a mate's Owen gun. Mike Heffernan and others from the 2/9th were located around Tokuku Pass, which was situated inland from Dagua on the rim of the Highlands. The narrow pass had been the scene of vicious fighting including artillery bombardment and air strikes from Australian Beaufort bombers. Lieutenant 'Bert' Chowne had posthumously been awarded the Victoria Cross for charging Japanese machine gun positions during the fight. It was now a scarred landscape of exploded trees and flattened jungle foliage.

The Commandos manned an outpost at the pass some distance from the established infantry units that occupied the area. Between the two was 'no man's land', always with the potential for the Japanese to sneak in and create havoc. As a consequence, the 2/9th still patrolled an area that was littered with booby traps, despite the fact that Japan had surrendered a few days earlier. On August 18th, with the war over, nineteen year-old Mike Heffernan was on a clearing patrol responding to reports of possible Japanese activity in the area. On what should have been a straightforward patrol, Mike tripped a booby trap and was killed by the blast from the grenade. A teenager who had only been in New Guinea for a few weeks, he was to be the Commandos' last casualty of the war.

Some said that it was an enemy booby trap while others reported it to be one of their own. One account related to Phillip was that Mike had dropped his Owen gun and activated the device when he bent down to retrieve it, before standing upright again and saying apologetically, "It's my fault. I dropped my weapon". Then he collapsed. The details Phillip received later were scratchy, but the fact was that Mike was now dead. That was enough. He had known him since they first joined the Air Force at Kingaroy and both had re-mustered into the Army and the Commandos at the same time.

As Phillip sat in his tent and contemplated bad news once again, he realised that the attrition rate had been relatively high among the 'Canungra Cannibals' who had arrived in recent weeks. Of his relatively close group of eight mates that had shipped out with him, three were now dead and he'd had a couple of 'scrapes' as well. However, it was the waste of Mike's death that was particularly hard to swallow as the enemy had already formally surrendered.

That surrender really took hold in the Karawop and Wewak area a few days later when General Adachi emerged from the jungle and laid down his arms. The beleaguered remnants of his once mighty force also straggled out of the jungle; starving and beaten. They emerged in large groups or as pairs or even singly. Some were in shorts, some trousers, bedraggled with their small cotton caps atop their heads and under the cover of a white flag. Phillip had been trained to hate and mistrust this conniving enemy when he was at Canungra and the past few weeks had only intensified his feelings towards them.

The ultimate humiliation for General Adachi came when he ceremonially surrendered his sword and signed the surrender at Cape Wom airstrip near Wewak on September 13th. Some of the members of the 2/10th were shipped down by barge to witness the surrender of the Japanese 18th Army to Australian Major-General Horace Robertson. Like his men, General Adachi attempted to maintain a level of dignity dressed in uniform with rows of ribbons, riding boots and spurs. But, on closer inspection, the dark brown uniform was dirty and hanging loosely on his withered frame, while the boots were unpolished and the spurs rusting.

Under the gaze of the 6th Division who had battled so hard, Adachi handed his

Samurai sword to Robertson over a small wooden table on which the surrender documents lay. It was the final act in a campaign that had seen Adachi ultimately lose ninety per cent of his men; many of them perishing due to malnutrition. As he flew out of Wewak on board a RAAF Tiger Moth biplane, his war was over. He was sentenced to life imprisonment for war crimes committed under his command, but within two years would take his own life in a prison camp on Rabaul.

The war had now ended and the last remaining Japanese dribbled out of the jungle. On one occasion a couple did surrender in novel circumstances by wandering into the back of a Betty Grable movie one evening. The first Phillip and Ron Wells knew of the surrender was when a 'dust up' started in the back of the tent. Far from being a disagreement between diggers, it was a group of Australians setting upon their foe who had apparently been sitting quietly in the back row for some minutes! However, that was about as exciting as life was to be over the next few months.

Conscious of maintaining discipline and morale, more sporting competitions were held and a school was established to prepare the men for civilian life. Compounds were built to hold the Japanese prisoners-of-war, with many shipped to nearby Muschu Island.

Phillip would spend a good deal of time by the water where Bill Elliott taught him to swim. This was a critical skill to pursue another pastime; fishing with hand grenades. With food still in relatively short supply, Phillip and his mates would hurl grenades into the shallows to catch fish. Following the explosion, the stunned fish would float to the top of the water where the boys of the 2/10th would dive in, throwing the fish to the shore. It was a case of the 'quick and the dead' as the local New Guinea natives were also very adept at entering the water and salvaging a meal to cook.

Food was welcomed from any source, although when Phillip and Ron Wells wandered back into camp one day, they were warned off a rotting pig by the medical orderly that had accompanied them. The animal had been dead for some time, and parasites had begun to eat some of its flesh, but this didn't overly deter Phillip as he eyed the pig. The orderly's words of "Don't even think about it, Zuppie!" had faded in Phillip's ears by the time he had dumped his gear and headed back to the pig with his bayonet in hand. He butchered it up, steering clear of the obviously tarnished flesh, salvaging a good deal of acceptable meat which he carried back to camp. That night a very thoroughly cooked meal of pork was enjoyed by all; even the medical orderly.

Never the greatest at correspondence, Phillip hardly ever troubled the very limited mail service. In contrast, his mother would periodically write to inform her youngest of the latest happenings in Toowoomba and about the family. One such letter contained pleasing news about Ivan who had now recovered after being shot in combat earlier in the year. His mother wrote that Ivan had been awarded the Military Medal and, while she was unsure of its standing in the Army world, she was sure that it was a great honour. She had seen a copy of the citation for the award and it had been printed on the letterhead of the Office of the Governor General.

The citation said that Ivan had been wounded near Bougainville back in February. He had been manning a Bren gun when his platoon had been attacked by a large party of Japanese armed with mortars, machine guns and hand grenades. They attacked Ivan's position for over an hour and he repeatedly fought off the Japanese even after he had been shot through the chest. He ignored the wound and continued to fight until finally he collapsed on the Bren. By that stage the fight had been won. Phillip was proud of his cousin and subtly reminded that he had missed the real action by only a matter of months. Then he laughed. He too had been 'wounded' under fire, while manning his Bren, by his own hot shells. Well done, Ivan.

Phillip maintained his passion for flight and continued to flick through the Pilot's Flying Manual whenever he had the chance. He would scrounge a ride whenever a truck was heading up to Dagua and spend the day crawling over the wrecked Japanese aircraft that littered the abandoned airfield. There were light-twin engine bombers and a few single-engine fighters with kunai grass already growing up through them.

Some were mere shells, engineless corpses of aeroplanes, while others had survived quite intact. Into these he would clamber and flick switches and move levers, often with his flying manual on his lap to assist in identifying the various components that were all engraved in Japanese. He could push and pull the cockpit's control stick and watch the movement of the control surfaces on the wings and tail, always imagining the air flowing over the aeroplane and how it would respond in flight.

His biggest trek in search of aeroplanes saw him venture to Tadji, just to the east of Aitape. It was home to 100 Squadron RAAF and was a base for their Beaufort bombers which had been so active throughout the campaign. The squadron had worked in co-operation with the Commandos on numerous occasions before Phillip's arrival and the two units still shared a bond from that time. As he wandered around the airfield he came across a wrecked Beaufort in among the jungle scrub, the result of a landing accident early in 1945. It had been stripped of many parts for use on other Beauforts, but remained fundamentally intact. This time, as Phillip sat in the cockpit with his manual on his lap, he was interrupted by a RAAF officer who queried what he was up to. When Phillip explained his situation and showed him the manual, the officer enthusiastically escorted the young man to an operational bomber and showed him through it in detail. Phillip was overwhelmed as the pilot explained every detail to him and answered his long line of questions. In his heart he knew that he still desperately wanted to fly.

As the weeks passed by, Phillip would venture up the track and explore the jungle, always wary that a stray Japanese could still be encountered. Along the jungle paths he would discover abandoned foxholes and gun pits and marvel at the bush-craft used by the enemy to conceal them. Occasionally he would happen upon a body beside the track, sensing the stench well before he ever encountered a body. If he ever did sight a body, inevitably it was decomposing and in some tortured, contorted posture. Such sights unsettled some, but they never really disturbed Phillip. He thought no more of it than the carcass of the dead cattle littered about the farm in drought. For him it was more the smell of rotting flesh and guts intermingling with the gaudy scent of those damned frangipani flowers that seemed to irritate him. At times one smelt as vile as the other and he thought that the blooms may just as well have been coated in blood for he could not distinguish a difference.

At times, as well as bodies, he would discover items that he would salvage and stuff into his kit bag, mementoes of his time in New Guinea. A water bottle and a Japanese jacket were a couple of items with the small lightweight jacket actually comfortably fitting his slight frame. In its pocket he found two medals, engraved and undoubtedly identifying the owner. One still bore the ribbon, while the other had lost it somewhere along the line in the campaign.

His most treasured item was a Japanese sword that bore marvelous handiwork and seemed to be a grade above most of the swords that he'd previously seen. Its owner had seemingly hailed from a family of status and this weapon had finally ended its historic journey in the distant jungles of New Guinea. The top of its handle was engraved with flowers while the blade itself was finely etched along one edge. The handle was criss-crossed with tightly bound chord while the guard at its base was metal and once again etched, but this time with a basic pattern. What remained of a red tassel also hung from the handle and seemed to be more ceremonial than a way of attaching the sword to a belt.

Back in his tent, Phillip cleaned the sword and water bottle to a more presentable state. At the time, trade was underway with the natives in various goods ranging from baskets and spoons to model canoes. Another enterprising man was engraving Japanese water bottles and selling them to his fellow soldiers. Phillip cast his eye over his handiwork and figured he could do an equally good job. He traced a rough outline from a completed bottle and then sat down with a darning needle and began to scratch a pattern into the lightweight metal.

First he etched the outline of an Australian Commando, complete with beret and a simplified 'Rising Sun' badge. He filled the background with unfurled Australian and British flags, while below the Commando's torso the words "2/10 AUST. COMMANDO SQN" were displayed with equal pride. At the top, just below the bottle's spout, he personalised the bottle with his own details, "TPR. P. ZUPP QX62143 NEW GUINEA". Along with his sword, jacket and medals, he packed the bottle for the journey home, whenever that may come.

A highlight for some of the troops came when their beer ration of two bottles was handed out, normally in conjunction with pay day. For Phillip beer held no real allure and he would generally give Bill Elliott his ration, until the amber fluid

The Japanese water bottle etched by Phillip.

was handed out on one extremely hot day. This time Phillip drank the cold beer and by the time he was through his first bottle, the non-drinker was well and truly intoxicated. He giggled and swayed and recounted one of his many 'dirty ditties' as the lads lined up to have their pay book signed. There was a deal of mirth in the queue as 'Zuppie' always had the knack for getting a chuckle out of them and now the sight of him with a beer under his belt just added to the humour.

When he came to the front of the queue, he stepped up to receive his pay from Lieutenant Griffiths. Before anyone could stop him, he reached up and put his arm around Griffiths' shoulder and slurred, "Thanks Griffo, old mate!" The giggling turned to silence as they all awaited the officer's response to this outlandish break from procedure. Fortunately for Phillip, Lieutenant Griffiths had a sense of humour and he began to laugh with the assembled men erupting shortly after. For Phillip's part, he staggered back to his tent, lay down and promptly rolled off his bunk on to the ground face first where he proceeded to sleep for the next few hours. It would be a number of years before he ever had another drink.

General Blamey, 'Old Tom', who had addressed Phillip at Cowra, had taken the salute at a Parade at Wewak at the end of October. Resplendent in their uniforms with contrasting black berets and white webbing belts and boot-top gaiters gathering in their trousers, the Commandos cut an impressive picture. Their commander had addressed them and congratulated them on the completion of the Aitape-Wewak campaign. He explained that everything would be done to return them home as soon as possible but shipping shortages were making this a challenging task. Inevitably and rightfully, the longest serving would have first priority to sail home. Unfortunately for Phillip, he was one of the most recent arrivals in New Guinea so his return to Australia was still a good way off.

Phillip was seriously considering his options as sitting around New Guinea didn't seem to hold much allure. The end of the year was fast approaching and there was no sign of a boat to take him home. Both he and Bill had been transferred to Wewak, while Ron Wells lay in hospital critically ill with malaria. When Bill was transferred to Rabaul, in New Britain, Phillip wondered what was to come next for him. Even should a boat pull up to the dock tomorrow and take him home, what was there? Every man and his dog would be laying down his arms, taking off his uniform and looking for a job in the real world.

An Uneasy Peace

War weary Japanese prisoners of war at Karawop.

Ever since he was old enough to enlist, all Phillip had known was the order and routine of the military. They fed and clothed him and all they asked in return was that he do what he was told. Already his time in the Army and Air Force had shown him more of Australia than he'd dreamt of seeing, taken him across the oceans to New Guinea and shown him the exhilaration of flight and the tension of combat. In two years, he had lived. At nineteen, he'd grown as a man and already outlived three mates who had been cut down in the prime of their lives.

He cherished life as only those who have risked it can fully appreciate and longed for the adventure to continue. There was nothing back at home except for a shrinking Army and a dreaded life on the land. Bill was off to New Britain but now there was another option on the table and Phillip liked the sound of it. In the wake of the war's end, men were now needed to make up a force to occupy the defeated nations and play a role in the restoration of stability and begin the rebuilding process. With the offer of continued service in the Army and further travel abroad, Phillip wasted no time in volunteering for the new task force. In a matter of days he was re-mustered into the 67th Battalion and this would form the core of one of the first units to depart New Guinea and join the newly formed British Commonwealth Occupation Force (BCOF).

He now readied his kit bag for another sea voyage and prepared to depart. He was not going home, and he was not going to war, but he was leaving for a war zone that defied the imagination. He was destined for Japan. He was destined for Hiroshima.

A studio portrait of Phillip in Japan 1946.

Chapter Twelve

Hiroshima

Long before the shooting had ceased in New Guinea, Australia's military and political leaders had been jockeying for a seat at the post-war table, keen to prevent any resurgence of the Japanese military. The Australian Army had also been left behind in New Guinea, Borneo and the Solomon Islands as MacArthur led the Americans through their bloody island-hopping campaign northward to Japan. With its extensive and, at times, pivotal role in the Pacific War, Australia both desired and deserved a significant say in the future of the region. General Blamey had signed the historic surrender document aboard the USS *Missouri*, but now his country postured for a new role.

Consequently, the British Commonwealth Occupation Force (BCOF) was born. Its role wasn't to act as a military government in Japan. That was left to the Americans. The BCOF was in Japan to ensure that the terms of surrender were enforced and that their capacity to make war was thoroughly disabled, once and for all. The BCOF would draw more than 40,000 personnel from Great Britain, India, New Zealand and Australia with the latter making up about a third of that number. Within their contingent, the Australians sent units from the Army, Navy and Air Force and it was from the 34th Infantry Brigade that Phillip's 67th Battalion was drawn.

Such political jousting and military logistics were far beyond the scope of a soldier's lot and Phillip knew very little of what lay ahead. For weeks he and his mates waited at Wewak, packing gear and stores for the sea voyage ahead, knowing they were bound for Japan but little more. In December, his twentieth birthday had come and gone without any fanfare and when 1946 dawned he was keen to be on the move. His time came in February when he moved down to the beach at Wewak and boarded a landing barge in a reverse performance of his arrival seven months earlier. Phillip looked back at the coastline as the barge lurched towards the troop ship and once again he was struck by the panorama of devastation; the flattened vegetation and towering palms stripped of their foliage. War had been here but it had visited his destination too.

As Phillip shipped out this time, there were no friendly faces waving farewell from the docks, just the New Guinea coastline and the Army hardware upon its beaches, shrinking with each passing mile. He had been there for only a matter of months, but as he looked back he knew that three of the mates he landed with would never be shipping out. Two of them still lay in the graves that he had dug them in the middle of nowhere and the image of their bodies and that final patrol still sat uneasily with him. He couldn't help but feel that he was leaving them behind.

His voyage would initially take him to Morotai. The small island was only four days by boat from Wewak and had been the scene of fighting until the war's end. Like New Guinea, many of the Japanese ultimately fell victim to malnutrition and starvation. By the time of Phillip's arrival in February 1946, the island had become a major staging point for the BCOF as men gathered for the journey north.

Phillip found Morotai a welcome place of transit and a relief from the ship's pitching decks. In some ways it seemed almost idyllic with its clear waters stocked with fresh fish and fruit that could be picked from the tree if you knew where to look. However, many of the Australians didn't share his perspective. Some had been waiting on Morotai for months and they were keen to move on either to Japan or Australia. They had been mildly entertained by the occasional lecture on Japan, its ways and its language as well as the ongoing war crimes trials but, overall, the wait had worn very thin.

By comparison, Phillip was bound for Japan only a week after his arrival in Morotai. This time there wasn't any clambering up or down nets, but a civilised boarding of a Victory ship by staircase. The advance party had left some weeks before, now this main convoy of vessels was to deliver the first substantial body of soldiers to Japan and Phillip was among their number.

The Victory ships were crewed by American Merchant Mariners and crammed around one thousand Australian personnel on board. These carriers of cargo and men were only lightly armed with an anti-aircraft gun fore and aft and a series of machine guns that were manned by naval personnel. As they steamed out of Morotai, the week-long voyage started well until, after two days, the convoy entered a 'Typhoon Triangle' off the Philippines. In gale force winds and rolling seas, the calm, crystal waters of Morotai became a distant memory. Below, on the troop deck, the noise of soldiers vomiting and the acrid smell allowed the nausea to spread like a contagion, affecting one and all. Phillip fought the rising urge to release the contents of his stomach every time the vessel pitched and heaved in the wild seas.

Every time the ship's propeller left the water, the noise level and vibration intensified to a backdrop of groaning metal plates. In a quest for fresh air, Phillip made his way above decks and cracked open the watertight door between the vessel's wild rolling motion. The waves were enormous and the Victory ship's stern rose high into the air as it rode the swell before pitching down into the next valley between the waves. For a boy from the bush on his third time at sea, this was a baptism of fire.

Finally, they cleared the region of hostile weather and a degree of normality returned to the voyage. By contrast, the Seto Inland Sea, separating the Japanese islands of Honshū, Shikoku, and Kyūshū, was beautifully calm, in part shielded by the surrounding terrain, Phillip thought. The air was still and icy and his breath turned quickly to fog as he exhaled and surveyed the scene around him. Everywhere, from the quiet morning waters, jutted jagged rocky islands and outcrops with picture-postcard lighting that totally belied the fact that war had recently ravaged this place.

As the city of Kure approached, Phillip was staggered by what he saw. As he had approached Wewak there had been abandoned guns and trucks, but here a mass of rusting, sunken warships littered the harbour having been attacked by the Americans the previous July. Once proud battleships now sat aground with the water lapping over their silent guns and their towering superstructures leaning, as if set to topple. A large cruiser had been beached by a desperate captain, and in the rock face were dark, hidden caverns which had once housed submarines, but now only hosted echoes. Like an elephants' graveyard, these once enormous beasts now lay lifeless with their guns silenced forever.

But it had not always been so. Kure had been home to the might of the Imperial

Japanese Navy. It had also been a secretive naval dockyard and once produced the world's largest battleship, the *Yamato*. Displacing 72,000 tons, armed with eighteen inch guns and a top speed of 27 knots, she had been the flagship of the Navy and led the fleet at the Battle of Midway. However, the *Yamato* too had now been silenced and lay on the ocean floor two hundred miles away.

The Victory ship moved through the eerily still waters, weaving past the haunted wrecks while ghostly jellyfish drifted just beneath the glassy surface. For a place that had seen such violence, it was very still as the Australians readied to disembark with their shuffling and shouted orders the only noise that disturbed the apparent peace. Phillip stood with the others, formed up in their uniforms, complete with kit bags, white webbing and disembarkation cards tucked into the band of their slouch hats. His first steps on Japanese soil were a few paces across to the back of a waiting truck.

The truck rattled its way inland to his new home at Kaitaichi. The town lay midway between Kure and Hiroshima and snow lay on the ground as he climbed from the back of the canvas-covered truck. It was bitterly cold and the wind cut through the young Queenslander with an icy edge that he'd never felt before. They were now situated at the location of the Nippon Steel Works which had its own barracks attached to house workers. This series of timber-framed one and two storey buildings seemed to have miraculously escaped any damage during the war and looked to be ideal accommodation for the Australians.

An Australian flag flapped in the breeze as if to offer a welcome to the new arrivals as they trooped into the barracks and sorted out their bunks. It was the first time since Mount Gambier that Phillip was not living under canvas and the prospect of four walls and heating was a welcome development given the harsh winter outside. Adjoining the barracks was a large vacant area, ideal to serve as either a parade ground or football field as circumstances dictated. Across the way were more barracks and some of these still housed Japanese workers that were employed in various tasks in the rebuilding process.

That night the barracks fell silent at an early hour as the exhausted men slept on land for the first time in more than a week. It had been a long day and yet in the early hours Phillip awoke and, half asleep, propped himself up to look out the paned window behind him. At first it was hard to focus, but then he was aghast to

The T-Bridge used as the aiming point by the 'Enola Gay' to drop the atomic bomb over Hiroshima.

see a mass of ash falling from the sky. "The Yanks have dropped another bomb!" was his first thought. He jumped from his bed and moved his face closer to the glass and watched each and every speck of white waft down to the ground; the white snow-covered ground. Only then did he know for sure that this was not another bombing raid, it was snow drifting down and blanketing the parade ground and barracks. Half-naked, he slipped on his boots, crept downstairs and out of the building, determined to experience snow falling. There he stood, a twenty year old soldier from Queensland, up to his ankles in snow, arms outstretched and mouth open catching snowflakes. The jungle of New Guinea was so very far away.

Days later he ventured out for the first time to see the devastation of Hiroshima first hand. Rugged up in his woolen winter uniform, he watched as the damage slowly but surely increased as he moved through the blast's perimeter towards Ground Zero. At first the evidence of fires that had burnt the wooden structures to the ground was present, while major buildings of brick, concrete and mortar only possessed damage to the roofs and were missing the glass in their windows. Then the landscape disappeared. Flattened.

Nothing but rubble, strangely frosted by the latest snow, as far as the eye could see. Among the rubble, starving, feeble men and women fossicked for anything of use. Their faces lowered, they wore clothes like pyjamas with sacks on their backs into which they cast bits of timber for firewood. Occasionally a masonry archway would still be standing, or the walls of a gutted building, but these were the exception. Tramcars were no longer on their deformed tracks and Army vehicles were the only form of transport to be seen. All the while, in this bitter cold, the survivors were scraping together a way to survive.

As Phillip walked around Ground Zero, he was amazed that anything had survived the detonation of this bomb at such close range, although he was led to understand that it exploded before it hit the ground. He stood on the T-Shaped Aioi Bridge that had served as the aiming point for the Superfortress and cast his eyes through 360 degrees. Flattened, but how? He knew nothing of the atomic bomb or radioactivity, only the 200 and 500 pounders that could be released from the belly of an Avro Lancaster. How big was this bomb? He couldn't grasp how one strike could so completely evaporate an entire area.

A short distance away stood a lone building topped by a skeletal dome. As he wandered among its ruins he could see that there was nothing inside. All of the floors were gone and now only the shell remained, but he was struck by the fact that this building by the river could be standing at all, for in every direction all he could see was destruction.

Eerily, he saw rows of headstones and they seemed untouched. In the same area, the outline of a tree was etched on the remnants of a wall and yet there was no tree. He rubbed his fingers on the wall and could feel the difference in texture where in one instance flying particles had struck the wall while in the shadow of the tree the wall had been sheltered. What force would that take? Where was the dirt and dust that was thrown up to create this macabre etching? These were forces and munitions he could not perceive.

He could see why the Japanese had surrendered when two of these bombs had been dropped on their cities. No nation could defend against this weapon, it was futile. Yet he was glad the Americans had done what they had done as it had undoubtedly saved Allied lives. He had seen how fiercely the starving Japanese had defended an irrelevant patch of New Guinea jungle, even when the war was over. He could only imagine having to try and land soldiers on their sovereign soil and claim victory inch by bloody inch. The war in the islands proved that it would have been a bloodbath. He made his way back to the barracks once again contemplating

HIROSHIMA

Bayonet fixed and on guard in Japan.

the sheer power, absolute destruction and devastating aftermath that this lone bomb had caused.

By comparison to the starving Japanese, conditions at his Kaitachi base were fit for royalty. The food was more than reasonable and the showers were heated in an area that would cover two basketball courts and hose down a good many men at once. All in all, it was a relatively comfortable existence for the 6th Battalion of which Phillip was a member of number 4 Platoon, Headquarters Company. They were all part of the 34th Brigade under the command of Brigadier Ronald Hopkins. Next in line was his company commanding officer, Major Ian Ferguson, a no-nonsense soldier who had served in New Guinea, earning the Military Cross during a counter-offensive on the Kokoda Track.

Gradually more men began arriving at Kaitaichi. Many had come straight from Australia having completed their infantry training too late to be deployed to the war. Army life called for the routine tasks to be performed. Boots and brass were highly polished and the white webbing was kept white with regular doses of 'Blanco'. Rifles were kept clean inside and polished on the outside from the woodwork to the brass butt plate. There were parades and inspections that included Lieutenant-General Horace Robertson, the overall commander of the BCOF and the man that had taken General Adachi's sword and surrender at Wewak the previous year.

However, the BCOF was also there for a purpose and the duties that befell the 67th Battalion included destroying Japanese military equipment, active patrolling and assisting in the post-war rebuilding of the shattered nation. The Americans had already accounted for a lot of the Japanese war machine, but a good deal still remained stored in tunnels deep within the hills. As the year moved on and the days became warmer, the pursuit of these arms became a slightly better task as the tunnels afforded some respite from the heat that had moved in to replace the bitter winter.

One such ammunition dump existed on Ninoshima Island, a couple of miles off-shore within the inland sea and a short ride aboard a small wooden sampan. It had previously been used to house naval munitions, high explosives and a military hospital in the one tunnel. Now emptied of ordnance, each magazine consisted of three-foot-thick cork-lined walls and was sealed by heavy steel doors. Now, instead of ammunition, it was home to Phillip and his platoon in the role of prison guards for soldiers who had stepped outside the rules.

Punishments such as denying leave and confining a soldier to barracks were for lesser offences and carried out 'in house'. For more significant matters, a soldier could face detention, or 'field punishment', and these were conducted at dedicated facilities under the watchful eye of specially trained military guards. In their absence, the trustworthy '4 Platoon' was roped into the duty and sent off to Ninoshima Island where they would live in their own dormitory bunker while prisoners would be confined at a rate of ten per magazine. By day the prisoners shifted dirt and performed other laborious tasks designed to motivate them to return to their unit. Phillip initially seethed at receiving the duty but soon learnt that it was actually quite an easy task and away from the prying eyes of senior ranks. The 'prisoners' were well behaved and the bunker was the coolest place in Japan to take refuge from the heat. It wasn't a bad job after all.

Due to the shortage of just about everything, the black market was an ongoing source of trouble for the BCOF. Against this backdrop an order came down from General Douglas MacArthur, the Supreme Commander for the Allied Powers in Japan. The order stated that to stem the illegal trade of Japanese Samurai swords, and as an act of good faith, all swords were to be handed in. In many cases these swords were family heirlooms that dated back centuries and the authorities dictated they must be returned to their rightful owners.

Phillip was compelled to comply with the order and reluctantly drew the sword from his kit bag. It irked him that a sword found in New Guinea fell under the same banner as the illegal trade of war booty but, nonetheless, his first duty was to obey a lawful command. He handed the sword in as per the directive, however he genuinely wondered if it would find its way to its proper home or simply be hung above the fireplace of a quartermaster who never saw a shot fired in anger.

Not long after Ninoshima Island, Phillip and his platoon moved inland by truck with a six-pounder anti-tank gun in tow to Hara-mura to participate in a field firing exercise. It was a pleasant relief to be firing a weapon and undertaking some Army-orientated activity for a change. As 'Number Two' Phillip was the loader and after each firing the gun would jolt back amid a cloud of dust and a deafening blast that he could only offset by placing his hands over his ears. It was hot, hard work after Ninoshima Island, but a satisfying day for their gun group, landing five shots together on a four foot square target at 900 yards. Alas, the fun came to an end prematurely when a senior citizen from a nearby village appeared at the range with a used projectile that had apparently skidded down his main street.

Just before Christmas, Kaitaichi was struck by a late evening earthquake that forced the barracks to be evacuated. Phillip and his mates rushed out and down the stairs as the building and staircase rocked. After a minor pile-up of bodies at the base of the stairs they gathered to watch the arcing power lines and dimming lights, still unsure of what had actually occurred. Soon the disturbance subsided and they all returned to their barracks, none the worse for wear.

Throughout his stay in Japan, patrols were conducted by the Australian platoons into the hills with the dual purpose of seeking out other munitions while offering a visual presence of force to the Japanese. While there was occasional tension at political rallies that the platoon oversaw, Phillip never struck any trouble on these hillside patrols. In fact, he was often struck by the beauty of the landscape away from the scenes of destruction in the cities. The people seemed reserved and courteous as the troopers wandered through their precinct with guns in hand. In fact, it seemed to Phillip that the Japanese had now well and truly accepted their fate. From what he'd witnessed, even the defeated Japanese soldiers that disembarked at Kure generally dispersed without event, although there were a few of instances when tempers flared and tensions rose. But there was nothing of consequence.

Never was their defeat more apparent than when Phillip took leave and ventured

Live firing at Hara-mura (Phillip is at far right)

beyond his duties and the limits of Kaitaichi. On one occasion as he travelled by train to Tokyo he noted a Japanese woman having difficulty in opening one of the train's windows which appeared to be jammed shut. Phillip stood up and walked towards the woman and she sunk into her seat, sliding away from the approaching soldier. Despite his best efforts, he was unable to budge the offending window and offered the woman a smile and some very poor, very broken Japanese. He then drew his bayonet from its sheath to wedge beneath the window and jemmy it open using the increased leverage.

His blade had hardly left its scabbard when the woman fled from her seat and others also moved quickly away while some cowered where they sat. In their eyes Phillip saw genuine fear. To them he was not a lone soldier, but a white devil who was going to carve them up singlehandedly. He raised his hand and slowly stowed the blade to put the wary civilians at ease, but it was to no avail as the tension continued and they all disembarked the next time the train came to a halt.

Tokyo had also received a battering from the air by the American war machine, however, whereas Hiroshima had been apparently flattened by brute force, Tokyo and its surrounds had been systematically burnt to the ground. A rain of incendiaries had fallen from the bellies of the bombers, igniting the predominantly wooden city. The residential areas with their wood and paper construction were a tinderbox and were effectively wiped out. The number killed in Tokyo was undoubtedly comparable to Hiroshima, but had resulted from a series of raids rather than a single flash.

However, unlike Hiroshima, there were some substantial buildings in the city that had survived relatively unscathed and, by 1946, offered good accommodation. While the soldiers were housed in the Ebisu Barracks, there was an officers' facility at the Marunouchi Hotel. Conversely, the Imperial Palace had been significantly damaged by the American air raids and it was from its concrete basement that Emperor Hirohito broadcast his surrender speech to the Japanese people. Now the remnants of the Imperial Palace were constantly surrounded by a series of guard posts comprising American and Australian soldiers in full dress with rifles and bayonets. In due course Phillip had his turn on guard and took in the history that lay behind him that spiked a thirst in him for more knowledge about not only Japan, but the vast world beyond the Darling Downs.

Back at Kaitaichi, even if he wanted to read, there were not that many publications available. So Phillip continued to thumb through his atlas and read and re-read the Pilot's Flying Manual whose pages were showing increasing signs of wear. Just as he had done in New Guinea, he managed to find his way to an Australian airfield to peruse the aircraft on display. By far the most attractive were the single seat Mustang fighters of 77 Squadron RAAF who were also a contingent of the BCOF stationed at Iwakuni. He would often see the sleek fighters in formation overhead and was impressed by their speed and intoxicated by their sound, but seeing them close up was a particular thrill.

Their massive four-blade propeller, driven by a Rolls Royce Merlin engine, could push the Mustang to more than 400 miles an hour and with enough range to help turn the tide of the war in Europe. Now they were here in Japan with their gleaming silver flanks only interrupted by the red, white and blue roundel of the RAAF. Phillip would sit and watch as one Mustang after another took off in a stream and pondered what might have been had he stayed in the Air Force.

Again, a kindly pilot took to the land-locked soldier and walked him along the flightline to step up onto the wing. As Japanese workers tended to the aeroplane,

Phillip eyed the dials and levers in the cockpit and the gunsight that sat on top of the instrument panel. "How much fun would it be to wheel around the sky in one of these?", he thought and imagined the freedom that would come with such an aeroplane. On the way back to Kaitaichi he couldn't help imagining that very act and promised himself that, one day, somehow, when this war was finally done and dusted, he would learn to fly. It seemed like a dream, but the young digger was determined.

So another birthday passed with December and 1947 arrived without fanfare, although he did try his hand at skiing. February marked one year in Japan and he felt that he'd seen about all there was to see. As he contemplated returning home, he once again was faced with the reality of what awaited him beyond the Army. The truth was that he had no idea, but he couldn't avoid the inevitable forever either. As he put plans in place to return home and leave the military, he knew that he would miss the stability and security of the only life he had known for the past three years but the time had come.

In May he said his goodbyes and boarded HMAS *Kanimbla* at Kure where he had first arrived in Japan on that ghostly morning in 1946. Many of the derelict ships remained but they were no longer strange to him, merely the backdrop to this chapter of his life, just like the hills he patrolled and the flattened city of Hiroshima. In his time in Japan he had seen so much. He had been on guard outside the Imperial Palace from where Hirohito surrendered, stood beneath the very spot where the atomic bomb was detonated, played prison guard to some military rascals and felt snow on his face for the first time.

Now he was going home.

A sketch of Phillip drawn by a Japanese street vendor.

Deck life aboard the HMAS Kanimbla, bound for Australia.

Chapter Thirteen

A Restless Year

The *Kanimbla* docked in Sydney thirteen days after it had left Kure. The next day he made his way by train to Redbank in Queensland where he had first traded his Air Force blues for khaki in 1944. The next day he was discharged and a civilian for the first time in his adult life.

There were no queues, no medical examinations and a minimum of paperwork. He had served in the military for nearly four years and yet he was discharged in a matter of minutes. He knew that his life was about to change but the speed of what had just occurred caught him off-guard. Now he stood outside Redbank, still in uniform and with his kit bag slung over his shoulder, but no longer a soldier.

Without the usual vices associated with youth, he had spent very little of his pay during his time in the services. His only expense stemmed from the fact that he had nominated his mother as his 'allottee' with the Army and regularly sent money home to her. Otherwise, the funds had simply accumulated, religiously stamped into and signed off in his 'Soldier's Pay Book' month by month. At a time when the average civilian wage was around eight pounds per week, Phillip had the grand total of four hundred and forty five pounds, eleven shillings and eight pence to his name. It was more than a year's salary, so there was no financial pressure on him to make any rash decisions. For now, it was time to go home to the farm.

As he approached the property at Middle Ridge he could see his father ploughing a paddock with one of his horses. The land was on a steep incline and looked like the first good rain might wash half of his father's labour down the hill. 'Bill' was yelling something at the horse out of frustration and was too busy man-handling the plough to see his son approaching. Phillip unceremoniously, and without prior notice, walked into the house for the first time in two years. His mother maintained her composure but hugged her son with obvious joy which was always an act that he didn't quite know how to reciprocate.

In a quiet moment, he passed his mother a sizeable chunk of his Army pay, knowing that times were tough at home and that she would manage it responsibly. His father then came into the house and the three exchanged stilted conversation. Phillip related a few anecdotes from Japan while his mother listened and his father cursed about the farm. Within the first few minutes Phillip knew that he couldn't go back to farming for good, but spent the next few weeks helping his father ploughing and mending fences. It was an easy way to move onto a life beyond the Army, but he knew that he couldn't stay for long.

Something had fundamentally changed within him and he knew it. When he left Middle Ridge the first time he was a boy on a big adventure. Now he was a man who had lived that adventure. He had been the skinny, dumb kid, the butt of jokes at the foundry, but now he had grown into a muscular form and was far worldlier than those that had once ridiculed him. He was unsure what life had in store for him, but he knew he was no longer going to be bullied or pushed around by anyone. He had returned from active service and he wasn't going to take shit from anyone ever again.

He had seen so much and travelled so far that now it was almost incomprehensible to stay in one place, settle down and have a normal life. He had tasted the world beyond the Downs and he wanted more but he didn't know how to pursue it. His brother had settled back into life after the Navy and even married a Land Army girl, but there was no one for him. He had some inkling towards one Toowoomba girl, but no idea how to follow through.

The frustration simmered within him from his first days as a civilian. In New Guinea he had seen combat and lost mates and even in Japan he had lived a life fully armed and wary of the surroundings and its people. The Army had organised his life, clothed and fed him and in return he had been the best soldier he could be. However, beyond the khaki lines, his skill set as a Commando with the ability to kill and maim was not highly in demand in a nation looking to move on from six years of war.

He was restless and knew that he would have to move on again soon. He used some of his accumulated wealth to purchase a Matchless 350cc motorcycle. It was his pride and joy and over the next few weeks he taught himself to ride it,

Another load of sugar cane, cut by hand.

falling off and stalling it more times than he would like to count. As soon as he was competent to ride he packed together a few belongings and set out for North Queensland. He had heard that hard work and healthy rewards were to be found in the sugar cane fields so that was to be his first port of call.

He took to the road on his Matchless and grew increasingly confident at riding. Day by day, he built up his speed and cut the corners just a little tighter on the rough country roads. He would sleep by the side of the road at night and stop at small towns along the way for a feed. He was entering the cane country when he failed to sight a sizeable rock emerging from the surface of the road, hitting it at an angle and at speed. The front wheel cranked sideways and the Matchless flicked beneath him, hurling Phillip face first into the dirt as the bike bounced along behind him. In short sleeves and without a helmet, skin flew off him but the major impact was taken by his chin.

Everything finally came to rest in a cloud of dust and there he sat on the side of the road with his new bike in a ditch. He surveyed the damage to the Matchless and it seemed minimal, however he had taken a fair bit of skin off his arms and his chin hurt like hell. He wriggled his jaw without complaint, but blood was streaming from his chin where a deep gash had been carved out by the rocks and the road. He rinsed the wound with a water bottle and stemmed the flow with a handkerchief, but boy it still stung.

He hopped back on the motorbike and rode to the next town. He had covered nearly 800 miles on dirt roads and now he was sore, hot, tired and covered in blood. He parked his bike on its stand and for the only time in his life, Phillip walked into a pub of his own volition and ordered an ice-cold beer. The barman surveyed his damaged customer and, recognising the tell-tale khaki pants he was wearing, asked him where he had served. Phillip provided him with a brief answer and then asked about work in the cane fields. The barman gave him a name and told him to ride on to the township of El Arish where he would most likely find work as a cane cutter. Phillip only drank a mouthful of the beer, remembering his pay day misadventure in New Guinea, before he settled for a few glasses of water.

He washed up and rinsed his shirt before making his way a little further north. The shirt dried in minutes as the warm air swept by and shortly he found the cane field at El Arish that the barman had steered him to. With the fields desperately short of labour, experience was not required for this hard, filthy work, just a strong back and arms. At three times the average wage, the money was good, but the conditions were tough.

Cutting cane was brutal manual labour. Armed with nothing more than a cane-knife, the cutters would swing the long handled blade to sever the tall cane at its base. They would then gather up the cut stalks and load them into one of a series of small box trailers towed behind a tractor. For hours on end the cutters would bend over and hack at the cane, stand up, bend over, pick up the heavy bundle of stalks, load them, walk back to the cane, bend over and start again. Adding to the task was that, prior to harvesting, the sugar cane is burnt off. The crop is set alight in order to burn off the straw, the tops and leaves from the cane stalk which makes up a quarter of its bulk. As those fires would burn up into the night sky, Phillip would be in awe of the sheer volume of flame and the towering pillars of smoke. However, next day, reality would set in and he would now be called upon to cut the blackened cane. As a result, he would become covered in soot and the cane syrup would run down his bare, black back as he hoisted a load of cane over his shoulder.

Already scratched by the foliage, bees and all manner of insects would then land on his sugared flesh and sting him at regular intervals. Beneath his feet, huge brown snakes that had not perished in the burn-off would slither past or over his feet. He quickly became expert at swinging the cane knife and slicing the snakes in two. They were long days that ended with Phillip retiring to barrack-like accommodation in a single room wooden building with no power, a water tank and dirty laundry hanging on the verandah.

In the few hours of downtime, Phillip would read prolifically on a range of subjects from world history to geography and, as always, his Pilot's Flying Manual. Then it would be time to sleep and start all over again. When one cane-field was harvested, it was onto the next, so Phillip packed up the Matchless and rode east to Mourilyan where the process was repeated day after day until the end of the season. By December of 1947 he had saved a good deal of money and was ready for a short break back home.

Phillip rode this motorbike between work in various cane fields.

When he arrived in Toowoomba he slipped unannounced into Fred's home one night and went to sleep on the verandah, only to be discovered the next morning. Fred's wife Hazel cooked him a hearty breakfast before he headed down to see his parents and help his father with odd jobs around the property. However, it was not long before he became restless once again. Fred and his cousins had all settled down with homes and families but none of that was on the horizon for Phillip. As mysteriously as he arrived, Phillip would disappear again and take to the road working at any laboring job he could find.

Early in 1948, he re-appeared in Toowoomba without notice. Again he spent time with Fred and the family, playing games with his young nephews Billy and Johnny and calling upon his sister Alice. He enjoyed his time there, but was still unsettled and agitated and had to move on again after a few weeks. This time he convinced Fred to join him. There was wheat-stacking work at Horrane, not far west of Toowoomba. The money was good and the season was in full swing, so Fred climbed on the back of Phillip's Matchless and the two brothers set out for the wheat fields.

It wasn't long before Fred was hanging on for dear life as Phillip opened up the throttle on his two-wheeler. His little brother seemed to be in control of the motorcycle but was absolutely impervious to the fact that they could come off at any second on these sub-standard roads. The back wheel bumped and skipped and, as Phillip corrected, Fred held on a little tighter. It was a ride to remember and the two brothers stacked wheat at Horrane and then moved onto Bongeen to do it all over again. By the time they arrived back at Toowoomba eight weeks later they were cashed up and the brothers both bought new motorcycles; Fred a BSA and Phillip a new top-of-the-range Norton 350cc. The Norton was his pride and joy and he couldn't wait to show Fred what it could do on the open road so the two brothers set off on a ride beyond Gowrie Mountain. Clear of Toowoomba, the two were cruising along when a Chevrolet overtook them at speed, showering them with stones as it pulled away. In a heartbeat Phillip took off after the brazen driver, leaving Fred in his wake. Fred cringed at the break-neck speed of his brother's Norton as its back wheel skipped left and right searching for traction.

Fred gave up the race and let his brother go ahead, but saw him pass the Chevrolet and return the favour, kicking up a shower of rocks as he disappeared over the crest of a hill. When Fred finally caught up to Phillip he was leaning against his bike as it rested on its stand and drinking from his water-bottle as if to say, "What kept you?" Fred could see that Phillip had a thing for speed, but wondered if it would cost him his neck at some point.

A couple of weeks later, Phillip was gone again without a word. Fred could see that his little brother was becoming a drifter, floating from shed to shed, job to job. He had barely stood still since he'd returned from Japan and the war and Fred was beginning to wonder if he ever would. Phillip was wondering the same thing as he set course for the cane fields once again, stopping to camp the first night on the banks of the newly constructed Somerset Dam before beginning the long trek north to Ingham.

He picked up cane cutting where he had left off the previous season. Still he read prolifically and still his bank account grew. He started to contemplate learning to fly. It wasn't cheap, but maybe another good season and he could afford it. He considered getting an education or re-enlisting, but the Air Force had scaled back since the war and there weren't any aircrew jobs going even if he could apply. Phillip knew he couldn't live the rest of his life bouncing between laboring jobs and he longed for the stability and order of the military. He was at a loss what to do so he just continued to do what he knew as the days ticked by; cut the cane, stack it and cut some more.

He didn't know it when he woke up on August 2nd 1948, but his life was about to take a major turn. He had a few hours off that morning and uncharacteristically took to kicking a football with a young cutter in his crew. A stray kick saw the ball fly high and land in the water tank at the end of the barracks so Phillip clambered up to retrieve it. What he saw when he looked in the tank was disgusting. The top layer of their drinking water was full of dead animals ranging from rats to a possum and all manner of filth. He yelled a description of the slime to his mate below, laughing as he threw the ball down.

This innocent action raised the ire of one of the senior blokes who came running across to Phillip and told him to shut up. He got close up to Phillip's face and screamed that there were blokes off the night shift trying to sleep and his yelling and shenanigans would wake them up. Phillip half-heartedly apologised and went to move away, but the bloke couldn't let it go. When the former Commando bristled up and squared off with his accuser, he backed down, mumbling something about, "...all you bloody war heroes" and turned his attack on Phillip's young mate for no reason. That was enough and Phillip bore down on his antagonist until he skulked away, still muttering as he left.

Fuming, Phillip jumped onto his Norton and rode out of the cane fields at speed. He had been simmering since he'd come home from Japan and now the valve had just been cracked. Enough was enough and he knew exactly what had to be done and where he had to go. It had crossed his mind, as he had ridden northward, but now the idea had crystallised into a plan. The Air Force still had a significant presence in Townsville and he was going to re-enlist. He'd had enough of civilian life and now couldn't wait to sign on the dotted line once again. With his level of education there no chance of enlisting as aircrew, but he was going to throw his hat in the ring to train as an aircraft mechanic if the RAAF would have him back.

The recruiting officer interviewed Phillip and thought that he was a suitable candidate to become a flight mechanic. From there on Phillip knew the drill; forms, queues, police and medical checks. He was now 25 pounds heavier than when he'd first enlisted in 1944 and all of it was muscle born of Commando training and cane cutting. His application went smoothly and within a few weeks he was advised that his application to enlist as a trainee flight mechanic had been successful. His new life was on its way, but there was one last order of business with his old one that he had to take care of.

In the weeks since the flare up with the senior cutter, both men had been caught up in a tense deadlock. The senior man had tried to use his standing to needle Phillip at every opportunity and bully him in the same manner that the adults had done at the Toowoomba foundry so many years before. All the while, Phillip had absorbed the abuse, knowing that if his Air Force application was successful, he was on his way.

Now that he had the green light, he resigned his position at the cane shed, cashed in his pay, collected his bedroll and strapped it to the back of the Norton. He then sought out the other cutter and asked him to say anything that he had to say to his face. The offender went silent and simply stood there. "I bloody thought so" was Phillip's simple response as he turned to walk back to his motorbike and leave.

Phillip had just started to turn when he sensed something bearing down on him; it was the handle of a cane knife that struck him hard above the right eye. He didn't flinch and stood his ground, his lack of reaction causing turmoil in the mind of his attacker. Before the man could take a second swing, Phillip cut loose and released every bit of pent up frustration that existed from the foundry to the bloody patrol at Mashuan. The other bloke had no idea, but he had just let the top off a bottle that was looking for somewhere to explode.

Phillip's first blow struck him in the throat with the sickening crack of cartilage. As the cutter reached for his airway, he left his stomach unguarded and Phillip landed a second fierce blow. Doubled up and gasping for air, he realised that he had picked a fight with the wrong bloke and looked up helplessly at Phillip; but there was no mercy to be found there. Phillip's third blow smashed into his face, sending him crashing to the ground; unconscious before he hit the dirt. Phillip looked down at him for a moment before turning and climbing on board his Norton.

Phillip did not say another word as he rode off, leaving behind the past year of his life.

Phillip with his nephew, Bill Zupp, 1948.

Phillip poses with a pair of over-sized RAAF wings. Townsville 1948.

Chapter Fourteen

Back in Blue

Phillip felt like he had come home as he was issued with his new Air Force uniform. He was so excited that he had one of the staff take his photograph with a huge pair of Air Force wings to mark the occasion, despite the obvious swelling above his eye. The first that his family knew of him rejoining the ranks of the military was when he made a whistle-stop in Toowoomba to gather a few belongings on the way to his new posting at Wagga Wagga.

Located in the Riverina region of New South Wales, Wagga had been the site of a RAAF Flying Training School (FTS) during the war, as had many of the airfields in the area. Far from the front lines to the north and characterised by good weather and low terrain, western NSW produced a good many of the pilots that went on to serve in combat. Now RAAF Station Forrest Hill at Wagga was responsible for training recruits in the trades associated with flying operations. The RAAF School of Technical Training (RSTT) had taken on its first course of apprentices in January of 1948 so, when Phillip arrived in September, the school was still a relatively new establishment.

He was now among the new breed of aviation apprentices as he settled into the Ground Training School (GTS) to learn everything there was to know about an aircraft's engine and airframe. Phillip threw himself into his training, studying for long hours and thoroughly enjoying the practical aspects of what made aeroplanes tick. As his thirst for knowledge was being quenched and aeroplanes buzzed over the barracks, he was in his element. He was also reminded that the past year had been a waste of time, with one exception.

Unlike many of the younger apprentices, he had prior military service, so the marching, parades and discipline were a case of 'here we go again'. However, he'd held a series of jobs and possessed a bank balance to show for it. Now he was learning about aircraft and living on an airfield with a civilian flying school a short walk from his barracks. The planets had seemingly aligned for him to follow his ultimate dream and learn to fly.

His only concern was whether he could balance his technical studies with those required to become a pilot. He had only been on course for a couple of weeks and already the desire to fly was starting to burn him up inside. That weekend, as he pondered his options, a lone biplane became airborne outside his window, gently rolling into a turn and disappearing slowly into the distance. His mind was made up; he was going to learn to fly.

Without delay he left the barracks and walked over to Eric Condon's flying school. Eric met the young budding pilot with a shake of the hand and took him out to look at a Tiger Moth parked on the grass. Phillip climbed into the biplane's cockpit and Eric ran through the various 'ins and outs' of the fabric-covered trainer. Phillip pushed the control stick to the left and right, fore and aft and watched the control surfaces respond, just as they had in the wrecked Japanese aircraft in New Guinea. The difference was that this was an operational aeroplane and he now had the chance to take it into the sky. Despite his outward appearance, Phillip was overwhelmed and signed up for his first lesson on the spot. He couldn't wait until next week.

By day he attended classroom lessons and sessions in the hangar, breaking aeroplanes down into their most basic components and building them back up again. By night he studied his course notes and then, when that was completed, he would read through every detail of the small book of DH.82 Tiger Moth Handling Notes that Eric had given him. In between he would find time to eat and sleep, but very little else.

When the next Saturday rolled around, he could not get out to the aeroplane quickly enough. Eric walked around the Tiger Moth with him and demonstrated the pre-flight inspection that must occur prior to every flight. He then showed him how to swing the propeller by hand to start the engine and bring the aircraft to life. It was a skill that he had already been shown at the training school so it was a very convenient overlap of his studies. Finally, Phillip donned a leather flying helmet and climbed into the back seat.

Eric checked that his student's seat belt was securely fastened and plugged the

Forlorn warriors. Lines of Bristol Beaufighters await their ultimate fate at Forrest Hill in 1948.

clear plastic tubes running from the helmet's earpieces into the instrument panel. Adjacent to this was a black rubber funnel that was connected via tubes to the instructor's helmet in the front cockpit. Communication between the front and back cockpits was achieved by yelling into the funnel with the voice travelling down the tubes and into the ears of the other pilot. It was primitive, but it worked. Eric then strapped into the front cockpit and a third person moved into position to swing the propeller.

The two switches controlling the magnetos and engine spark used to ignite the fuel were mounted outside the cockpit, but within easy reach. One was flicked up to make the system live and then, with a flick, the propeller was swung, the spark lit the fuel and air and the engine coughed and then fired into a steady rhythm. The second switch was now flicked up and the wheel-chocks that stopped the aircraft from rolling were pulled away. Phillip's first flight was set to begin.

Eric moved the throttle on the left hand side of the cockpit to get the aircraft moving. Without brakes and only a small skid at the back, handling the Tiger Moth on the ground was in many ways the hardest part. The visibility for Phillip in the rear cockpit was virtually zero and the aircraft was taxied by constantly zig-zagging to maintain some sort of view ahead. Eric told Phillip to keep his hands and feet lightly on the controls to feel what it was like to taxi the aeroplane. Then he yelled to Phillip that he now had control and Phillip responded by yelling back, "Taking Over!". The Tiger Moth now weaved under his hand and the gentle movement of the rudder pedals beneath his feet. He was concentrating incredibly just to steer the aeroplane on the ground. What would it be like to fly?

Eric took control once again and eased the aircraft to a stop. He increased the power on the engine and flicked the magneto switches one by one. He checked the controls and the trim setting and the hatches and the harnesses, there seemed so much to remember, then finally they were set to go. Pointed into wind, Eric instructed Phillip to follow his control inputs as he took the aeroplane into the air as Phillip's heart was almost beating out of his chest.

With the control stick pulled fully back, Eric moved the throttle smoothly forward and the engine responded in kind. The needle on the tachometer indicating the engine revolutions steadily increased and then stabilised and the airspeed indicator left the stops as the speed ticked over; 20 knots, 30 knots, 40 knots. But Phillip's eyes were outside the cockpit. Soon after the aircraft began to accelerate, Eric moved the control stick forward to an upright position and the Tiger Moth responded by lifting its tail-skid off the ground to now roll across the airfield solely on its two smooth balloon-like tyres. Now the airflow from the propeller was whipping past his windscreen and Phillip could feel Eric lightly pushing on the left rudder pedal. They were really moving and he could feel that the aircraft wanted to fly. Then it did.

The rumbling of the tyres on the ground was replaced by the light buffeting of the air. The controls became lighter as the ground fell away beside him and the individual blades of grass blurred and then merged into a single green blanket. Ahead was the back of Eric's helmeted head, but beyond that was the translucent wooden disc of the spinning propeller and the bluest sky he had ever seen. The air base and his barracks sat just off the wingtip as Eric turned the aircraft up and away before lowering its nose and wings and steadying the Tiger Moth in level flight. Then he waggled the stick and uttered the words, "Handing over". Phillip almost choked on his response but managed to voice down the Gosport tube, "Taking over", and waggled the stick in acknowledgement. He was flying!

He tried his utmost to keep the Tiger straight and level, but it seemed a little

Phillip's first civil flying log book.

akin to balancing atop a ball at first. Eric encouraged him to relax and let the aeroplane do the work, to be light of hand and subtle with the inputs. Little by little, Phillip edged the aeroplane around the sky, hanging on every word that Eric spoke. Amid the effort, he allowed himself the pleasure of looking down upon the fields of the Riverina with its roads and rivers. He had never felt such absolute joy as he ventured into a turn to the left, watching the horizon tilt and his wingtip trace a line along the earth.

The hour went by too quickly as they returned to Wagga and Eric reclaimed control for the landing. The RAAF station grew closer and he could make out his barracks and the rows upon rows of rotting warplanes still waiting to be scrapped. With Eric moving the throttle back, the engine became quiet except for a slight 'Pop! Pop! Pop!' as it slowly turned over. For all intents and purposes, the Tiger was now a glider as it sailed down towards the landing field and the blanket of grass once again become tufts and then individual blades. Bit by bit, Eric pulled the stick back and the nose of the aeroplane rose until it sat there, very slow and on its haunches. Just as Phillip felt that the aircraft had lost its energy and could not continue, the rumbling of the wheels upon the earth returned and they were down.

After the propeller kicked to a halt and all noise had ceased, Phillip paused for a moment and breathed in what had just happened. The dumb kid from the foundry had actually flown an aeroplane. Not just seated in an aeroplane as a passenger, but he had pushed and pulled, pitched and rolled and, for a matter of minutes, he had been a pilot. His dream was coming true. Eric caught a glimpse of his protégé and brought him back to reality with instructions to flick his magneto switches off and undo his seat belt. As always, Phillip followed orders well and did as he was told before taking off his helmet and goggles and climbing from the cockpit.

That night in his barracks, there was an extra task for Phillip to complete. He dipped his nib pen in the ink well and wrote the first entry in his 'Pilot's Log Book'. "October 16. 1948. DH82 Tiger Moth. VH-BEO. Air Experience. One Hour." He found it difficult to comprehend that he was actually learning to fly.

It almost proved to be a distraction to his technical studies, but still he applied himself to all of the tasks assigned and began registering marks consistently around ninety per cent and impressed his instructors with his knowledge and enthusiasm. Throughout each week he was the diligent apprentice and then each weekend he would climb aboard the Tiger Moth with Eric Condon and play the role of the student pilot. There was very little time for frivolity, but that didn't bother Phillip as he really felt that his life was going forward. Life was very good.

Each weekend he would take to the skies and learn a new aspect of flight; climbing, descending, stalling, turning, take-off and landing. Little by little he grew more competent and was consistently able to leave the ground and return the Tiger Moth safely to earth. After eight hours of guidance under Eric's watchful eye, the instructor decided that it was time to let his student loose. On the morning of December 11th and with no prior warning, Eric instructed Phillip to bring the aircraft to a halt after a series of nice touch-downs. He then climbed out of the cockpit, removed the control stick from the front cockpit so it couldn't be fouled and secured the belt across the now empty seat. He yelled at Phillip to fly one take-off and landing and then come back to see him when he was finished. He patted Phillip on the shoulder, stepped away from the aircraft and gave a smile and a 'thumbs up'.

Phillip had committed all of his checks, airspeeds and procedures to memory, now all he had to do was fly those figures and mimic the take-offs and landings that he had just been flying with Eric. There was no time to be nervous. There was only time to focus on the task at hand. He taxied away and completed his pre-take-off checks before lining up, taking a breath and then opening the throttle. The Tiger skipped into life, accelerating crisply. He eased the stick forward and

Tiger Moth VH-ATF in which Phillip flew his first solo flight on the 11th December 1948.

was impressed by the outlook before him without an instructor's head to obscure the view. When the aeroplane whispered to him that it was time to fly, he answered by pulling gently back on the stick. His first thought was how well the aeroplane was climbing without the ballast of another human being on board. His second thought was "I'm flying. Really flying!"

It was his hand alone that guided the Tiger through the air; his eyes that scanned the sky for other aircraft; his feet that squeezed the rudder pedals; and his hand that enticed the biplane into a climbing turn. As he reached one thousand feet above the ground, he lowered the nose, now parallel to the airfield but in the opposite direction to the way he took off. He meticulously completed his pre-landing checks, saying the words out loud even though there was nobody to hear. As the landing field passed behind his left shoulder, he turned towards it and reduced the power. 'Pop! Pop! Pop!'

He picked his point to touch down and, with one eye on that point and one eye on the airspeed indicator, he steered the Tiger Moth back to earth. He crossed the fence of the airfield with his house in order and made sure that everything was straight as the earth crept up towards him. When his peripheral vision prompted him, and the feeling in his backside urged him, he eased gently back on the stick, asking the Tiger to cease flying. It answered him just as the wheels and tail-skid skimmed the grass, washing off speed and settling back down upon the airfield.

He rolled to a halt and then carefully taxied towards his waiting instructor whose smile was almost as broad as Phillip's. He had just flown alone through the sky.

That night he dipped his pen in the ink well and wrote a new entry in his logbook. "December 11. 1948. DH82 Tiger Moth. VH-ATF. FIRST SOLO. Thirty minutes."

Trainee mechanic by day and pilot by weekend and night, Phillip continued to manage the workload well. He was thrilled to crawl over an Air Force Vampire fighter jet when it arrived and could only imagine what it would take to fly one at such speeds. The cockpit was a maze of instruments compared to the basic panel in his Tiger Moth. That same month Eric arranged for a number of the aero club's aircraft to fly to nearby Lockhart as part of a goodwill visit. It was the day before Phillip's twenty-third birthday and Eric invited him to come along for the ride. Once at Lockhart the aircraft flew a series of joy rides, including the Club's Wackett trainer.

Phillip thought it strange as the two-seat Wackett readied for take-off when two passengers climbed aboard to share the one rear seat. After the low-winged trainer had reached only about 150 feet above the ground it appeared to be terribly slow and its nose terribly high. In a second, the Wackett's nose dropped and the left wing lowered as the aircraft fell to earth. It hit the ground heavily in a cacophony of noise and dirt. Phillip and the other aero club members raced towards the crash site as one of the passengers pulled the badly injured pilot from the front cockpit.

Clear of the aeroplane, the risk of fire was very real and Phillip joined the others in finding a fire extinguisher. Their efforts were only moments too late for, as they approached the broken aeroplane, it caught fire and, with its load of fuel, soon became a fireball forcing everyone back. He knew that there shouldn't have been two passengers in the back seat and, as he learned more about the theory of flight, he learned just how lethal such overloading can be.

Another weekend when he had finished flying, Phillip was 'recruited' for a secondary role by Eric who had acquired an Avro Anson from the RAAF. Eric had asked the commanding officer at the air base where he could purchase some spare engines to which the reply was "Help yourself!" as the officer pointed out the window towards the rows of abandoned aeroplanes. Now Phillip sat with his instructor and budding airline baron in a flat bed truck driving towards the perishing hulks that were waiting to be smelted down and reborn as saucepans.

Row upon row of fighting planes sat there; Vultee Vengeances, Beauforts and the beautifully lethal Bristol Beaufighter. There were hundreds of them, all exposed to the elements and stripped of their armament. Occasionally one still bore the markings of missions flown against the Japanese painted on its nose, a reminder of a more valiant time. Now they were mere ghosts of their former selves with tales to tell but only the encroaching weeds there to listen.

Finally, the two came upon a couple of very old, very damaged, Avro Ansons with their engines still in place. They removed the engine cowlings and then proceeded to back the truck up, placing the flat tray beneath one of the engines. With a reasonable amount of effort and absolutely no finesse, they cut through the engine mounts and dropped one engine and then another onto the back of the truck.

Phillip's own flying continued to progress and in January he ventured beyond the confines of the airfield, and take-offs and landings, to learn how to navigate. His first cross-country flight was a simple hop across to the township of Young and back; about an hour of flight time each way. His flights gradually increased in duration over the weeks, visiting other townships such as Naranderra and Temora. He was seeing so much of the countryside as he acquired the skill of navigating by map, watch and antiquated compass. Interspersed were sessions of aerobatics in the old biplane that he found particularly enjoyable and not once did he feel any of the nausea that had plagued him in the back seat of the Ansons on his navigator's course. In fact, the aerobatics only further emphasised the sense of freedom, unburdened in any of the three planes and looking at the world below from angles and perspectives that he could never have hoped to imagine.

By April he was ready and Eric assessed his student as safe and proficient to hold a Private Pilot's Licence. Phillip was now the holder of licence number 5231 and was free to fly anywhere, even Toowoomba if he had the time and money. However, the demands of his flight mechanic course had been intensive since February and he had to be satisfied by shorter jaunts to Goulburn, Albury and across to Jervis Bay. There, on the coast, he would buzz the beach and marvel at the cliffs to one side and the pounding ocean to the other. It was pure freedom and he knew in his heart that he would not be happy until flight was his vocation.

His final exams to graduate as a mechanic were drawing near and all indications were that he would be successful. But now a fire was lit deep within Phillip and it could not be doused by anything short of success. He had now more than tasted the skies, he had felt at home there in a way that he had never known on the ground. He wanted to go where Hinkler and Smithy had gone. He wanted to soar amongst the cumulus and fly even farther and faster, leaving the world in his wake. He dared to dream once and now he looked down upon the world with that dream realised. Now he aimed even higher. He wanted to be a pilot in the Royal Australian Air Force.

The seed had been planted in Phillip's mind when the Vampire jet made its visit to Wagga and he had clambered over it in absolute awe. The sheer speed and brute power of the screaming aircraft made his Norton sound like cracking a matchstick. Everything about the jet intrigued him both aerodynamically and in an engineering sense and the respect the pilot received as he climbed down from his cockpit was a far cry from his own bush beginnings. To wear Air Force wings and fly such machines was the pinnacle as he saw it.

It was a long way between aspiring to be aircrew and actually being selected. In his favour, he had been more than holding his own on his course and he now held a Private Pilot's Licence. Weighing heavily against him was his lack of formal education compared to other candidates, the fact that the Air Force had been downsizing since the war and the issue of only gaining A3B medical status the first time around with the RAAF. That only permitted him to fly as a 'combatant passenger', such as a navigator or air gunner, although his subsequent medical status had been adequate to serve as a Commando in New Guinea.

Weighing up the options, and figuring that he had nothing to lose, he applied for aircrew training. Excitedly, he completed the form, but found there were a lot of blank spaces where he had nothing to offer. The reply was quick in coming, he had not been successful. He was disappointed, but not distraught, and vowed to keep trying.

He expended even greater effort towards his studies and continued to accumulate flight time, believing that both could only enhance his prospects. When May arrived he was rewarded by achieving a 'Pass with Special Distinction' on his flight mechanics Course and was posted to RAAF Rathmines. At Rathmines he would complete the practical phase of his training with a squadron. In this case it was the recently reformed 11 Squadron that operated Catalina flying boats in a search and rescue capacity.

However, he had no sooner arrived at Rathmines than he applied for aircrew training again. This time he was more particular with the form stating that his Air Training Corps passes had previously been recognised as a satisfactory level of education. He also highlighted that he now had 55 hours of flight experience and a Private Pilot's Licence. His recent 'Pass with Special Distinction' must also work in his favour so he was far more confident when he submitted the form for a second time. That confidence grew when there wasn't a rapid-fire rejection.

A week later he was called to the office at Rathmines to be interviewed regarding his application. Across the table sat Squadron Leader P.J. McMahon DFC, the commanding officer of 11 Squadron. McMahon had originally seen action in World War Two flying amphibious aircraft off HMAS *Manoora* before commanding a Catalina squadron. For a man in his early thirties, he could have written a book on flying boat operations.

Despite his air of confidence, McMahon was not intimidating. He spoke with the young aircraftsman and probed why he wanted to become a pilot and why he thought he might be suitable. Phillip was a more confident candidate than when he'd been asked these questions in 1944 and the answers were succinct and fair. McMahon was impressed with the youngster and respected his past military service, but still his education presented a glaring hole in the application.

The Air Training Corps passes might have been adequate in wartime, but the world and the Air Force had moved on. They could afford to be more selective and the reality was that Phillip hadn't even sat the exams to mark the completion of his primary education. McMahon remarked on Phillip's zest and drive and his apparent suitability even though he'd only been with the squadron a matter of weeks.

When Phillip opened the response regarding his selection for aircrew training, it was again in the negative. This time he was bitterly disappointed. Even so, for the next three months he kept his head down and his tail up. He listened intently and did exactly what he was told as he came to know the Catalina intimately. His ongoing assessments and results were good, and he was honestly enjoying the work, but he could not shake the bug to become a pilot.

Some weeks later he was perusing the notice board when he saw a call for servicemen to retrain, or re-muster, as pilots. His heart sank a little, fearing that the flood-gates would open and applications would pour in and push him further down the queue. Then, as he stood there, he sensed a presence behind him. Turning, Phillip snapped straight when he realised that the shadow belonged to Squadron Leader McMahon.

The Commanding Officer immediately recognised which notice Phillip had been reading and asked if he was going to reapply for aircrew training. Phillip stated that he would, although he had to be honest that he didn't like his chances. Squadron Leader McMahon started walking away but not before saying, "You just never know."

Phillip had not even submitted the application when the paperwork arrived. He was instructed to pack up and make his way to Point Cook, Victoria, the home of No. 1 Flying Training School and the birthplace of the Royal Australian Air Force. He read the letter a couple of times to check that there wasn't a mistake. He could hardly contain his excitement. He was sure that Squadron Leader McMahon had something to do with it and he would never forget the chance he had just been given.

Vampire. One of the Air Force's fighter jets made a brief visit to RAAF Forrest Hill in 1949.

No. 4 Pilot's Course. Phillip stands to the far right in the middle row.

Chapter Fifteen

Air Force Wings

The Royal Australian Air Force's base at Point Cook had come into being before the First World War as part of Australia's vision of establishing a Flying Corps. The airbase sat to the south-west of Melbourne on the shores of Port Phillip Bay in a relatively remote, low-lying area. When Phillip arrived in late August 1949, it initially seemed like so many other military bases with a guardhouse, a parade ground, a Mess and accommodation. It wasn't long, however, before he sensed that it was very different to his previous postings.

Tiger Moth and Wirraway training aircraft were continually passing overhead while, on the ground, trainees marched between classrooms in formation with their arms swinging high. Other cadets could be spotted in full flying gear and the officers in dress uniform inherently wore a pair of wings and a chest full of ribbons earned in the most recent world war. The ground oozed history and the air was drenched in flight. Point Cook may have been the Air Force's spiritual home, but Phillip also felt that it could very well be his.

He was assigned a room in the two-storey wooden barracks and soaked up the excitement as the 55 candidates settled in and stowed their gear. This was only the fourth intake of aircrew trainees in the four years since World War Two and every one of the young men felt privileged to be there. Yet they also knew that their journey had only just begun as only fifteen of their number would be selected for the highly coveted pilot's course. The remainder would become navigators, wireless operators or possibly be summarily scrubbed from aircrew training.

Over the next six months the trainees would be instructed on every aspect of basic flight and assessed in every manner imaginable. The ground training would be intensive, covering a broad range of around twenty subjects that drew in everything from English, mathematics and physics to airmanship, aerodynamics and engines. The trainees would be progressively rated on their work before final examinations would take place. Of course, there was also more drill and marching. By now Phillip had joined the armed forces three times and each time he had effectively been a new recruit, destined to 'square bash' around the parade ground. The yelling, marching, shining shoes and 'panic night' room inspections were now just par for the course.

When the ground school had been completed, then began a critical phase for those aspiring to a position on the pilot's course; flight grading. Each trainee would be given ten hours of flight training in the Tiger Moth, culminating in a flight test. Based upon the combined assessment of their performance over the six month period, their future specialty would be determined. As the young men mingled, Phillip sensed from the outset that the competition would be fierce. There were some extremely sharp minds in the group; polished off with the sound education that Phillip had been denied. There were ten naval cadets, destined to claim a few spots on pilot's course and, like him, a number of chaps had previous military service and had been re-mustered.

Phillip was finally issued with his own copy of the Pilot's Flying Manual, five years after he had acquired his well-worn copy at Mount Gambier. He set about studying from the very first day, aware that he had a great deal of work to do to reach anything near an equal academic footing with the others. In the absence of any common areas in the barracks, the halls became a standard meeting place and the noise that emanated from these conversations was about the only distraction to Phillip's studies.

Point Cook did not even boast a village in 1949, so on weekends a group of the cadets would often venture into Melbourne for lunch and a movie on Saturday as only churches and the zoo were open of a Sunday. Just outside the airbase's gate was the 'Greasy Spoon', a small café where the monotony of Mess food could be occasionally broken. For Phillip, there was no urgency to break the routine, and the Air Force food was fine by him, so more often than not he would remain in the books, endeavouring to make up for lost schooling.

To his advantage was the fact that he had already had a pilot's licence, and that must surely be of use when he reached the flight grading stage, but he had to get there first. To aid his chances, Phillip made his way to Essendon Airport on some

Tiger Moths are prepared for their next sortie at Point Cook, 1950.

Saturdays when his course-mates made their way to the movies. Once there, he would hire a Tiger Moth from the Royal Victorian Aero Club and fly a series of take-offs and landings to keep his hand in at flying.

His diligence was recognised from the early stages of the course by both his instructors and his peers. They recognised that he was a little rough around the edges, in terms of schooling and etiquette, but there was no denying his drive and ability. He struggled at times with subjects such as English, but proved to be strong in aerodynamics, mathematics and physics. These were the results that the instructors paid significant attention to.

By the end of the initial ground school phase of training at the end of 1949, Phillip had done more than enough to progress. He had been positively assessed in both character and proficiency and was cleared to progress to flight grading where he hoped that his previous experience may just provide the competitive edge he sought.

With the arrival of 1950, the dynamic within the course shifted just a little from Phillip's perspective. Whereas he had bordered on feeling inferior in the academic stakes, he now believed that flight grading was his best chance to impress the instructors. He had sixty hours flying Tiger Moths and had kept current on his weekend visits to Essendon. Over the next ten hours of flying with his air force instructors, he would concentrate on flying their way; the military way. Instructors were always on the lookout for the non-standard habits brought in by trainees with previous flying experience.

The flight grading was to consist of ten hours flying with a progress test at the halfway mark and a final test when all of the hours had been flown. For Phillip, it was a slight reprieve from the rigours of the classroom, although the briefings and study continued at breakneck pace when he wasn't in the cockpit. He could certainly fly, but this was a very different world.

In place of Wagga's pair of Tiger Moths, were rows of mostly silver machines uniformly painted with yellow bands about their fuselage. Rather than being the ultimate craft, the Tiger Moth was the first, but critical, stepping-stone on the military pilot's journey. To guide Phillip initially through this phase of 'make or break' was Warrant Officer Scott. Recognising his pupil's previous experience, Scott wasted no time getting Phillip back into the high workload environment of the circuit area to perfect his take-offs, approaches and landings. Phillip's five hour test with Flight Lieutenant Wes Guy went without a hitch but his eyes were firmly on the final grading test with Squadron Leader Glen Cooper DFC; the commanding officer of 1FTS at Point Cook.

In the wake of World War Two, the instructing staff at Point Cook boasted a wealth of operational experience. Cooper had been an instructor at 1FTS before the war and had seen action in New Guinea as a fighter pilot, earning the Distinguished Flying Cross. Flying Curtiss P-40 Kittyhawks, he had commanded 80 Squadron in New Guinea, which had been known as 'Cooper's Flying Circus'. Later, he commanded an entire Wing, and flew the legendary Spitfire, before being posted to Japan with the Occupation Force at war's end. While Trooper Zupp had been kicking through the ashes of Hiroshima, Squadron Leader Cooper had been one of those overhead flying the majestic Mustang out of Iwakuni.

Yet their limited shared history meant nothing as Phillip readied for his final test in the Tiger Moth. He had flown the second stage of his training with Flight Lieutenant Ken McAtee and he had smoothed the edges of the youngster in readiness for the big day. As Phillip climbed into the cockpit with Squadron Leader

Cooper that February morning, he felt more nervous than he had ever been before. Sidestepping booby traps in New Guinea or patrolling the hills beyond Hiroshima had held no great fears for Phillip, but the possibility of failure at this final stage of the selection process was pushing his stomach up into his throat.

With Cooper in the Tiger Moth's front cockpit, Phillip's forward vision was greatly impeded by the back of the commanding officer's head, but at least he couldn't see the fear in his eyes. As Phillip slid down further into his seat, however, and checked his parachute harness and pulled his belt tight, he began to relax. With

Vance Drummond, Jim Kichenside and Doug Robertson at Point Cook beside a Tiger Moth.

every thoroughly drilled action, his mind began to focus on the task rather than the occasion. By the time the propeller had been swung and the engine had burst into life, Phillip's mind was pre-occupied with flying the aeroplane and nothing else. As the wheels left the earth, he only cared about squeezing in just enough rudder and holding the aeroplane so steady in its attitude, that the airspeed indicator needle appeared to be frozen.

A disembodied voice would arrive in his helmet, asking him to complete all manner of exercises in the air. As he climbed and turned, stalled and glided, landed and took off, he only saw the horizon ahead and felt the aeroplane respond beneath his gloved hands. Through absolute concentration, Cooper all but disappeared and it was just Phillip, his Tiger Moth and Point Cook below. When the voice instructed him to make his next landing the last one, he merely responded and didn't consider whether that was a good or bad sign. That emotion only returned when the propeller had stopped and the fighter pilot with the DFC climbed out of the front cockpit once again.

The waiting now began. All of the candidate's flight grading results had to be collated and the assessments by their instructors factored into the equation. In the end, the final fifteen positions would be allocated to pilot training with the remaining number bound for East Sale and navigator training. When the results were announced, they were announced in alphabetical order; the bane of Phillip's existence. The fifteen trainee pilots selected were; Bear, Blackwell, Drummond, Gillan, Halley, Murray, Myers, Newson, Oborn, Robertson, Strawbridge, Thomson, Towner, Waugh and Zupp.

He'd made it!

As one of the final fifteen, Phillip now had a genuine chance to become an Air Force pilot. The first elementary stage of training would take place on the Tiger Moth before moving on to the speedier Wirraway and, finally, the twin-engine Airspeed Oxford. The next twelve months and 200 hours of flight time would see his wings stretched far beyond the confines of Point Cook and Port Phillip Bay. He would come to know his aircraft inside out and quite literally upside down. There would be navigation exercises across Victoria, simulated engine failures, flight without any guidance other than the biplane's handful of dials and, of course, aerobatics. It was to be the greatest challenge of his young life, but the Gods of good fortune continued to shine down upon him.

Phillip's primary flying instructor and mentor over the next year would be Warrant Officer Alan 'Blue' Philp. Like his student, 'Blue' was a Queenslander and also had family on the Darling Downs. Slightly taller and lither than Phillip, 'Blue' derived his traditional nickname from his ginger hair and fair complexion. Importantly, his manner put Phillip at ease and for him it was just one Queensland country boy teaching another how to fly an aeroplane.

Even so, there was no place for complacency or time to relax. The workload was high and Phillip knew in himself that he wasn't one of the gifted pilots. He was more a product of enthusiasm and sheer bloody-mindedness. Nor was this a light-hearted business. Trainee pilots could very easily be killed and a reminder was evident early in Phillip's training. Having recovered from spinning the Tiger Moth, 'Blue' pointed out the crumpled wreck of another Tiger in a field west of Point Cook. As they orbited around the aeroplane, Phillip could see that everything forward of the front cockpit was a twisted mess. 'Blue' then told him that the pilot had survived, but had not fully recovered from a spin before the aircraft crashed into the ground.

Aerobatics in the Tiger Moth were more graceful than aggressive. In the absence of power, gravity was used to accelerate the aeroplane into a manoeuvre and, once there, any energy disappeared rather quickly. Rather than a loop describing a symmetrical arc in the sky, often the Tiger did well just to get to the top of the loop before politely continuing over the top in an ellipse and accelerating down the hill once more. With the need to fly precisely in order to preserve the precious inertia, the Tiger Moth kept Phillip honest. As he looped, stall turned and barrel rolled about the sky it called for significant pedaling and pushing of the control stick. All the while the wind whistled through the wires and brushed his cheeks.

By the nature of the controls, one used their feet in a Tiger Moth to keep the aeroplane nicely aligned with the airflow in balanced flight. A failure to do so greatly impeded the ability to climb adequately on a hot day but, more to the point, raised the ire of 'Blue' in the front cockpit who felt as if the aeroplane was flying sideways. Taken to the limits of Air Force training, Phillip found the Tiger Moth to be a challenging, but fair, aeroplane. It was also an aeroplane that was easy to fly badly.

The freedom to fly cross-country enchanted Phillip. The sight of houses and livestock slipping beneath his wingtip was something that he never tired of, however, the workload on these exercises was always high. For the breeze that romantically whispered past the open cockpit also had the potential to rip maps from the grip of the most vigilant trainee pilot. Finding the right balance between flying the aeroplane, knowing where you are and steering a new course on a very primitive compass made a flight interesting. 'Blue' would then up the stakes by calling for a low level leg across the countryside where there was no time to look down at charts and major landmarks could be lost behind the surrounding terrain. However, the sense of speed down low was much greater and Phillip yearned for more.

Along the way, Phillip would fly with other instructors to assess his progress. All his performances were progressively logged in a file that would never fall under his gaze and was known by the trainees as the 'Hate Sheet'. 'Blue' kept pushing him and Phillip kept responding. Where there was life, there was hope and Phillip was still alive and kicking. He had completed cross-country exercises on his own, undertaken formation training and was growing steadily closer to moving up to the Wirraway. He knew that it would be a quantum leap with a 600 horsepower radial engine up front compared to the Tiger Moth's 145 horsepower. The Wirraway had retractable main wheels, an enclosed canopy, more advanced instrumentation, a more complex propeller system and even the potential to carry weaponry. All of this was wrapped up in 6,000 pounds of aeroplane hurtling along at up to three times the speed of a Tiger Moth. He couldn't wait.

In May, Phillip returned from a solo session of Tiger Moth aerobatics to find Point Cook abuzz. One of the Wirraways had failed to return from a training flight and the pilot had been killed. Initial speculation suggested that the trainee pilot had flown into the ground while mock dogfighting with another trainee. However, there was also some speculation that the trainee had been attempting low level aerobatics near a passing train, spearing down to ground level before pulling up abruptly and commencing a rolling manoeuvre, only to nose over into the ground at high speed. The other pilot witnessed the tragedy and then had to gather himself to safely return to Point Cook.

The riot act was read to all of the trainees and 'Blue' followed up with some well-chosen words for Phillip. A few days later, the sobering sight of trainee pilots carrying the coffin of a course-mate sent an even stronger message to those on No.4 Pilot's Course. Even so, boys would be boys when aeroplanes were involved and this wouldn't be the last accident or loss of life in training that Phillip would encounter and, just like combat in New Guinea, it would never be him that would catch the bullet, it would be someone else.

When the time came to graduate to the Wirraway, 'Blue' was there again to guide Phillip through it. By now he had taken a great liking to his instructor that was founded on real respect. Similarly, Phillip had bonded with the other members of his pilot's course. Previously, he had kept fairly well to himself, but through the shared experience, trials and tribulations of flight training, true friendships were growing. Away from flying he would take a boat out on Port Phillip Bay with Doug Robertson and Peter Waugh, occasionally attracting the low-flying attention of fellow trainees, or he and Bob Strawbridge and Vance Drummond would wander to the distant corner of the airfield and crawl over a rotting Spitfire or Hurricane.

AIR FORCE WINGS

Leather helmets, scarves and goggles in place, the Wirraway was the RAAF's advanced trainer in 1950.

Of a night the lads would chat and intermingle with the new course of pilots coming through. Ken Towner, Bruce Gillan and Vic Oborn were all becoming mates and the bond reminded him of those days at Canungra and of Les Turner and Ian Wharton, although surely these were different times. And yet they weren't.

For as Phillip and his course mates readied to fly the Wirraway for the first time in June of 1950, North and South Korea traded blows and went to war. Tension had been brewing on the Korean Peninsula since 1945 when Japan surrendered the territory they had previously occupied for 35 years. Initially, the United Nations moved towards re-unification, however, just as Berlin had been split into East and West in the wake of World War Two, Korea became divided into North and South along the 38th parallel of latitude. To the north of the 38th parallel existed Stalin-backed communist rule, while to the south, President Truman of the United States supported a democratic republic. The two world powers stared each other down and the Korean Peninsula was the stage. Stalin bet that Truman wouldn't risk nuclear war over such a remote peninsula and before sunrise on the 25th of June 1950, the North invaded the South. Stalin was wrong.

Basic geography may have suggested that Phillip's flight training was far removed from the machinations taking place on the Korean Peninsula, but this was far from the reality of the situation. The Royal Australian Air Force had maintained a presence in Japan since the end of World War Two as part of the BCOF and within days of the outbreak of war, the Australian Prime Minister Sir Robert Menzies had committed 77 Squadron to the conflict. The Australian pilots had been readying to return to Australia when they were thrust back into the front line.

The ramifications for Phillip and his fellow trainees were obvious. The RAAF was now at war and short of pilots due to the scaling back following World War Two. Now No. 4 Pilot's Course sat at Point Cook with another eight months left before they would graduate when they would be among the first in the breech for this new war. A new intensity came over the young pilots, particularly those like Phillip who had seen action before. The stakes were now raised to a new level and anyone who had perceived that this was anything less than a very serious business had their illusions absolutely shattered when Squadron Leader Graham Strout was shot down and killed over North Korea July 7th.

Strout had been flying a Mustang fighter at the time of his death and the CAC Wirraway was a very tangible stepping stone to such a fighter from the Tiger Moth. Its complexity of systems and handling over the Tiger Moth made it quite a sizeable transition to undertake. Whereas the Tiger had its solid wooden propeller, the Wirraway had a metal propeller with movable blades that enhanced performance and were controlled from the cockpit. Its wheels retracted into its single low-wing for improved performance although, on the ground, the Wirraway could be difficult to steer. For a Queenslander like Phillip, the enclosed canopy was a welcome means to keep the chilly Point Cook winter at bay.

Kitted out in his full flying suit, life jacket, parachute, flying boots and leather helmet, Phillip stepped up on to the Wirraway's wing and climbed into the front cockpit for the first time. Now 'Blue' would have to look at the back of his head for a change. He had sat in the aircraft at length previously and studied his pilot's notes until the pages were fraying. Now it was time to bring the Wirraway to life with the luxury of a starter motor. The procedure was baked into his brain. He could find every lever and switch blindfolded, the legacy of spending every spare moment running through his drills.

He adjusted his seat, checking that his forward visibility was sufficient. Check. Rudder pedals adjusted, unlock the controls and verify that their movement is unhindered, parking brake 'on'. Check. Master Switch 'on' to bring the electrical system to life and confirm that the wheels are selected 'down'. Check. Cycle the flaps up and down with the hydraulic pump and unlock the tailwheel. Check and ready to start. Fuel selector to 'Reserve'. Click. Operate the hand fuel pressure pump to read at least three pounds per square inch. Done. Six strokes of the fuel primer, then lock it. Push the starter button. Yahoo!

The nine cylinders of the Pratt & Whitney radial inhaled the mixture of fuel and air, coughing as the spark ignited the cocktail. Puffs of smoke belched back past Phillip's cockpit as the three propeller blades slowly turned before the cough became a throaty roar and the blades disappeared into a single constant disc ahead. The entire airframe seemed to develop a low harmonic pulse at that point as if a sleeping beast had been awoken. Phillip double-checked that the parking brake was set as the Wirraway seemed very keen to go flying with or without him.

Phillip muttered to himself, "Oil pressure up and rising, throttle set to 1,000rpm, Carburettor Heat 'cold', Gyros, suction and other instruments." He took a breath and checked outside that nobody was unwittingly walking towards this roaring beast. "Altimeter to 'zero', Compass Ring 'locked', Switches 'set' and harness secure." He checked that 'Blue' was also set to go and then he moved off gingerly, wary of the power at his fingertips.

He taxied the trainer out to the take-off area and completed his final checks of the aeroplane's engine and controls. Lined up on the runway, 'Blue' took over for the first take-off and told Phillip to 'follow him through' just as Eric had instructed him on that very first take-off at Wagga. With the propeller lever set to 'Maximum RPM' and the control stick fully back, 'Blue' eased the throttle forward to the gate and the manifold pressure gauge now indicated 32 inches of power, or 'boost'. The Wirraway responded, initially with a gentle roll, before accelerating into a full-blooded take-off.

'Blue' eased the stick forward, to raise the tail and bring the Wirraway up to its flying posture, and eased in some right rudder pedal to stop any tendency to swing in response to the giant propeller's torque. At 75 knots, the speed at which a Tiger Moth cruises aloft, the Wirraway took to the skies in its own right, accelerating quickly to 95 knots and then climbing away. 'Blue' touched the brakes, retracted the wheels, checked the mixture lever was still 'fully rich' and retarded the engine settings to 28 inches of boost with the throttle and then 2100rpm with the propeller. Flaps selected 'up', check for other aircraft and set course for the training area. "Handing Over!". The instructor's words rattled in Phillip's ears as he waggled the control stick and acknowledged. This was flying.

The wind was no longer waltzing between his wings and the breeze was no longer in his face. He was strapped in, low and tight, and belting along at 130 knots. He and 'Blue' would spend a few lessons getting to know the Wirraway in the training area before it was time to return to perfect take-off and landings. They would turn the aeroplane steeply; fly it so slowly that eventually it ran out of lift and stalled; they spun it and looped it and pretended that the engine had stopped and the only way to land was via a gliding descent. All the while, Phillip became more comfortable with the cockpit and what was expected of him.

In the training circuit where take-offs and landings were practised, everything seemed to happen quickly. On his first take-off, advancing the throttle, stopping the swing, taking flight, raising the wheels, setting the power and retracting the flaps, all happened at once. 'Blue' chuckled from the back seat as Phillip's arms and legs were everywhere converting this lumbering piece of land-based engineering into an airborne example of relatively modern aviation.

With sweat on his brow and 'Blue' in his ear, Phillip readied the Wirraway to come around and land once more. The trainee pilot rumour mill had this tabbed as the place most likely to mess up. If you touched the brakes too soon, she'd tip on her nose and if you let her get away from you directionally on the ground, she'd ground loop. In the latter case the tail would swing around in an instant and have you embarrassingly facing the wrong way with quite possibly a tyre wrenched off the rim and a damaged wingtip. There was no time to let doubt creep in. There was only time to complete checks and fly the aeroplane.

The airfield now sat just off the left wingtip, just the right distance away. Phillip completed his pre-landing checks and selected the undercarriage down. When the time was right, he throttled back and turned the Wirraway towards the runway. Finessing power and flap he brought the aeroplane into alignment with the field ahead. Crossing the edge of the field he smoothly reduced the power and raised the nose until the throttle was closed and the nose approached the angle it sat at when the aircraft was on the ground. Then, contact. He had nailed his first landing in a Wirraway! Just as the thought entered his head, the aeroplane started to bite the complacent trainee. Shifting left and right, it threatened to ground loop and spin Phillip around. He felt coarse inputs through the rudder pedals as 'Blue' showed the aircraft who was the boss. From that day forward Phillip knew that the flight wasn't over until the aircraft was tied down or in the hangar.

As the weeks passed by, he came to know the Wirraway on better terms. He was learning to fly and navigate it with reference solely to instruments, shrouded beneath a canvas hood and putting into practice the lessons learnt in the Link Trainer; a very, very basic flight simulator. The skill of instrument flying is hinged upon self-discipline. It is the self-discipline to ignore the body's natural signals and place one's faith entirely on the information being provided by the aeroplane's dials and gauges. It is also the self-discipline to continually ascertain that information through a regular scan of the instruments, avoiding fixation on any one dial.

To further challenge that discipline, 'Blue' would routinely disrupt a perfectly uneventful flight by ripping the aeroplane into some unusual attitude that saw it falling inverted from the sky or spinning to earth. He would then simply tell Phillip to recover. Thanks to his training, Phillip could ignore the horrendous situation, draw the appropriate information from the instruments and salvage the situation to return the Wirraway to stable flight. After one such recovery, 'Blue' told the student that another way of telling if your aircraft was inverted in these situations was that the "shit would be running out your collar"! Phillip laughed all the way back to Point Cook.

There were low-level sorties when he would terrorise sheep and dive-bombing practise when the Wirraway would hurtle towards the earth at what seemed like breakneck speeds with the airflow screaming past the cockpit. Taking the challenge one step further, cine camera gunnery sessions had the trainee pilots using each other as targets, firing film instead of bullets. In these sorties the pilots would learn how to estimate the range and line of flight of another aeroplane as they endeavoured to shoot it down. Then would come the art of deflection and assessing how far ahead of a target the attacker should lead with his aim to allow for the time the bullets will take to reach the target. Finally, there were 'quarter attacks' where the attacker would position offset to the rear of the target and make a firing pass. Phillip was in his realm combining flying with fighting. He had been a crack shot as a boy and through his Army years and now he was spitting fire from the front of an aeroplane.

He came to know the Wirraway as a strong aeroplane, far in advance of the Tiger Moth. With each flight he grew more and more comfortable with its vices and its attributes. In such a positive frame of mind, late one afternoon Phillip made an approach to land at Point Cook with a slight crosswind; no big deal. He flew the approach, touched down and was slowing down without fuss, already mentally retiring for the evening, when the Wirraway bit back. Without warning she took offence at his leisurely attitude and the puffs of wind from her beam. She teetered for a moment, threatening a ground loop, before suddenly falling off. Phillip was too slow and too timid with the rudder and the Wirraway hurled itself about its own axis. One wheel dug into the Point Cook turf, while the other wingtip reared into the sky and the horizon flicked wildly past his windscreen. By this time Phillip was fighting the aeroplane, but in reality he was just along for the ride. Then, as quickly as it had started, the Wirraway came to a halt amid flying clods of dirt.

He was now sitting off to the edge of the airfield with the radial engine still pounding out its beat. He had been the last arrival and the entire air base seemed deserted except for his heart pounding in his throat. He shut down the engine and climbed down from the cockpit expecting to see the tyre screwed off the wheel. It wasn't. He walked around the aeroplane and carefully checked it over only to find a few grass stains on one wingtip. He had literally come within inches of digging in and wrecking the Wirraway. He spat on the evidence and rubbed the stains thoroughly with a rag from his pocket until all that remained was a suspiciously clean patch of wingtip. He re-started the engine, thanked God and parked the aeroplane for the night.

The Wirraway was testing every trainee by this stage and night flying had now entered the training regime. This was a whole new experience, taking to the skies without any horizon available to tell the mind which way is up. A greater reliance was placed on the ability to fly on instruments as the night could play tricks and disorientate a pilot very quickly. For his part, Phillip was at home night flying. The stillness of the air, the stars above and the dim glow of the cockpit lights were like another world and one that very few had the ability to visit.

Taking off and landing by night were a challenge but, once the skill had been mastered, the trainees were sent out over Port Phillip Bay for some solo consolidation flying in the black abyss of the night. It was on one of those evenings that Phillip performed one of his most stupid acts in an aeroplane. The sortie had called for a simulated emergency landing gear extension followed by a series of turns before returning to Point Cook. The extension of the gear was straightforward and he was soon bored with turns to the left and right so he decided to get adventurous.

He pushed the Wirraway's nose down and accelerated the aeroplane to 170 knots. As it roared downwards, he heaved back on the stick to bring the aircraft up into a loop. At night. At the top of the loop, the Wirraway objected, shuddered and, low on airspeed, fell out of the loop. The aeroplane toppled from the sky as did every instrument indication in front of him. There was no horizon or shadows to tell him which way was up so he locked his scan on the instruments and desperately sought to extract the critical information. Nose down, speed increasing, left wing down. He processed the facts and used his hands and feet as 'Blue' had taught him to recover the Wirraway back to controlled level flight. Once under control Phillip found time to draw a breath. His heart was racing and he could feel the sweat beading on his cold skin. He couldn't work out what the problem was and then, all of a sudden, he felt sick to the core. In his foolhardy impatience, he had failed to close a valve after the simulated emergency landing gear extension. Despite selecting the gear to 'up', it had remained down. He had tried to loop a Wirraway, at night, with the wheels down! To make matters worse, he had exceeded the maximum speed for the Wirraway with the landing gear extended. Idiot!

He flew back to Point Cook and landed with his tail between his legs. He immediately sought out 'Blue' and confessed his sins, desperately angry and disappointed in himself. The instructor was not happy and let his young charge know it, but commended him on admitting that he had exceeded an aircraft limit. 'Blue' could see that Phillip's self-recriminations were far more severe than any punishment he could dole out, so he left the situation at that. Phillip was thankful, but wondered what had been written in his 'hate sheet' about such a stupid act.

Phillip knew that he wasn't the ace of the course and chastised himself for his complacency and stupidity. He was neither the first nor the last offender during the course of his training but was still angered by his stupidity. Another trainee's fall from grace was far more public when he failed to ensure that the flaps were locked 'down' when he made his approach to land. Flying too fast, the young pilot wasted valuable runway, landing well into the field and still travelling too fast. The runaway Wirraway scattered anyone in the vicinity as it speared off and headed towards the row of pine trees where it finally came to a halt, with a very expensive thud, just short of the instructors' parked cars.

These misadventures combined to give Phillip a wake-up call and a new focus. He envied the chaps that possessed that extra ability, blokes like his mate, Vance Drummond. Vance was a New Zealander who, like himself, had trained as a navigator in World War Two but was too late to see action. He had also been in Japan, as an interpreter for the New Zealand forces, when Phillip was there. Now the two were on the pilot's course together and Vance was showing that he had all the 'right stuff' to be a pilot of the highest calibre. The instructors spoke of Vance with the highest regard and when it came to Cine Camera Gunnery, he always seemed to have the edge in handling and a steady aim to come out on top. Even Vance, however, was not immune.

One Monday morning in October, as Phillip prepared his charts for an upcoming solo cross-country flight, Vance was starting his Wirraway and readying to depart along the same route. The flight was to depart to the southwest over Swan Marsh before turning north to Lismore and then returning to Point Cook. The flight time was a little under two hours, which would have Vance home around lunch time. However, midday came and went and Vance had not yet returned. He finally arrived home 24 hours later and he kept Phillip and the others on the edge of their seats as he told them what had happened.

The first leg had gone as planned with Vance turning to the north over Swan Marsh. His route to Lismore would then take him over Lake Corangamite, so Vance descended the aircraft to two hundred feet above ground level to traverse the lake. It was a still day and the surface of the lake was like glass but, while it made for a picturesque scene, it also made the task of judging one's height significantly more difficult.

Inside the cockpit, Vance still had to attend to managing the aircraft's performance, cross-checking his position and all the tasks that go with operating a Wirraway. Unfortunately, the Wirraway was not particularly user-friendly, with non-descript levers jutting out from every available space and no logical theme to the arrangement of instrumentation. The worst offender was the liquid-filled P8 magnetic compass that sat virtually on the floor, in front of the pilot but on the other side of the control column. This antiquated cylindrical navigation device was the size of a small fruitcake and would not have been out of place on the sailing square-riggers of the previous century.

As Vance crossed the lake, he checked his fuel stocks and then leant forward to synchronise his Direction Indicator with his compass. At this time he sensed the aircraft start to slightly nose over and responded by pulling back on the stick. No sooner had the aircraft responded to his input when it felt like all hell had broken loose. The aircraft vibrated violently and shook beneath him as he raised the nose further and slammed the throttle forward in search of full power. However, the vibrations continued and the aircraft refused to climb away. His propeller had obviously struck the water and now the bent, out-of-balance airscrew threatened to rip the engine clean out of the airframe. There was no other option and Vance prepared to ditch the Wirraway in the lake. He slid his canopy back and tightened his harness and eased the aircraft down onto the water. The tail struck first and then the belly of the aeroplane, hurling Vance forward in his harness and smashing his nose against the instrument coaming.

The next few moments were a blur and Vance found himself stripped of his flying gear and adrift at a distance from the aeroplane. Bleeding from the nose, he swam back to the submerged Wirraway and took refuge upon the tailplane which was only a foot beneath the surface. After nearly two hours of waiting, he was rowed ashore and checked out at the local hospital.

Phillip and the lads had hung on every word. Firstly, because Vance had inadvertently leant forward on the control stick and very nearly flown into the lake at speed, so a lesson was there to be heeded. Secondly, because this was the pacesetter of the course, Vance Drummond, and if it could happen to him, it could happen to anyone. Everyone realised just how close Vance had come to spearing in, but thankfully he had made it back in one piece. As Phillip flew across Lake

Corangamite a few days later, he could still clearly see the wreck of Wirraway A20-714 sitting forlornly on the bottom of the lake. It would remain there undisturbed for decades.

As 1950 drew to a close, the intensity of flight training increased. From instrument flying and night sorties to formation flights over Melbourne with smoke trails weaving patterns in the sky, there seemed to be a new challenge at every corner. Where 'Blue' had once occupied the rear seat of the Wirraway, Phillip was increasingly flying with more senior officers who assessed his every move. He was getting used to coming under scrutiny, accepting that this was all part of being a pilot. Finally, on December 12th he undertook his Instrument Rating test with Squadron Leader Coombes. It was his last flight in the Wirraway and a final test of his competency to fly without any reference to the outside world. There was even a couple of unusual attitudes to recover from and Phillip couldn't help but re-visit the night he tumbled from the sky over Port Phillip Bay.

After he had parked the Wirraway, the Squadron Leader shook his hand and congratulated him. Phillip knew he was now on the home stretch of the course with only his multi-engine aircraft training still to complete. As he felt the elation rise, he fought complacency with every fibre in his body. He had learnt that lesson the hard way. "One more step..." he told himself, "...don't blow it now."

Wirraway Formation. Phillip and his fellow trainees perform a flypast of Melbourne.

Phillip, Bruce Gillan and another trainee relax in the barracks at Point Cook.

1951 not only brought the new phase of Phillip's training, but more information about the conflict in Korea. Major battles were taking place at places like Chosin Reservoir and the RAAF were in the thick of it. Number 77 Squadron had been the first United Nations squadron into the action and had already lost six pilots killed in action. A particular body blow was the loss of the squadron's commanding officer, Wing Commander Lou Spence DFC. A highly regarded and respected leader, Spence had failed to pull out of a dive as he led an attack on a storage facility to the north of Pusan. News had also been received that 77 Squadron was to receive jets to replace their propeller-driven Mustangs. The new aircraft would be the British Gloster Meteor F8. It was powered by two engines so, as No.4 Pilot's Course readied to fly the twin-engine Airspeed Oxford, many couldn't help but wonder if it was a sign of things to come.

Phillip soon found that the Oxford was certainly no Meteor! In fact, it was flat out being a Wirraway. Despite two piston engines, it only flew at around the same speed as the Wirraway and lacked the manoeuvrability. It was an eight-seat aeroplane, designed for straight and level flight in a transport role. The second engine didn't even offer any real enhanced safety or redundancy, as the engines were fitted with fixed-bladed wooden propellers like a Tiger Moth. Should one engine fail, its windmilling propeller was actually a great hindrance and severely eroded the

An Airspeed Oxford sits off the wingtip of its squadron mate.

Oxford's performance. So poor was that performance in critical phases, such as take-off, that Phillip and his course-mates were taught to force land the aeroplane in the event of an engine failure as it was anticipated that the aircraft would not be climbing to safety!

Still, the Oxford was as good as it was going to get in pilot training. Once Phillip had learnt to fly the Oxford on two engines, he was taught to fly it at altitude with only one engine, or 'asymmetrically'. Flight Lieutenant Max Holdsworth had flown Kittyhawk fighters out of Milne Bay in World War Two and was a very competent, if not gruff, instructor. He was now in charge of the flight training on the Oxford and Phillip managed to avoid incurring the wrath of the combat veteran long enough to be certified to fly the Oxford solo.

On his final day on No.4 Pilot's Course, Phillip signed for Airspeed Oxford HN655 for some final asymmetric handling. His course-mate Johnny Myers came along for the ride knowing that this was their last flight as trainee pilots. Determined to stay out of trouble, Phillip practised his engine failures and a few steep turns; nothing more. When the Oxford's propellers stopped turning, the two young pilots both sat there for a moment reflecting on the significance of this innocuous flight. For the first time since they started eighteen months earlier, they allowed themselves to think they had passed. Indeed they had.

The results were promulgated and Phillip had met the required standard in all areas. He knew that he hadn't excelled, that was the realm of chaps like Vance Drummond who had topped the course. Even so, he was excited, proud and relieved to have made the standard. In his time on course, he had flown sixty flight hours in the Tiger Moth, 130 in the Wirraway and 25 in the Oxford. He had attended countless classroom lessons, sat numerous exams, scored highly on the rifle range, marched in parades through the centre of Melbourne and stood guard at night in the middle of the freezing Point Cook winter. He had gone from a landlocked novice to a qualified Air Force pilot.

On February 23rd 1951, Phillip stood on the parade ground at Point Cook, formed up with the other fourteen men who had become his family. One by one, World War One 'Ace', and current Chief of Air Staff, Air Marshal George Jones CBE, DFC presented the young pilots with their new wings. The other trainees generally had family on hand to witness their graduation but there was nobody there for Phillip. He didn't care. The runt of the litter, the kid from the bush, was about to receive his Air Force wings and that was all that mattered.

As the Air Marshal pinned the wings through his crisp khaki shirt, Phillip could feel every muscle in his body standing at attention. The Air Marshal uttered some words of encouragement which didn't register as Phillip was concentrating too hard on his salute and not tripping over. He fell back into the ranks of new airmen before, finally, the parade was over.

He could hardly believe it. It was the greatest moment of his life. The RAAF and Navy's newest pilots congratulated each other and vigorously shook each other's hands, and he was one of them. The celebrations continued into the evening and there was animated discussion about where each pilot would be posted and what aircraft they would be flying. Would they fly fighters, bombers or transports?

Into the bushes. An errant Wirraway came to rest among the trees at Point Cook after an incident on landing.

Would they be called upon to fight in Korea?

Finally, the wave of excitement subsided and the course-mates prepared to settle in for the night. Phillip had disappeared for a short time before re-appearing proudly in his sleepwear. Vic Oborn, Bob Strawbridge, Bruce Gillan and Ken Towner cheered their mate as he walked towards them in the corridor. 'Zuppie' had sewn a pair of Air Force wings on his pyjama shirt and in that simple act he had summed up just how they all felt. They were on top of the world!

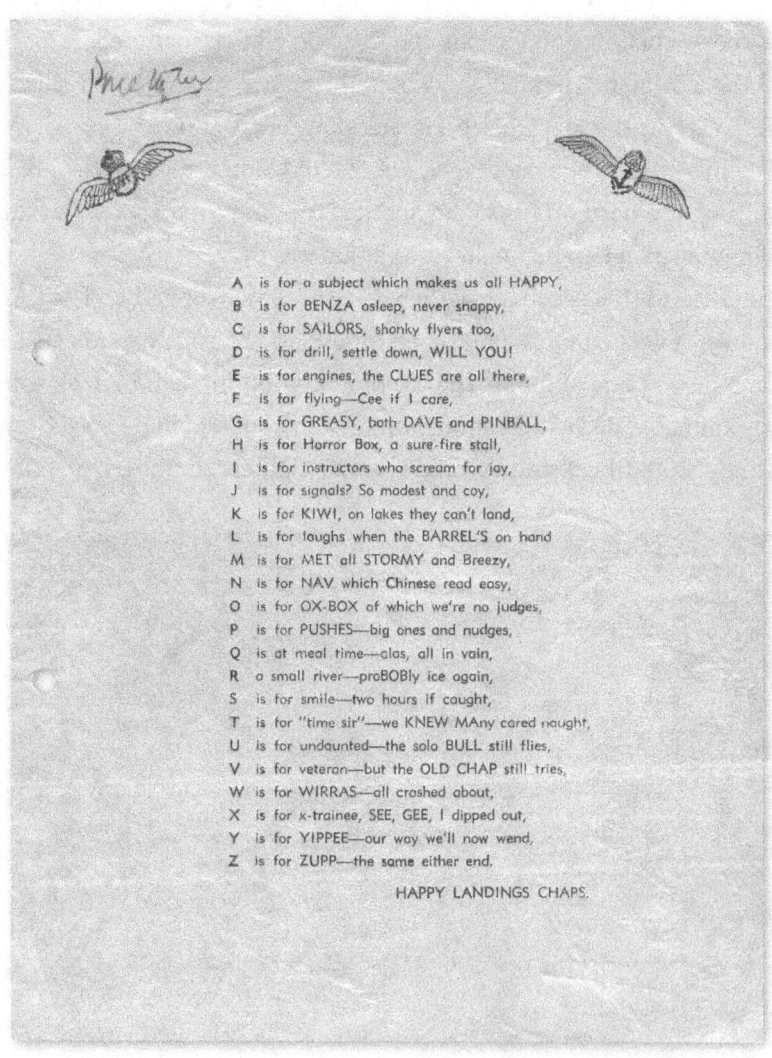

No. 4 Course Humour. Phillip's thinning hair is referred to on the pilot's course souvenir.

Air Force Wings

The Chief of Air Staff, Air Marshal George Jones CBE DFC, presents Phillip with his wings in 1951.

Phillip operated the sizeable Avro Lincoln for a single day before he was posted to fly CAC Mustang fighters.

Chapter Sixteen

A False Start

Within a week of receiving his wings, many of Phillip's questions about his future were answered. He had been transferred to No. 82 Bomber Wing, based out of RAAF Base Amberley, in Queensland, to fly the giant Avro Lincoln. The Lincoln was a substantial aeroplane with its four Rolls Royce engines and was a direct descendant of the famous Lancaster bomber. It was a major step up from the Airspeed Oxford on all counts.

He was genuinely thankful to have graduated from pilot's course but had dearly wanted to fly fighters. The fast, aerobatic, single-seat machines were the pinnacle of flight as he saw it and it was also the fighter pilots who were most likely to see action in the Korean conflict. He was slightly frustrated but knew the Lincoln would still provide an immense challenge. Furthermore, there was a jet on the way to the squadron later in the year; the Canberra bomber. These were exciting times with or without a fighter to fly.

He had no sooner arrived at Amberley as a brand new sergeant pilot than he was shown to his quarters, issued with his Lincoln 'Pilot Notes' and tasked to fly his first training sortie. Despite being very close to the family farm at Toowoomba, he knew there wouldn't be time to visit there just yet. Once again, he set about studying his textbooks and preparing for his first flight which was to be an epic cross-country. Phillip also managed to crawl over the Lincolns parked on the flightline and, just like training on the Wirraway, he spent hours sitting there, orientating himself with every switch and mental checklist.

Previously, the furthest Phillip had ventured from base was in the little Wirraway on flights which were of about two hours duration and travelled 100 miles from Point Cook. Now he had been scheduled to fly south from Amberley to Armidale in NSW, back to the north to Longreach in Queensland, and return to Amberley. By his first estimates it was distance of around 1,500 miles for the round trip and about seven hours of flight time.

His instructor for the flight was almost as daunting as the flight route. Flying Officer Davis DFC had received his Distinguished Flying Cross flying Lancaster bombers over Europe in World War Two. He had flown in combat, been decorated for his deeds and was obviously right at home in the massive Avro bomber family. Unsure of what to expect, Phillip decided to cover his bases by studying for the flight in every spare moment and listening intently when the time came to brief the mission. There was no ground school taught on the Lincoln and the only manual was the small A5 Pilot's Notes which covered the bare basics in fifty pages. They were Royal Air Force notes and Phillip discovered that one of the first steps in bailing out of a Lincoln involved "loosening one's tie". Wearing a tie in combat? Very British, Phillip thought.

When he first met Davis in the flesh, he was caught off-guard. The Flying Officer's reputation had preceded him, but Davis was actually only three years older than Phillip. As with so many veterans of war, he seemed many years older than his age, exuding a level of knowledge and confidence that belied his relatively young years. Phillip knew that he had matured through his experiences in World War Two, but the air about Davis was of another level.

The Lincoln was built around the same design philosophy as the Avro Lancaster and that aircraft had a lone pilot. Everything of consequence in the Lincoln was within reach of the man sitting in the left hand seat and only that seat was furnished with a full panel of flight instruments. The co-pilot seat was a small fold-away seat that facilitated having another pilot there to operate the wheels and flaps and any other secondary tasks called for by the pilot in command.

Davis showed Phillip around the aeroplane and explained the external aspects of this tailwheel gargantuan. They then ascended the ladder into the Lincoln and readied for departure with Davis in the left seat and Phillip looking on in the right. One by one they started the four Rolls Royce Merlin engines among a cacophony of coughing and smoke until the four 1,700 horsepower powerplants harmonised into a dull roar. The airframe exuded sheer power as Davis opened the throttles and moved the Lincoln from its parking position towards the runway at Amberley.

In the absence of checklists, all procedures had to be committed to memory and learning these checks had consumed many hours for Phillip over the past few days. As Davis rattled off the checklist, Phillip mentally followed his instructor through every sequence. When everything was in order, the lumbering Lincoln lined up and Davis smoothly advanced the four throttle levers in the centre of the instrument panel. With his short stature, Phillip could hardly see over the nose, but the tremendous noise and the sight of the massive engines out his window gave the entire exercise a real sense of power.

Ever so gradually, the tail rose from the ground and as the speed passed 100 knots, Davis eased the Lincoln into the air at which time it transformed from an unsteady crate into a graceful giant. Davis called for Phillip to raise the landing gear and, a few hundred feet later, to retract the flaps. The power was then eased back and the engines' piercing roar became a reassuring drone as the Lincoln climbed away to the south.

Levelling out, Davis handed over to Phillip to get a feel for the controls. There were no flight instruments in front of Phillip, so he flew visually, cross-referencing to the dials on the far side of the cockpit. After the Wirraway and Oxford, there just seemed to be so much aeroplane trailing behind him as the sun beat down through the vast Perspex canopy over his head. For the next thirty minutes he managed to fly relatively straight and level, with the greatest challenge being to keep the four propellers synchronised. When they all spun at the same RPM, a single solid tone was emitted. However, should they spin at different RPM, a loud warbling sound resulted, permeating the airframe and annoying everyone therein.

After an hour of flying and discussing various traits of the Lincoln, Davis took command of the aeroplane once again and landed at Armidale. The time on the ground was minimal as a long day was still ahead with the next leg to Longreach spanning nearly 700 miles. Once again Phillip supported the take-off by raising the wheels and flaps and setting the power settings for Davis. When they levelled out, Davis again handed control of the Lincoln over to Phillip. This time, however, he no sooner had control of the aeroplane than Davis unstrapped from his seat and stood up. "Are you happy?" he asked, receiving a nod and a word in the affirmative from the new pilot. "Then give me a call when we get close to Longreach, okay?" He then got down on the floor and crawled beneath Phillip's seat down into the nose section of the aeroplane. Once there, he leaned back and nodded off to sleep.

Phillip sat there stunned.

Phillip was at once grateful for the hours he had spent sitting in the parked Lincolns at Amberley. He then looked around to see the navigator hard at work on his plot. He looked back to the front and tweaked the levers a little to keep the propellers in sync. Thankfully, the aeroplane was very stable beneath his hands and required very little manipulation on his part, but what now? He reached down and grabbed his Lincoln Pilot's Notes and opened them on his lap, thumbing the index between scans of the horizon and the instruments.

His first thought was what if something went wrong; perhaps an engine failure. He ran through the actions in his mind and considered that the slewing, or yawing, of the aircraft would have to be arrested by pushing on the opposing rudder pedal. Then there was the issue of securing the failed engine. He would have to shut down the failed engine and stop the propeller spinning. By pushing the correct button, the propeller blades on the failed engine would then be turned edge on to the airflow, or feathered, to minimise the resistance to the air, or drag. Then would come the job of taking care of the engines that were still working, although hopefully in the real case scenario Davis would already be back in his seat and flying by this stage.

But for the moment, here he sat alone and at the helm of this massive machine. With all of twenty hours flying the tiny Oxford, he was now steering the Lincoln inland as the navigator checked his progress. For the next few hours he alternated between admiring the amazing scenery below and running through his Pilot's Notes. When Longreach loomed ahead and the top of the descent approached, he yelled as subtly as possible to Davis that it was time to resume command. The senior man smiled and reversed his contortionist's manoeuvre before resuming his seat.

"How'd it go?" he enquired. Phillip replied in conjunction with the navigator by briefing Davis of their location, fuel status, estimated time of arrival and anything else that he thought was relevant. At this time Phillip thought he caught the navigator giving Davis the thumbs up and a positive nod, but he couldn't be sure. The veteran then brought the aircraft in to Longreach effortlessly and departed for Amberley with equal ease. Phillip was struck by just how Davis made the operation of the aircraft look simple, knowing full well that every time the undercarriage or

A False Start

flaps moved, so did the balance and trim of the aeroplane. Davis corrected with anticipation every time and the Lincoln never wavered an inch.

Once the aircraft was in the cruise for the 600 mile run home to Amberley, Davis handed over and slipped down into the Lincoln's nose once again. Phillip took control and ran through his checklists and notes, just as he had done for the preceding few hours. When they finally arrived back at Amberley, they had been flying for seven and a half hours and Phillip felt exhausted physically and mentally. It had been a long day. Davis congratulated him on a sound performance as they walked away from the flightline. He recognised the fatigue on his co-pilot's face and arranged to debrief the flight the next day. That next few days, however, held more in store for Phillip than a simple debrief.

Without warning, he received orders to transfer out of Amberley as soon as possible. Transport had been arranged for him to fly to Canberra where he would join No. 3 Tactical Reconnaissance Squadron. Once there he was to commence conversion training onto the Mustang. His dream had come true. By some good fortune, he had been granted a slot for fighter training and potentially a chance to fly jet fighters.

He almost felt guilty when he broke the news to Davis, although the senior man already seemed to know of the transfer. Phillip attempted to restrain his excitement as he had grown to respect Davis greatly in their few days together. Davis had been a mentor but had also cast enough rope out to his trainee to build his confidence very quickly. Phillip parted company with 82 Wing and his instructor, sure that their paths would cross again. Sadly, they never did. Flying Officer Francis Noel Davis DFC was killed only a few years later when his Canberra bomber crashed into the runway at Amberley on a training sortie. There were no survivors.

Mustang – low and fast.

Chapter Seventeen

Mustang

As Phillip made his way to Canberra, he wondered what had caused the Air Force to have a change of heart. He had mentioned to Air Marshal Jones after the graduation that he wanted to fly fighters. He'd also raised the point with Flying Officer Davis at Amberley. Heck, he'd probably told just about everyone of his preference to fly fighters. Or perhaps it was as simple as an administrative error that had sent him to No. 82 Wing in the first instance. He honestly didn't know, but he wasn't going to question his good fortune either. Once again, he'd been given an opportunity and he was about to run with it.

In fact, he had been given a string of opportunities since he had re-enlisted in the RAAF. After his childhood years had been plagued with disappointment and relative disadvantage, his time in the military had offered a direct contrast, particularly these recent years in the Air Force when the door had been cracked open for him despite his lack of a formal education. Honest, hard work had been the prerequisite and it had in turn been recognised and rewarded. As far as he was concerned, he never wanted to be a civilian again and there was nothing that was likely to change his outlook. For the moment, however, his sole focus was on dedicating every fibre in his being to making the grade as a fighter pilot and 3 Squadron was that first step.

His mood was further brightened when he touched down at Canberra as he was surrounded by the familiar faces of Bruce Gillan, Ken Towner, Bruce Thomson, Vic Oborn and Ken Murray. A number of his No. 4 Course mates were also on the way to becoming fighter pilots and their unity seemed to strengthen at every turn. Vance Drummond, Bruce Thomson, Johnny Myers and Doug Robertson were all headed along the same path and they all anticipated the road would eventually lead them to Korea.

Phil seated in a No. 3 Squadron Mustang at Canberra, 1951.

Canberra did not possess the jagged snow-covered peaks of the Korean landscape, but it was still a suitable location to begin moulding the young fighter pilots. There was rising terrain to the south as the hills grew into the Snowy Mountains and the valleys between them offered dead-ends and limited space to turn around. The weather at Canberra could also sit low to the ground, simulating the challenges of low-level navigation that would confront them in Korea.

The squadron was equipped with Mark 22 CA-18 Mustangs, the Australian-built variant of the famous World War Two fighter. As the Mustang only possessed one seat, some Wirraways were on hand to assist with the conversion training as well as serving in the role of an instrument and night-flying trainer. A fleet of single-engine Auster Mark IIIs would be used to train the Army pilots bound for Korea. The Auster was a slow, high-winged, two-seat aeroplane, more akin to a trainer than a combat machine. It served as an Air Observation Post (AOP) that required the pilot to fly at low level and direct artillery fire and ground-attack aircraft on to targets with precision. Unarmed and vulnerable, the Auster pilots performed a critical role with danger always close. Phil came to know one of the Army trainees during this time. An athletic officer that towered over Phil, Lieutenant Bryan Luscombe was a member of No.16 AOP Flight. He was tasked to learn the skills required to orchestrate the battlefield's firepower alongside the Mustangs above and the artillery units below.

The role of Phil and his mates in the Mustang would be to identify and attack ground-based targets. However, they would also hone their air-to-air skills in their time at 3 Squadron. This all lay ahead of them, so for now the first step was to master the Mustang and this was no mean feat. The Mustang was a purebred fighter. With sleek lines and a new-technology wing, its speed, range and lethal firepower had helped deliver Allied air supremacy over Europe in the previous war. Just as the Wirraway had been a leap from the Tiger Moth, the Mustang now represented a step up from the two-seat trainer.

Flying Officer Bruce Wilson and the commanding officer Flight Lieutenant John Hubble started Phil's re-familiarisation with the Wirraway and it wasn't long before they were pushing the trainer to its limits. To get him comfortable with the long nose and obscured forward vision of the Mustang, he began flying it from the rear seat. To acquaint him with the higher speeds associated with landing a Mustang, they had him landing the Wirraway without using flaps. The Wirraway was an old friend, but he was now flying it very differently for the Mustang was a very different aeroplane.

Even as it sat at rest on the ground, the Mustang exuded grace. Of all-metal construction with a sleek, low wing, its long nose housed a twelve cylinder supercharged Merlin engine that turned a daunting four-bladed propeller. A clear, streamlined 'bubble' canopy replaced the slab-sided greenhouse cover of the Wirraway. The Mustang's maximum speed was around 400 knots, it could fly at over 40,000 feet and had enough fuel to stay aloft for more than nine hours. It had six machine guns mounted in its wings and the ability to carry rockets, bombs, napalm or just about any other ordnance a fighter could be asked to deliver. The 3 Squadron Mustangs also had the capability to lay a cover of smoke on the battlefield.

When the initial training was complete, Flight Lieutenant Don Hillier signed the paperwork that released Phil to fly the Mustang. Only a couple of years older than Phillip, he had flown fighters in World War Two and knew the excitement his student was feeling. Now, on a calm Canberra morning, the flight lieutenant stood on the wing as Phil meticulously recalled all of the pre-flight sequences from memory. The clearance was given to start the 1,400 horsepower engine and Phil brought the Mustang to life. As the four flat blades slowly turned, the fuel vapour searched for spark, the blades now at an ever-increasing speed. The exhaust stacks punched out a burst of smoke that caught a ride in the slipstream and wove its way into the still open cockpit. Fuel, air and ignition then combined and the whirring blades replaced by a massive spinning disc and an objectionable cough by the throaty roar of twelve cylinders leaping in to life. He moved the fuel mixture lever to 'run' and checked that the oil pressure was off the stops and rising. The Mustang was now alive.

Hillier stepped from the wing and gave Phil the thumbs up that he was clear to go. Unknowingly, with that gesture, Hillier had cleared Phil to enter a world that he had dreamed of since he was a boy. From the day that he had laid on his back in the paddock as those Bristol biplanes roared overhead the Toowoomba farm and for the hours that he had turned the pages of 'Every Boys Book of Fighting Planes', this had been his burning ambition. He may as well have dreamed of going to the moon as a boy from the farm with no particular schooling, but his faith never faltered. Now, as he sat alone in the cockpit, there were no bullies to ridicule him, nor naysayers to admonish his wasteful dreaming. He was about to become a fighter pilot.

He opened the throttle and left the other parked Mustangs behind, taxiing out to the runway's end. He wound the canopy closed and the sound of the Merlin faded a little into a background hum. Cocooned in his bubble of Perspex, Phil ran through his mental checklists and readied both he and his magnificent steed to take flight. Now, there was nothing left to do. The time had come and he was cleared to take-off.

Lined up on the Canberra runway, he leaned his head a little to the left to see past the nose of the Mustang and held the control column all the way back to keep the tailwheel locked and straight. As he smoothly advanced the throttle lever, the aeroplane responded in an instant and came to life, rolling ever more quickly. He gave a second push on the throttle to check it was all the way forward and glanced down at the gauges to see that the engine was indeed punching out full power as he sank into his seat under the acceleration.

The massive amount of torque was trying to swing the Mustang around to the

No. 3 Squadron Pilots. Sergeants Phillip Zupp and Ken Towner stand at either end. Jim Flemming is without his hat, while Harry Browne-Gaylord is third from right.

left, but Phil countered with his right foot pushing the rudder pedal. He eased the stick forward, releasing the tailwheel lock and lowering the nose. He could now see ahead. He was tracking straight down the runway and accelerating at an incredible pace. In a moment the aircraft was snapping at the air, anxious to be unbridled and free to fly. Phil pulled the stick back to grant it's wish and the fighter leapt into the air.

He quickly moved his left hand from the throttle and raised the wheels, giving the Mustang its head and passing 150 knots before throttling back and climbing into the sky like a homesick angel. Mount Majura dropped away beside him as he pointed the nose up and left the world behind. He had never felt such exhilaration. The power and responsiveness that now answered his two very humble hands took his breath away as he wheeled to the left and right enroute to the heavens. He craned his head around and could see Canberra sitting just off his tail, a growing maze of roads and buildings around a magnificent lake.

For nearly an hour he waltzed around those southern skies, almost not believing that it was really happening. He looped and turned and rolled and stalled with absolute ease and a reserve of power. There was no struggle to create energy for the aeroplane to manoeuvre. It oozed performance out of every single rivet. Whether he was upside down looking at the quilt-work of pastures below, or heaving the Mustang into the tightest of turns and mushing into his seat under the force of gravity, he was smiling the broadest grin beneath his oxygen mask.

The minutes passed without any hint of sympathy, eating at this magical moment. Phil knew he had to return to earth, but he wished that he and the Mustang could stay up there forever. He rehearsed the approach and landing, flying a practice approach on the way down. When he joined the circuit pattern at Canberra his mental checklists were voiced faultlessly once again, justifying the hours of rehearsal on the ground.

Lined up to land and with the landing gear and flaps fully extended, the runway awaited, as did an audience of his course-mates no doubt. The long nose of the Mustang had returned to spoil the view ahead and as he crossed the airport fence with 100 knots on the clock and slowed even a little more, the nose continued to rise. The runway had now virtually disappeared and his eyes and mind began to draw upon the visual cues in his periphery. The grass seemed to separate into individual blades and Phil knew the ground must be here somew… *Thump!* There it was and he was on Terra Firma. He thought to himself, "Keep it straight. Stick back. Slow down. Almost come to a halt before you turn off. Don't ground loop it now, Zuppie."

The landing had been more of an arrival than a finely judged transition from flight, but it would do him. As Hillier shook his hand as he stepped off the wing, he knew the landing had satisfied the flight lieutenant as well. Now he couldn't wait to write the entry into his logbook; 'Mustang A68-82'. The chatter among the young pilots was rapid as they were all becoming Mustang pilots by the day and Phil now shared their excitement and sense of achievement. They also knew that this was only the very first step. They had taken the Mustang into the skies for an hour and safely returned to earth. Now they had to learn to do it consistently and how to use the Mustang effectively as a tool of war. Certainly, they had flown the Mustang, but they had a long way to go to become fighter pilots and training was still a dangerous business.

They were reminded of just how dangerous when news of Flight Lieutenant Bruce Wilson's death became known. Wilson had left Canberra to convert to jet fighters at Williamtown, not long after he had flown with Phil in the Wirraway. Details were sparse, but it appeared that Wilson and another pilot in a pair of Vampire fighters had gone into a high-speed dive and never recovered. The reason for the accident was not known but the aircraft had hit with such velocity that the first Vampire was totally destroyed, buried in a river bed, while it appeared that Wilson may have tried to pull out at the last moment, but it was all too late.

The Korean War was another ever-present reminder of what lay ahead. The RAAF, in the form of 77 Squadron, was playing a pivotal role but it was losing quality airmen as a consequence. These were pilots who had been well versed in the Mustang, while a number also had World War Two combat experience. Phil and his mates represented the next generation. They were staring down the barrel of flying in battle almost as soon as their training was completed as 77 Squadron was now re-equipped with the Meteor jet fighter and a steady stream of new pilots was called for.

Phil's 3 Squadron was seeking to instill the fighting qualities required as well as the bare handling of the aeroplane. Central to its role was readying its pilots for combat. Among the instructors at Canberra was Flying Officer Jim Flemming who had been one of the first pilots to see action in Korea. Jim brought to the table first-hand experience and the challenges facing the young fighter pilots. It was not a case of hearsay. Jim had flown among the threatening terrain, he had seen the rapid advance of the North Koreans and been part of the heroic defence of the Pusan Perimeter that had been a pivotal moment in the war and one of 77 Squadron's finest hours.

Phil came to know and respect Jim and listened intently to the advice he had to offer. He also tagged along at every opportunity to fly in the Auster with Flemming figuring that every hour he could spend aloft and in the company of an experienced instructor could only serve to better him as a pilot. Whether it was a tactical reconnaissance exercise, or just a cross-country flight in the little Auster, Phil was the first to strap in and go for the ride. Similarly, when any of the Wirraways needed to be test flown after maintenance, he was the first to raise his hand for the job. Phil recognised that he was still far from the leader of the pack among his course-mates and that enthusiasm and application were his best allies in making the grade.

Another old hand was actually training alongside Phil at this time. Only a year his senior, Flight Lieutenant 'Harry' Browne-Gaylord had flown Spitfires and Hurricanes during World War Two under the name Henry Brown'. 'Henry' had flown fighter-bomber missions with the Royal Air Force's 145 Squadron in the Italian theatre and been awarded the Distinguished Flying Cross for his efforts. Even so, at the end of the war, there was no permanent position available for him and he subsequently left the Air Force.

Now, with the Korean War in full swing, and known as Mark Astil Baren Henry Aytack Browne-Gaylord, or 'Harry', he had re-enlisted in the RAAF. With a broad boyish grin and a thick crop of dark wavy hair, 'Harry' had the air of the debonair fighter pilot that could be found on recruiting posters. He brought with him combat experience and 1,000 hours of flight time to the benefit of the trainee fighter pilots. Once again, Phil made a point of listening to a voice of experience and would pair up with 'Harry' when it came time to take the Wirraway flying for 'instrument flying' practice.

Slowly but surely, day by day, he came to know the Mustang better. The training was thorough and diverse. One day he would take the Mustang to 30,000 feet to handle the aeroplane at the higher altitudes. The next day he would be making mock low-level ground attacks. Whenever he did take the Mustang to the higher altitudes, he would inevitably spin the aircraft back down from there; an exercise he thoroughly enjoyed. Strapped in as tight as possible, he would slow the Mustang to a speed where it no longer wanted to fly; the point at which the aircraft would stall. He would then bring the stick back briskly towards his stomach to ensure it stalled and, by opposing the other controls, the Mustang would flick into a wild rotation about the horizon. As the world flashed by outside, the aircraft fell back towards the earth and the needles on the cockpit's instruments wound down at an incredible rate.

Putting any amusement park ride to shame, the Mustang's spin was far more vigorous than the gentlemanly descent of the Tiger Moth. Woomf! Woomf! Woomf! Around the fighter went time after time losing a thousand feet with every turn and in the blink of an eye. The sun would flash past every second and

Phil counted the rotations by each flash of blinding light. He held tight, focused on holding the aeroplane in the spin. When enough was enough he would reverse the rudder pedals, push the stick forward and recover into a dive from which he would fly one more loop just for good measure. It was not all about solo aerobatics, though.

The skill of formation flying was critical to the fighter pilot. Flying in close proximity to fellow aircraft had been a function of combat flying since World War One as a means of mutual defence and concentrating firepower in attack. Now Phil and the other pilots practised formation flying until it became second nature. There was no room for hesitation or fear of the other high-speed fighter sitting only feet away. At times the pair would sit so close that the individual rivets on the other aircraft were as discernible as the look on the other pilot's face. On other occasions multiple Mustangs would form up in battle formation or in a 'finger four'.

He had fallen in love with the Mustang but he knew that flying the aircraft was only half the battle. Now he needed to learn to apply the aeroplane in its role as a fire-breathing weapon of war. In order to achieve that he too had to move to another level. He needed to become a fighter pilot.

The Auster Mk. III after Phillip's forced landing with John Hubble.

Chapter Eighteen

Fighter Pilot

The pace at Canberra was intense. There was dive bombing, night flying, rocketing, instrument flying and more air-to-air cine gunnery. The Army would play their role in tactical reconnaissance exercises, scampering across open fields while the pilots aloft would endeavour to accurately report their position and where they were headed. Mustangs would then roll in on the tanks and soldiers for mock attacks with the results filmed and analysed at a later time.

Low flying was a major skill to be mastered before setting course for Korea and Jim Flemming was given the task of training Phil. At first Phil baulked at the incredibly low level that Flemming was able to fly his Mustang with confidence, but the instructor edged his trainee lower and lower. After more coercion and training, Phil started to feel more at home down in the weeds. In fact, he grew accustomed to it under Flemming's tuition and, ultimately, low level flying became a great source of enjoyment. On one occasion, it led to trouble.

Phil had taken to making his shadow disappear over Lake George. This would involve descending lower and closer to the surface of the lake until he was so close the Mustang's shadow was lost beneath the aeroplane. He was playing the game with Ken Towner one morning and was determined to be the winner. Lower and lower he let the Mustang down until Ken baulked and held his Mustang level. Phil continued lower until he was sure that the tips of his spinning propeller blades must surely be only inches above the water. He held it steady, looking well ahead for any birds that might ruin his day, happy in the moment for beating Ken.

Unfortunately, by being so low over the lake, the Mustang was leaving a very visible trail of spray behind him; very visible to Ken Towner, but equally so to the senior officer who was passing overhead. The two were called in by the commanding officer and reprimanded. Flight Lieutenant John Hubble reminded his sergeant pilots that, while low flying was a necessary element of their training, putting a Mustang into Lake George was not! Phil confessed to being the lower of the two Mustangs and couldn't help but feel that he'd put himself in Hubble's gunsight; a case he worsened a short time later when his Mustang's propeller hit a battery cart while he was being marshaled by ground crew. That one earned him a severe reprimand and a five pound fine!

Phil couldn't believe it. He was always the quiet one in the background and now he had come to the attention of the commanding officer, not once, but twice. Still, Hubble had been very fair with him and recognised that he was a genuinely keen airman with a sound history of very good conduct. He just needed to look a little more before he leapt.

The going was tough all round and the weather also intervened at times. While tasked with a dive-bombing exercise, low cloud and rain in the area made flying a challenge and the ability to fly at altitude impossible. Rather than abandoning the flight, it was changed to a 'skip bombing' sortie that called for a low level deployment of the bombs. From only a few hundred feet, the bombs would be released and, like skimming rocks on a pond, allowed to skip along the ground towards the target.

As Phil and Ken Towner set out on the sortie, it was obvious that finding the target would be a challenge in itself. Flying low, wedged between the ground and the overcast, the pair of Mustangs roared towards the bombing range. As ground features flicked beneath them, the spits of rain grew heavier upon their Perspex canopies. The combination of the thrashing rain and the growing pressure to successfully bomb the target made Phil wonder what actual combat was like. Here he was over friendly territory on a training mission, but his heart was racing and he was beginning to sweat. Another road flashed beneath them; target ahead.

Their formation was loose but he was still very aware of Ken's Mustang bouncing up and down out of the corner of his eye. They were on time and the target now lay ahead. His thumb moved to the bomb release button on the top of the control column. Wait, wait, bombs away! The practice bombs fell away and bounded away towards their destination. Phil and Ken immediately set course for home as the weather seemed to be coming lower. Phil loved flying in the nap of the earth but, with the ability to see ahead severely hampered by the rain showers, it

A trio of Mustangs await their next sortie at Townsville.

was not quite so much fun. Finally, the pair came across a major road and hooked onto the centreline like a pair of semi-trailers clinging to the asphalt. Moments later the air base loomed over the nose and they knew they were home, but both wondered how tough Korea was going to be. Phil also wondered if this episode of low flying had come to anyone's attention.

By June 1951, there were numerous training exercises looming on the horizon and even escort duty for the transport aircraft returning the body of Prime Minister Ben Chifley home to Bathurst. In contrast, the flypast to mark the Jubilee of Parliament House was designated 'Operation Australia Fair' and Jim Flemming had been training his sergeants hard in tight formation flying. Unfortunately, the Canberra weather again closed in and, despite a vast array of Navy and Air Force aircraft gathered, the flypast was cancelled.

For the moment, it seemed like one step forward and two steps back. The weather had played havoc with his training schedule, while some of Phil's No.4 Pilot Course-mates had advanced. Vic Oborn, Bruce Gillan, Ken Murray and Bruce Thomson had already left for Williamtown, New South Wales, weeks earlier and were undertaking their Mustang operational training there before they converted on to jets. Phil and Ken Towner wondered if the weather was being kinder to them at the more northerly air base and, crucially, would they get to Korea before them.

Things changed for the better later in the month when they met up with their course-mates for a live firing exercise based out of Williamtown. Previously they had rolled onto the tail of a fellow Mustang in a quartering attack and opened fire with nothing more than a camera. For the first time, they were going to be firing at an actual target, albeit not another Mustang. The target was a large banner, or drogue, towed a good distance behind a twin-engine Beaufighter. To calculate the pilot's results, the bullets of each aircraft were dipped in different coloured paint that would leave identifying marks on the drogue.

As Phil positioned the Mustang high and offset to the rear of the target for a quartering attack, he checked one last time that his guns were off 'safe' and ready to fire. Then he rolled the aircraft over and down towards the drogue for the first attack, his gaze fixed through the Gyro-gunsight ahead of him. He closed on the target at speed and slowly rotated his throttle grip to adjust the six glowing diamonds that surrounded the target through the gunsight. When the ring of diamonds clipped the edge of the drogue, he squeezed the trigger on the front of his control column.

The Mustang came alive with the vibration and clattering of the firing guns. As empty shells flew back in the Mustang's wake, incendiary-tipped .50 calibre bullets, tracers, danced towards the target to assist Phil in his aim. The target jumped around in the gunsight for a second and then it was gone as he dipped beneath the drogue and left the attack behind. It had all happened so quickly and opened a new perspective to the cine-gunnery where only frames of film were fired.

Back on the ground scores were compared and it was evident that it was harder than it looked with only about five per cent of the bullets hitting the target. Inevitably the conversation drifted back to the subject of Korea and Bruce Gillan told Phil that it was likely they would be in action by October. Ken Towner and Phil both slumped at the information, knowing they had been assigned to take part in a major exercise in Townsville that was coming up. The queue to fly the limited number of Vampires was growing too so Phillip couldn't guess when his turn would come and remembered the disappointment delays had caused him in World War Two. He and Ken didn't want to be left behind but both pilots were assured that the exercise would constitute much of the advanced Mustang fighter training that their mates were undertaking at Williamtown.

As they prepared to depart on the exercise, the gunnery practise continued in earnest. Phil developed a particular liking for ground attack where he was firing on relatively stationary targets as opposed to the dancing drogue. The excitement of shooting was interspersed with the methodology of navigation. In company with 'Harry' Browne-Gaylord, Phil led a pair of Mustangs around NSW before climbing to 25,000 feet for the last leg where the map reading was significantly different.

A week later he climbed into the Auster to fly to Richmond Air Base with the C.O., Flight Lieutenant John Hubble, who had recently been awarded the Air Force Cross. The Auster had only just departed Canberra that morning when, three miles north of the airfield, the engine coughed twice and then fell silent.

Hubble immediately took over control and set the aircraft up to glide as Phil double-checked that his harness was as tight as possible. The ground below was hilly and heavily timbered with only a few clearings that may serve as a landing field in a pinch. Hubble turned toward one of the clearings and prepared to put the aircraft down, slowing it down and lowering the flaps. Phil could see tree stumps and rocky outcrops everywhere and hoped that the boss had picked a good line between them. He had.

The Auster contacted the earth firmly on all three wheels and scooted across

Flight Lieutenant Waller's Mustang on the beach at Halifax Bay.

the clearing. Hubble kept control, weaving past a dead tree and a jagged piece of granite jutting up through the grass. The aircraft bucked and banged its way along the ground and had slowed a good deal when the ground suddenly fell away and the Auster pitched down into a dry creek bed. Like a moat that it was unable to bridge, the Auster's wheels collapsed and its nose pounded into the dry bank on the other side. Amid the crumpling of the metal nose section, Phil and Hubble were thrown forward in their harnesses as the aircraft came to an abrupt halt. With dust still hanging in the air, the two pilots unstrapped and got clear of the aircraft before it could become engulfed in flame.

But the Auster did not catch alight, it just sat forlornly in the dry ditch. Its wheels had folded up and its nose cowling had seen better days, but overall it was in reasonable condition. With a good deal of daylight and knowing exactly where they were, Phil and Hubble walked a few miles to the roadway where an Army vehicle collected them and returned them to the base. In the wake of the bush landing, Phil never flew to Richmond that day but instead readied a Mustang for the long flight to Townsville in North Queensland and 'Operation Barrier Reef'.

Four pairs of Mustangs departed Canberra for Townsville at two-minute intervals. The bulk of the squadron personnel had already left on board a Dakota transport aircraft while a twin-engine de Havilland Mosquito accompanied the Mustangs as a communications relay. Only ten minutes out of Canberra, Ken Towner's engine began to run rough so, with 'Harry' Browne-Gaylord beside him, he turned around and landed. The other three pairs set course and cruised along the Australian seaboard at 25,000 feet.

For more than four hours the Mustangs tracked northward, ultimately arriving minutes apart at Townsville. The exercise over the next month was at a frantic pace with all aspects of their trade tested. There were photo-reconnaissance sorties and tactical recce flights over Aitken Road and Charters Towers. There was the spectacular live firing of eight rockets in a pass at Rattlesnake Island and dive-bombing with two 250lb semi-armour-piercing bombs being dropped on targets. Night formation sorties were flown and a string of air-to-air attacks on a drogue towed behind a Beaufighter over Halifax Bay. On one attack, Flight Lieutenant Waller's engine failed and he landed his Mustang on a beach. Unfortunately, the aircraft was unable to be salvaged before high tide inundated the prized fighter.

Operation Air Force. Phil captures a photo of the Fly Past team. (Standing L to R) Towner, Hill, Hubble and Hillier (Kneeling L to R) Turner, Browne-Gaylord and Turnbull.

By the time Phil returned to Canberra he was becoming comfortable with his lot as a fighter pilot. The exercise at Townsville had been a concentrated period of true fighter flying using real bullets and bombs. A usual, he had generally acquitted himself with a middle-of-the-pack performance, although the exercise had highlighted a strength in his repertoire; ground attack. His rocket attacks on ground targets had scored highly and this had not escaped the attention of his instructors. More importantly, in his mind, the results had implanted a seed of self-belief.

It was now September 1951 and Korea loomed large in his consciousness as each day the newspaper spoke of some new land battle or the efforts of 77 Squadron. The grapevine of pilots returning from the war left no doubt that the Australians were having a tough time. They were pitted against the highly manoeuvrable MiG-15 fighter jet flown by Chinese pilots, although there were strong suspicions that some cockpits contained experienced Russian aviators. Up against the MiGs, the Australian Meteors fought hard but were at a disadvantage against the faster, newer generation fighter with its swept wings.

There was no doubt the air war was in full swing and Phil and Ken knew their involvement was potentially only a matter of months away. They would often listen to the old hands; Don Hillier, 'Harry' Browne-Gaylord and 'Val' Turner, all of whom had flown fighters in World War Two. The tales of aerial combat held no trepidation for the new 'bods', just a sense of anticipation of playing their part. It was youthful confidence blended with a sense of adventure, although Phil had some idea what real combat was about. However, this time it would be different. He would be trading the mud for the sky, khaki for blue.

Their time at Canberra seemed to be nearing its end and formation flying in the Mustang became the main duty. 'Operation Air Force' saw Ken and Phil involved in a six aircraft display over Sydney and a fortnight later 'Operation Wedgetail' flew over Melbourne. Resplendent in white overalls and ties, the war seemed a world away as they posed for a photograph before the Sydney flight. It was smiles all around as the sandy-haired Don Hillier made faces behind the kneeling 'Harry' Browne-Gaylord. But the reality was that the war was not very far away at all and more than one of their jovial team was destined to die on the snowy slopes of Korea.

Chapter Nineteen

Jets

By mid-September Phil was finally on the move again. In the preceding six months at 3 Squadron he had flown 150 hours and learnt the fundamentals of being a fighter pilot to the satisfaction of those in command. Hubble had noticed his young pilot's strength in ground attack and rated him highly in his final assessment. However, he had also not forgotten Phil's earlier disciplinary breaches including his low flying episode over Lake George and warned that, "... his thoughts do not keep abreast of his actions". Phil knew that he had to try even harder as it was now time to move onto RAAF Williamtown air base on the NSW coast and the home of the Air Force's fighter operations.

By the time he and Ken Towner arrived, their other mates from Point Cook were already on their way to Korea. Vance Drummond, Bob Strawbridge, Bruce Gillan, Ken Murray and Vic Oborn had been posted to 77 Squadron and Bruce Thomson was soon to follow. It seemed as if all of No. 4 Course was in Korea and Phil's impatience stirred. These were good friends, and he felt that he should be with them, and lamented the delays in his training. He'd spoken to Bruce Gillan before he left and he had warned Phil that the first order of business at Williamtown was to report to the commanding officer. The C.O. would then confirm his willingness to serve in Korea if needed. Phil was more than ready and the two then shared Bruce's long-standing joke that he'd only joined the Air Force to learn to fly and become an airline pilot. He hadn't read the fine print about getting shot at.

Williamtown was a hive of activity as it struggled to keep pace with the demand for new fighter pilots in Korea. Along the flightline sat the familiar forms of Wirraways and Mustangs, but it was the shining silver jets that caught the eye. It was the Vampire that had taken his breath away with its arrival at Wagga when he was a trainee mechanic and now he was set to fly one. The small single-engine de Havilland Vampire looked to be little more than a cockpit pod with two booms extending to the rear where they were joined by a horizontal tailplane. It sat level on the ground with a wheel beneath its nose, rather than the tail, and, most significantly of course, there was no sign of a propeller.

Despite the apparent simplicity, the Vampire was the stepping-stone to the Gloster Meteor, the aircraft that Phil would ultimately take into combat. However, first he had to transition into the realm of high-speed flight. This was no simple matter as the 'Jet Age' had only recently dawned in the Royal Australian Air Force. Vampire numbers had only grown over the preceding two years and there still weren't any two-seat trainers on strength. As a consequence, new Vampire pilots bordered on being test pilots with their first jet flight being flown solo.

Phil's first week at Williamtown was spent flying the Mustang above 30,000 feet in mock aerial combat using cine cameras. At these high altitudes the air was thin and not conducive to the harsh manoeuvring of dogfighting in the piston-powered Mustang. It was a mix of aggression and finesse to put the aircraft where it needed to be without getting too slow and starving it of the airflow over the wings that was needed to produce lift.

The Vampire also had its problems with the air through which it flew, although its issues were a function of its higher speeds. The little fighter jet used to reach a critical speed when it passed through the air at 78 per cent the speed of sound, or Mach 0.78. At this speed, certain curved portions of the airframe actually accelerated parcels of air to the speed of sound, creating shockwaves that severely buffeted the aircraft. Subsequent control then became a significant problem and a number of Vampires and their pilots had been lost. The Jet Age had dawned but it came with a new set of challenges.

The Vampire loomed large for Phil. True to their word, his Mustang flying at Williamtown was abbreviated and he was being fast-tracked towards the jet. Every minute he spent on the ground was used to saturate his brain with the intricacies of the 'Vamp'. He would scour his notes from Point Cook on jet engines and aerodynamics, immerse himself in the Pilot's Notes and sit blindfolded in the cockpit locating every switch and lever by touch. With only single seat Vampires available, he would have to satisfactorily display his competency to one of the squadron's senior instructors before he could take the jet into the sky.

JETS

Phil sits off Ken Towner's wing in his Mustang. The two would ultimately see service together in the skies over Korea.

These senior instructors of 75 Squadron were a force to be reckoned with. Flight Lieutenant 'Brick' Bradford DFC had flown fighters over New Guinea in World War Two and had already completed an operational tour in Korea flying Mustangs. Flight Lieutenant 'Freddie' Lawrenson DFC MID had flown Hurricane and Kittyhawk fighters and received the Distinguished Flying Cross for continuing a ground attack sortie after his canopy had been blown off by ground fire and he was wounded in the face. A highly regarded veteran, Lawrenson would be killed in Korea on Christmas Eve the following year.

After eight hours flying the Mustang at Williamtown, Phil was told on a Friday afternoon to be prepared to fly the Vampire on Monday. After an intensely studious weekend, Phil met Flight Lieutenant Ian Parker, a tall, lean affable instructor with a crop of fair wavy hair. Like Phil, Parker hailed from Toowoomba, albeit on the other side of the tracks. The flight lieutenant had attended the Grammar School while Phil had been scraping out the insides of furnaces. Like so many instructors, Parker had a maturity beyond his years that was borne of experience. In reality, he was only two years older than Phil, but he was already an old hand in the new age of jets.

Parker listened intently as Phil answered every question and demonstrated the required actions in the tiny cockpit of the Vampire. In turn, Phil hung on every word that Parker shared with him. To complicate matters, the early RAAF Vampires did not possess an ejection seat for the pilot to use in an emergency. They ran through the bail out procedure again and Phil couldn't help but think that it involved a fair dose of luck. Reduce speed, jettison canopy, roll inverted, undo harness and fall from the aircraft. Primitive! With the instructor satisfied with his student's knowledge, it was time for Phil to fly the Vampire.

Methodically, he brought the Rolls Royce Nene engine to life. It sucked in gutfuls of air through the intakes before spewing it out as scorching thrust from the single exhaust behind the cockpit. Inside, it seemed strange with different smells and different sounds to absorb. There was no huge spinning propeller disc ahead and that unobscured view was totally alien due to the nosewheel arrangement. Easing the throttle forward, the 'Vamp' increased its whining and began to slowly roll forward.

He bumped along the taxiway, keeping straight through use of the rudder pedals. It was a dream to handle on the ground compared to the tail-draggers he had previously flown, but how would it handle in the air, he wondered. At the end of the runway Phil sucked in his own gutful of air. A week of study and an hour of questions and now he was set to take this jet into the sky all alone.

Trim, Neutral

Fuel, L.P. Cock 'On', HP Cock 'On', Booster Pump 'On'.

Flaps, Set.

Dive Brakes, 'Off'.

For all the reading of systems, learning of airspeeds and practising of drills, the next few minutes still remained a mystery. To find out what lay ahead, he advanced the throttle fully forward with his left hand and held the spade-grip of the control column in his right as the whining engine increased in its pitch and power. Releasing the brakes, the result was immediate. The Vampire accelerated down the runway faster and faster as he was pushed further into his seat. Without the long nose of the Mustang out in front, he felt like he was sitting on the handlebars of a bicycle with nothing in front of him, but, boy, was this bike moving!

In a heartbeat, he was through 80 knots and gently raising the nose. Through 110 knots and the 'Vamp' leapt into the air. He retracted the landing gear quickly before the increasing speed and rushing airflow could prevent the wheels from coming up. Initially, everything seemed wrong. There wasn't a long nose in front of him to set an attitude against the horizon, forcing him to cheat by looking at the artificial horizon on the instrument panel. Then he checked his power setting and the blood drained from his face.

JETS

Phil's first jet flight was in the de Havilland Vampire. Solo.

The Mustang would punch out 3,000rpm on climb out and the Vampire's indicator looked different as he throttled back for climb power. It was only showing 1,000rpm! Quickly he cross-checked his instruments and they all told the same story. Going up, going up, going up and quickly. The engine hadn't failed and the instrument wasn't reading 1,000rpm; it was reading close to 10,000rpm! Phil was not so much tearing up the sky as being pushed into the stratosphere by the immense propulsive force of the jet engine.

The altimeter was winding up like a crazed clock as the Vampire ate up altitude at an alarming rate, climbing higher and higher. Compared to the Mustang, the Vampire seemed so quiet and light to the touch. Getting into the air felt wrong but, now he was up and away, he was free to take in the view afforded by the Perspex bubble above his leather helmet. The outlook was unobscured except for two intakes, or 'elephant ears', behind the cockpit. Ultimately these scoops would be identified as the culprits that led to the fatal controllability problems and they would be repositioned beneath the aircraft.

All too soon his first solo was over and he rolled the Vampire back towards Williamtown. He hurtled back to earth with the same sense of freedom and simplicity. A single throttle lever was all that was needed. There was no propeller or fuel mixture levers to manage. To slow down, he simply closed the throttle and deployed the dive brakes to spoil the smooth passage of air over the wings.

In the circuit pattern, and preparing to land, the aircraft was further slowed as the landing gear and flaps were extended. With the runway ahead, the airspeed sat at 100 knots with power at the ready in case the approach had to be abandoned. Parker had emphasised that the Nene engine took a while to wind up when power was called for and idle thrust close to the ground was a risky combination.

In the absence of a long nose, the view of the runway ahead was unimpeded. Finally, he needed to remember that this was a nosewheel aeroplane, so the aim was to touch down on the main wheels and then gently lower the nosewheel to the pavement. His aiming point stayed steady in the middle of the tiny rectangular front windscreen, the morning sun at his back. Lower, lower, lower, the runway swept beneath him and, with a squeak and a subtle jolt, the main wheels touched down. Soon afterwards the nosewheel followed and the 'Vamp' rolled out to a slow taxi speed.

Clear of the runway, Phil raised the flaps and completed his checks as he made his way to the parking bay. Only after he had shut down the Vampire fully did it really dawn upon him. It had been his first jet flight, his first flight in a pressurised aircraft and his first landing in a nosewheel aircraft. Furthermore, it had all been achieved without an instructor beside him, although Parker was not far away as Phil slid the canopy open.

He congratulated his protégé and the quietly spoken Phil was caught between a stilted reply and the broadest of grins. Recognising that his student had hit Williamtown running and completed his Mustang training and Vampire solo in only a week, Parker gave him the next day off before the training began in earnest.

Firstly, there were the fundamentals of flying any military aircraft; take-offs and landings, missed approaches, low level operations and formation flying. It built a level of familiarity and confidence with the aeroplane without being a totally new skill set. He had already flown these exercises in Tiger Moths, Wirraways and Mustangs and now it was time to apply them to the jet. They were familiar with one exception; the 'Mach Run'.

Given the control issues and accidents the Vampire was experiencing at the fast edge of the envelope, new pilots were required to venture to the aeroplane's limits and bring it back from there. This involved climbing the Vampire to 30,000 feet before nosing over into a high-speed dive. Approaching the critical speed of Mach 0.78, the recovery called for closing the throttle and deploying the dive brakes to slow the aircraft to a safe speed. It was simple enough, but with Bruce Wilson's death at Karuah still fresh in his mind, Phil was wary of this seemingly sweet little jet.

With five hours experience in the Vampire, Phil departed Williamtown in formation for the climb to 30,000 feet. Ten minutes later they were there and readied themselves for the 'Mach Run'. Without looking, Phil reached directly behind the throttle and felt for the dive brake lever. It was the shortest of three levers extending back from the throttle box. The airspeed indicator was the top left of the six primary instruments and just outboard of that was the all-important Machmeter.

When it was his turn, Phil rolled the Vampire into the dive and accelerated towards the threatening Mach number. Plummeting to earth at over 400 knots, the needle on the Machmeter nudged closer to 0.78 and Phil felt a hum reverberate through the airframe. Without hesitation he closed the throttle swiftly and pulled the lever to extend the dive brakes and slow down the twin-boom bullet. It responded just as the instructors had assured him and he double-checked that the engine hadn't flamed out as it was known to fail on occasions.

With the 'Mach Run' completed, he had successfully conquered the first hurdle, but a good many still lay ahead. Now he had to take the Vampire and apply its speed and performance as a combat aircraft. To complicate matters, the Air Force wanted this to be achieved in only six weeks. Phil knew the real challenge was yet to come.

The MiG-15. 77 Squadron's adversary over Korea.
(Source: David Osborn via Alamy)

Edith Blight. The WRAAF Corporal that captured Phillip's heart.

Chapter Twenty

Getting Closer

It had become apparent that Ken Towner and Phil were running a parallel course towards Korea, but the young sergeant-pilots were not alone. As commissioned officers, 'Harry' Browne-Gaylord and 'Val' Turner had followed the same path from Canberra. Generally, the officers were one step removed from their non-commissioned counterparts, but 'Harry' and 'Val' were happy to bridge the divide of rank and mentor their young mates.

Phil and Ken had come to know 'Harry' Browne-Gaylord at 3 Squadron and listened to his recollections of flying Hurricanes and Spitfires in the Italian theatre of war. However, it was in their time at Williamtown that they came to learn more about Flight Lieutenant Valton Leslie John Turner DFC. He had flown the powerful single-engine Hawker Tempest fighter over Europe. As well as flying reconnaissance and ground attack sorties, he had been credited with shooting down four German fighters and two 'flying bombs' and, like 'Harry', he had been awarded the Distinguished Flying Cross. With his dark hair combed to a centre-part and a healthy moustache, Turner also looked like the copybook fighter pilot. A teacher by his civilian training, 'Val' had both experience and the ability to impart the knowledge of the lessons learned in combat. Once the Vampires had been put to bed, 'Harry' and 'Val' often guided their young squadron mates in what to expect in the months ahead.

In the meantime, the training maintained a relentless pace with four sorties sometimes flown in one day. From the outset, intertwined with the Vampire, were flights in the tried and trusted Wirraway aimed at honing Phil's instrument flying skills. Under the instruction of Parker, Lawrenson or Bradford, Phil would be confined to the darkness of a canvas cover, starving him of any external visual cues, and flying only with reference to the dials and gauges in front of him. The basics of instrument flight had been covered at Point Cook but this training was more intense. The next time Phil may be called upon to fly on instruments could be over Korea where the hostile mountains reached high up into the clouds.

There were also cross-country navigation exercises in which it was reinforced just how thirsty jet engines could be. Most efficient at high altitude, some flights were flown at 35,000 feet where the world below looked like a perfect match for the chart on Phil's knee. At other times, they skimmed among the ridge lines at 200 feet where navigation required an entirely different technique and he dare not look down at his chart. Ken and Phil could not help but find the humour in being encouraged to fly ever lower after their disciplinary episode over Lake George in the Mustangs.

Much of the fighter training was the same as he had flown in the Mustang up to now. Phil revisited air-to-air cine gunnery, air-to-ground firing and attacking a towed drogue. However, the speed at which these encounters occurred was startling with the target coming and going in the blink of an eye. The Vampire was armed with four 20mm cannons beneath the cockpit with two muzzles firing through flush openings either side of the nosewheel housing.

The targeting principle remained the same by putting the gunsight's central dot on the target's 'cockpit' and rotating the graticule control on the throttle grip until the ring of dots clipped the target's wingspan. When the target was nicely framed, depressing the button on the control column would bring either the cine camera or the four cannons to life.

Aware that their opponent in Korean skies would be the MiG-15, a good deal of time was spent dog-fighting and shooting at targets that were drawing away from them. The MiG had swept wings and a distinct speed advantage over the Meteor, so the instructors made every effort to refine their pilots' skills in air-to-air combat.

While the jet age brought increased speed and manoeuvrability, the human body wasn't designed for the high-speed turns that could be performed. In these gut-wrenching turns, the apparent force of gravity, or g-force, was multiplied and forced the pilot down into his seat and the blood away from his brain. The pilot's vision would fade to black and white before he lost consciousness, or blacked out.

As the air-to-air practice grew more intense, the manoeuvring became even more aggressive between the dueling Vampires. As the turns tightened, Phil would tense his gut muscles to keep the blood in the upper half of his body in an attempt to avoid blacking out. His short stocky build was suited to this punishment as it gave him a natural tolerance to g-forces. Being the shortest man in the room was finally an advantage.

On the gunnery range the four cannons would erupt beneath his feet, unlike the Mustang that spewed its fire from the wings. Each time his finger squeezed the firing button the vibrations reverberated through the airframe, drowning out the whistle of the jet engine until the guns again fell silent. Day after day he learned to fly and fight.

Phil also began to work in conjunction with ground controllers who gave a course to steer, or vectors, towards a target. Sometimes the target was a Mustang and sometimes a Lincoln bomber. He would roll in on the targets from above or make head on passes, breaking off the attack at the last moment, scaring the helpless bomber crews as they held their course.

Without even being aware of it, Phil's mindset was being trained to attack and be the hunter, not the hunted. An air battle can be over in seconds and the initiative can be lost in half that time. Between the heaving g-forces in the air and the experienced voices of 'Harry' and 'Val' in the calm of the evening, Ken and Phil were inching towards the combat they knew was coming.

On November 15th of 1951, Phil flew his last training sortie, a QGH approach to land when he was given headings to fly by a ground controller as he descended into Williamtown. Aside from his ten hours of Wirraway instrument flying, he had accumulated 32 hours in the Vampire, including forty minutes at night. His grand total of flying experience was 400 hours and he was assessed as 'Average' as a fighter pilot and cleared to proceed to Japan to train on the Gloster Meteor. 'Average' suited him just fine.

His next stop was RAAF Richmond, an air base to the west of Sydney. Here, his paperwork was organised, his medical clearances obtained and he was made ready for deployment overseas. As he and Ken moved between offices, he reflected on how civilised this process was in comparison to his Army enlistment and deployment. However, he had no sooner praised the RAAF when a major issue arose the day before he was scheduled to ship out.

He was informed that the documentation supporting his various vaccinations and inoculations had gone missing and that these papers were compulsory to complete the formalities. Phil was fuming. There was no way he was going to wave goodbye to Ken and wait in Australia while formalities were attended to. He stormed into the Base Headquarters office at Richmond and demanded answers with more authority than a sergeant could rightly claim.

The female corporal behind the desk offered up an unsatisfactory answer and Phil asked to be put through to someone in authority. The corporal dialed the number and handed the phone to Phil as her fellow office staff rolled their eyes at the livid pilot. As he sought answers from the other end of the line he reached into the bewildered corporal's drawer and, one by one, began taking lollies. The exchange became heated until Phil announced he was on his way to have the required needles for a second time if that would fix the problem, and slammed the phone down.

The dark-haired corporal bit her lip to hold in her laughter at the tantrum, still aghast at his forwardness in eating her sweets. He paused and looked at her and then said succinctly, "Sorry. Phillip Zupp. How do you do?" She looked straight back and said, "Corporal Edith Blight and I'm fine, thank you."

There was a moment's awkward silence.

His tone softened just a touch. "Corporal, would you like to go to the movies tonight?"

She said that she would.

That evening Edith could see Phil waiting outside the cinema that sat just beyond the air base's gates. Appropriately, the movie showing was 'Thirty Seconds Over Tokyo' which told the story of Doolittle's bombers striking back after the attack on Pearl Harbor.

Drawing nearer, she thought that he cut a fine figure in his dark blue uniform with a row of World War Two service ribbons on his chest just below his pilot's wings. Unlike the aggressive sergeant in her office, his body language reflected a nervous disposition. It was a far cry from the normally over confident pilots that passed through her office expecting her to swoon at their charm. She preferred nervous.

Phil tipped the peak of his hat as she approached before tucking it under his arm and apologising again for his earlier outburst. She laughed and asked if the

Getting Closer

second round of needles had done the trick. They had indeed, he assured her, and he was on his way to Japan the next day.

She knew all too well that he was leaving for war as her job was to process the documentation of the young men heading overseas. It was also her job to administer the files of the pilots killed in Korea and it was this task that ate away at her and tinged her heart with fear as she looked at Phil settling into his seat. As the lights dimmed the screen came to life and illuminated the faces of the audience. She studied Phil in the half light and wondered if he knew what lay ahead for him, unaware that he had already fought in the jungles of New Guinea and witnessed the devastation of Hiroshima first hand.

Similarly, Phil knew nothing of the pretty brunette beside him. She had served as a radar operator during the war, one of the 'Hush-Hush' girls. She had been engaged to a RAAF officer only to lose him weeks before their wedding when his bomber blew up over a target in New Guinea. Since then she had not let anyone get close. There had been friends, and even a marriage proposal, but her heart had withered when Frank had perished.

Now she sat next to another airman going to another war and the pain swirled inside her again. Phil caught her looking his way and smiled. She had never seen him smile and he looked like a mere boy when he did. She leaned over a little closer and wondered what the hell she was doing. In weeks Phil could be another name in an envelope on her desk. Another name on a cenotaph.

They enjoyed a cup of tea after the movie and danced around trivial subjects that kept the mood light. She avoided talking about Korea and he avoided talking about the Mitchell bombers attacking Tokyo. They had spent only a few hours together before it was time for Phil to walk Edith back to her barracks and say goodnight. Another couple was cuddling in a concealed spot beyond the reach of the moonlight, but there was no kiss goodnight for Phil. Edith simply asked him to write to her and she would to him. When he came home they would see where things might lead, but for now he had a war to contend with and she needed to mend a broken heart.

He tipped his hat again and bid her goodnight before turning and walking into the darkness. She smiled and waved. Inside she prayed where she stood that he would make it home alive.

Phil converted to the Gloster Meteor via the two-seat T.7 Trainer.

Chapter Twenty One

To War Again

This time war was different.

Phil looked from the window of his Qantas DC-4 aircraft as it made its way to Japan. Last time he went to war he had been crammed aboard a heaving troop ship surrounded by the stench of salt and sweat. Now the airliner cruised above the clouds without even a ripple in the air. The flight took a few days, stopping at Darwin, Labuan, off the coast of Borneo, and onto Hong Kong before the final leg across to Japan. Even so, there was a comfortable bed each night and food aplenty.

His final destination was Iwakuni, Japan, where 77 Squadron had operated from at the outset of the Korean War. Located only twenty miles from Hiroshima, Phil had been there before as a young soldier with dreams in his head and a Pilot's Manual in his kit bag. He remembered 77 Squadron and its Mustangs and now he was back, five years later, as a pilot with that same squadron.

Just as skilled Japanese mechanics worked on the aircraft, domestic staff were also from the local area. From the Mess to the two-storey accommodation block, everything was maintained in immaculate order by a more than willing population keen to work and rebuild their nation. Floors were highly polished, beds made as tight as drums and shoes never lost their shine. For the young boy from the bush it seemed like a life of luxury.

It was a different world beyond the airfield too. Much had changed since Phil first sailed into the ghostly inland sea in 1946 and walked through the rubble and devastation. Rebuilding had taken place and, where the Japanese once desperately foraged through the remains of a shattered Hiroshima, buildings were beginning to emerge. To Phil's untrained eye it seemed that about half of the city had been rebuilt, but a lot of destruction still remained. Still, the bare-domed building remained near the bombsite as a silent reminder.

In the present, the war in Korea was very real and struck close to home when Phil heard that Doug Robertson had been killed a fortnight earlier. His course-mate from Point Cook had been killed in a mid-air collision with another Meteor over Korea. Ken Blight had managed to bail out of his stricken jet, but Doug had gone down and was never seen again once he entered the cloud cover.

Phil showed Ken Towner around, explaining to him how little had remained five years before. He found an old bunker that he had explored as a young soldier and the two airmen walked inside. It had long been emptied, but for Phil it was the most tangible reminder of Hiroshima. Now Japan marked the start, rather than the conclusion, of his war.

His first step was to convert his newly acquired jet handling skills to the Gloster Meteor F.8. Unlike the Vampire, it possessed an engine on each wing and a conventional tail rather than twin booms. Like the Vampire, it possessed a bubble canopy although the pilot now also had the security of a Martin-Baker ejection seat. It had four cannons in the nose and could carry sixteen rockets under the wings. Its limited fuel stocks were supplemented by a belly, or ventral, tank that could prove the aircraft's Achilles' heel in ground attack. Still, he thought she was a beautiful looking machine.

The Meteor came with the benefit of a two-seat trainer, the T.7. A little different to the fighter, it still provided a wonderful means of bridging the divide between the two jets. Pilot Officer Ray Trebilco DFC was tasked with introducing Phil to the ways of the Meteor. Ray had been in Korea when the war broke out and was on his second tour. He had originally flown Mustangs and was one of the first to convert to the Meteor in July. He was a tremendous tutor.

Ken, 'Val' Turner and 'Harry' Browne-Gaylord were also undertaking their training and there was a sense of urgency to get them to Korea as soon as possible. Over the next two days, Phil flew two one-hour sorties with Trebilco covering take-offs and landings, aerobatics and the now familiar 'Mach Run'. The only twin-engine aircraft that Phil had flown previously was the antiquated Airspeed Oxford at Point Cook so the Meteor was a giant leap in technology and performance.

Critically, Trebilco versed his student well on flying the Meteor with one engine out of action. It was a reality that can occur all too easily in a combat environment and Phil practiced keeping the aircraft flying straight as the asymmetry of the thrust tried to slew the Meteor around. While he was able to achieve the required standard, Ray warned him that the Meteor was a very different beast when it was heavily laden with fuel and armament. In reality, the jet would struggle to maintain height fully loaded with one engine out. That day, Phil was cleared to fly the single-seat Meteor solo.

Strapping into the cockpit of the F.8, the array of dials in front of him was similar to the Vampire except there was two of everything where the engines were concerned. It looked like an old World War Two cockpit with extra instruments wedged wherever space could be found. Case in point was a newly fitted navigation aid, the radio compass. The dial was up high beside the gunsight, but the selector dial required the act of a contortionist to change frequencies.

The bubble canopy was actually opaque to the rear which struck Phil as strange, considering that's where a good many attacks would originate. However, with the bulky ejection seat behind him and the harness tight, it was still difficult to see back to the tail. Still this was a 500 knot aeroplane that he was about to fly and he relished the opportunity.

The battery cart sat nearby providing electrical power as Phil set about stirring the Meteor into life. With the throttles closed he felt for the fuel cocks beside his seat checking that the low pressure was 'on' and the high pressure (HP) was 'off'. After selecting the low pressure pumps 'on', he pressed the starter button and the first Derwent engine began to breathe. As the engine revolutions increased he gradually fed in the HP fuel cock until the engine was fully alight and self-sustaining. He then repeated the process until the Meteor had both engines at the ready. The ground crew disconnected the battery cart, gave him the thumbs up, and he was on his way.

Iwakuni was a hive of activity with fighters and transports taking off and landing at an impressive rate. When Phil's turn came, he lined up on the runway, rolling forward a little to make sure the nosewheel was straight. Pushing the two throttles forward with his left hand, the Derwents sent 7,000 pounds of thrust rearward and catapulted him along the runway.

At 110 knots he took to the skies, raised the wheels and flaps and accelerated towards 300 knots to climb away. Within three minutes he was passing 10,000 feet and eased the climb speed back a little. Japan fell away below him as he made for the coast and clear air to familiarise himself with his new steed. He pitched and rolled and felt the Meteor through his hands. It was power and freedom and his harsh childhood was a distant memory. Ripping open the atmosphere in a fighter jet had been beyond his wildest dreams. Now it was a reality.

Back on the ground, Ken shared Phil's excitement that night. Early the next day the two pilots were sent up twice more to fire their four cannons and launch their rockets in earnest into a small uninhabited island that was now pock-marked from the fury of fighter jets. Once the Australian pilots had unloaded their firepower and returned to Iwakuni they were officially Meteor pilots after a grand total of two days and five hours flying the single-seat F.8. Without delay, Phil was ordered to join Ken, 'Val' and 'Harry' and fly to Korea.

There was no time to celebrate. Phil's logbook was stamped, his file completed and his jet fuelled. His next flight that day would take him across the Sea of Japan and to war once again. His new home would be K14 Kimpo air base, fifty miles from the war's front line.

The Meteors departed Japan in a loose battle formation with Hiroshima to the right and the coastline ahead. As they levelled off for the water crossing, Phil looked around at his fellow jet pilots with one eye and his new alien cockpit with the other. Its switches and dials were still so new to him, yet somehow, within days, he would have to take the Meteor into battle. He knew that death may be lurking around the corner, but it was the thought of messing up and letting his squadron mates down that truly terrified him.

The Korean coast slid beneath the nose and Kimpo lay ahead. Their basic navigation aid's needle wandered about in the general direction of K14, but Phil continued to rely on the folded chart on his knee. The weather was grey and the four Meteors descended below the overcast occasionally encountering patches of drizzling rain. Then, through the murk, the 'Witch's Tit' came into view.

The 'Tit' was a peak near Kimpo air base and well known as the dominant landmark in the area. It had a light coating of snow on its upper slopes and Phil was reminded just how much colder the coming months in Korea would be. The Meteors contacted the air traffic controller, 'The Dentist', and were sequenced to land with aircraft returning from combat that were a higher priority and low on fuel.

To War Again

Phil flew 'Val' Turner's wing as Ken Towner hooked onto Harry's and the four silver jets rolled towards the runway in pairs. Concentrating intensely, Phil could not ignore the lines upon lines of aircraft parked on aprons and in walled revetments. Jets, propellers, fighters and transport aircraft were everywhere on this huge base that the United Nations airmen shared with the Americans. For the moment, though, only the runway mattered.

The runway was as long as any he had seen and its surface was covered in Pierced Steel Planking (PSP). The interlinked sheets of perforated metal were designed for ease of construction and all weather operation but, as his Meteor's wheels touched down firmly, it was the astounding noise of rubber on metal that really caught Phil's attention.

Exiting the runway, the new arrivals were marshalled to their parking spaces alongside the other Meteors of 77 Squadron. As the engines spooled down, the pilots wound back their canopies and breathed their first cold, damp Korean air. Beyond the flightline Phil could see familiar smiling faces from his pilot's course at Point Cook and his feet had no sooner hit the pavement than there were handshakes, smiles and jibes about finally joining them in Korea.

Reunited, there was a feel of old times and familiarity here on the other side of the world. Vance Drummond and Bruce Thomson showed Phil to their tent where there was a spare bunk waiting for him. There were four bunks, one in each corner, and Don Armit made up the quartet. In the centre of the tent was a pot-belly stove, fuelled by a rubber hose connected to a drum of diesel located outside. Wood was a precious commodity and broken down crates were rebirthed as shelves and cupboards while makeshift walls were made of longer planks. It was basic, but it was home.

Settled in, the four new arrivals made their way to meet the commanding officer, Wing Commander Gordon Steege DSO DFC. Phil had heard of Steege's pedigree as a fighter pilot having flown during World War Two in both North Africa and the Pacific and being credited with eight aerial victories. He had rejoined the RAAF at the outbreak of the Korean War and had been at the helm of 77 Squadron for three months. As he stood across the room from his new commanding officer, Phil waited for some inspiring words to be forthcoming from his boss, but there was nothing.

Steege seemed ill at ease and asked each of the new pilots about their backgrounds, flying and otherwise. He was relieved at what 'Harry' and 'Val' related but seemed disappointed when Phil and Ken confirmed their limited experience. The old fighter pilot thumbed through the files on his desk, periodically looking up to survey the young men in front of him. In the end, he simply advised them to be careful and do exactly as they were told. They were then dismissed.

That evening Phil met up with Bruce Gillan, Johnny Myers and Bob Strawbridge. Inevitably, the conversation turned to the realities of aerial combat and, eventually, to the seemingly lacklustre attitude of the commanding officer. The conversation dropped in volume as they discussed Steege's reservations about their task. Their adversary, the MiG-15, was a superior fighter capable of flying close to the speed of sound. The number of air-to-air encounters with the Russian-built jet had been growing. Steege knew this and was concerned about his young inexperienced pilots engaging the MiGs in their old technology 'Meatboxes'. Nearly twenty pilots from 77 squadron had already been shot down and they had been yet to bring down a MiG.

Steege had implemented more defensive taskings for his aircraft; an airfield defence role where men and machines maintained a state of readiness to scramble into the air at any time. More and more such roles and patrols eroded at the normally offensive nature of combat operations and with it the pilots' morale was slowly chiselled away. Even so, the young pilots were keen to fight and any genuine concerns regarding their Meteor were soon forgotten as the night deteriorated into bouts of laughter and reminiscences.

As he settled down in his bunk, the pot-belly stove continued to provide life-saving warmth as the temperature outside dived. He could hear Vance, Bruce and Don's breathing slow and deepen as they fell asleep while his mind still raced wondering what lay ahead.

It was November 30th 1951 and Phil's first night in Korea. Within 24 hours his world would be a very different place.

Chapter Twenty-Two

A New War Begins

The new arrivals attended a briefing on escape and evasion tactics, should they be shot down, some basic language skills and the operational procedures at K-14 Kimpo. Aside from their own squadron's Meteors, they shared the base with a broad range of American units and aircraft. B-26 bombers, F-86 Sabres, C-46 Commandos, P-51 Mustangs, the list went on. The squadron worked alongside the USAF's 4th Fighter Wing under the command of Colonel Harrison Thyng, a highly experienced fighter pilot and ace in World War Two who had also become a jet ace in Korea. Highly respected, his silver swept-wing Sabres wore distinct yellow bands on their fuselage, fin and nose in an effort to distinguish them from the MiGs in the melee of a dogfight.

Following the briefing, Steege had made it known that he wanted his new pilots to be very familiar with the Meteor before they launched into the fight. That meant more training in formation flying, 'cine' gunnery and flying on instruments. Phil could understand the need as he still wasn't comfortable with the Meteor, but it was frustrating as he saw Gillan, Thomson and Drummond readying for a real operation the next day.

They had been tasked to participate in a twelve-aircraft fighter sweep while Phil was rostered on two sessions of instrument flying and making approaches to land using the radio compass. For more than two hours that day Phil climbed above Kimpo, spoke to 'The Dentist' and descended back to K14. Despite the repetition, he began to feel more at ease with the Meteor. The speeds, the power settings and the lie of the horizon in different phases of flight started to feel familiar. There was even time for an aerobatic manoeuvre or two.

Gloster Meteor F.8 A77-911 in its revetment at K-14 Kimpo.

After the second flight he returned to his tent, which was now empty, and laid down on his bunk to sleep. Sometime later he checked his watch and wondered where the lads were. They should be back by now. He was sure that he'd heard the distinctive sounding Meteors arrive over the top a while back. Finally, the tent flap drew open, but it wasn't Bruce or Vance, it was Steege.

He jumped to rise to his feet, but Steege raised his hand to reassure his young sergeant pilot. Hardly making eye contact, Steege sat on one of the vacant bunks and said nothing for a minute. When he did look up, Phil saw a deep weariness in his eyes. He looked old and tired and not like the decorated steely-eyed fighter pilot that he was.

He explained that the fighter sweep had gone terribly wrong and the twelve Meteors were attacked by MiGs in far superior numbers. All three of his tent-mates, Vance Drummond, Bruce Thomson and Don Armit had been shot down and their whereabouts were unknown. Steege paused again and then instructed Phil to pack his gear and change tents as he didn't want him staying there as the sole occupant. As quietly as he had entered, Steege rose slowly and left the tent and the stony silence within its four walls.

Phil looked around at his mates' beds. Razors lay on the shelves, a shirt hung on a makeshift hook and a magazine was open where the last page had been read. Like a still life painting, the pilots' last moments in that tent had been frozen in time and now they were somewhere, dead or alive, in North Korea.

Memories of New Guinea came flooding back. Turner and Wharton had been butchered on their first patrol before he had ever had a chance to fire his weapon in anger. Now, he felt that same fire in his belly and the helplessness of not being there as he had years before in the steaming jungle. Perhaps Vance and the boys were still alive? Perhaps they had ejected. What had led to three aircraft being lost on a single fighter sweep?

Phil pulled on his boots and walked down the tent-line until he found Bruce Gillan. The young pilot that wanted to fly airliners had survived the fiercest of dogfights over Korea that had claimed three of their friends. Bruce was still staggered by the speed at which the battle had started and finished and the frantic melee that had taken place in between.

He explained how they had been flying around 20,000 feet when they sighted up to forty MiGs above them. The enemy fighters were upon them in an instant and Don Armit and Vance had been the first two aircraft to fall under attack. Aircraft were breaking left and right as trails of vapour and fuel criss-crossed the sky around them as the Meteors attempted to fight off the swarm of MiGs. Bruce saw a number of Meteors diving with MiGs on their tail and one trailing a huge stream of fuel. Other pilots reported explosions in mid-air and Bill Middlemiss' aircraft was damaged leaving his critical flight instruments reading zero.

Somehow in the chaos, Bruce Gogerly had brought down a MiG, the first for 77 Squadron. That was about the only positive news Bruce could share as he hadn't seen any parachutes, although he was still hopeful that at least one of the missing men was alive. The two pilots reassured each other that hope was not lost and remembered how Vance had survived the Wirraway crash when they were training at Point Cook. They half-chuckled at the memory, but there was no concealing the fact that Bruce was shaken by the ferocity of the combat. He kept saying, "One minute they were there and then they were gone."

Phil walked back to his tent, not allowing himself to dwell on what had happened.

It wasn't in his nature and New Guinea had reinforced the futility of reflection. This was war and it was life and death, not lines in a movie. It was the ultimate definition of finality. It wasn't a moustached Clark Gable slaying the enemy. War was young men barely out of high school dying in the most horrendous fashion and committing unspeakable acts. Dwell on them at your peril. Do the job and move on was the only way that Phil knew how to function.

In the larger scheme of things, the losses had virtually guaranteed that the squadron would now stay close to Kimpo, far from the lurking MiGs reaching down from north of the Yalu River. The American F-86 Sabre-equipped squadrons would be left in the interceptor role to duel with their communist foe. The Meteors would defend the airfield or fly Combat Air Patrols, better known as 'CAPs'. In this role they would cover downed pilots but mainly they would patrol at 25,000 feet to offer support for the American Sabres returning from the fight low on fuel and ammunition. At other times they were on standby to be scrambled against unidentified aircraft, but these nearly always proved to be friendly fighters.

For the fighter pilots of 77 Squadron it was frustrating, but out-gunned by the MiGs at the higher altitudes, it was a role they would have to get used to. It was also apparent that Steege was not keen for his young pilots to be unnecessarily thrown into a fray that had the odds stacked against them. The squadron motto was 'Swift to Destroy', but their mission now seemed to be in conflict with those words. Instead, in December 1951, the pilots modified the lyrics of 'All I Want for Christmas' and their voices could be heard of an evening emanating from the bar at the club. 'All I want for Christmas is two swept wings'.

A New War Begins

The tents at Kimpo accommodated four pilots and were reinforced with whatever timber could be scavenged.

A pair of Meteors become airborne at K-14 Kimpo.

Chapter Twenty-Three

Hard Lessons

Despite the warnings and general gloom, Phil was keen to become an operational squadron pilot and his opportunity arose at evening briefing when he was rostered to fly Meteor A77-368 the next day in company with the experienced Flying Officer Wal Rivers DFC. Rivers was on his second tour of duty having originally flown Mustangs with the squadron before converting to the Meteor. Now he was back, with a new pilot in tow and snow on the ground again.

The purpose of the first sortie was a familiarisation flight to acquaint Phil with the terrain, roads and towns to the north of K-14 and the bomb line. However, instead of an orientation flight, the order was given without notice to scramble to intercept inbound unidentified aircraft. Phil was surprisingly calm as he followed Rivers to the flight line where they had readied their aircraft earlier. The veteran pilot seemed to offer an air of confidence and it filtered down to his wingman. Still, as Phil grabbed the handhold on the side of the Meteor and began to hoist himself up towards the cockpit, there was no mistaking that his time had come.

Stepping down into his seat, the ground crew began to secure the stiff half-frozen straps around the young pilot. Phil's icy fingers struggled with the buckle of his leather helmet for a few moments before it was finally fitted. Gloves, oxygen mask and goggles. The precious minutes seemed to be slipping away as he looked across sheepishly at Rivers who was ready to go and now gave the signal to start engines.

With the canopy closed, Phil brought the two Derwent engines to life and began his pre-take off drills as Rivers moved forward. Phil followed his leader to the runway, lining up together as a pair with Rivers ahead and to the left. The two pilots brought their engines to take-off power without delay and accelerated down the runway at K-14. Easing into the air through 100 knots, Phil reached down with his left hand to select his landing gear 'up' with one eye locked onto his leader. The silver Meteors climbed into the blue Korean sky as Rivers checked in with 'The Dentist' and the controller responded with a course to steer to intercept the unidentified aircraft.

In a matter of minutes, the two fighters levelled off at more than 20,000 feet. "Godfrey Leader Level. Oxygen on high. Gun switches to fire and test." Phil throttled the engines back to 11,600 rpm and held the Meteor level. He checked his oxygen setting, flicked the safety catch on the control column to fire and squeezed the trigger. The four 20mm cannons in the nose of the aircraft erupted sending a shudder through the airframe, and black puffs of cordite smoke into the airflow, as Phil nudged his Meteor back in behind the leader.

In the next instant a flock of tumbling sparrows seemed to fly past Phil's cockpit. He wondered what business the tiny birds had being at such an altitude when it dawned on him. They weren't birds, they were the shell casings being ejected from Wal's Meteor as he tested his cannons. He felt both stupid and sick. He had tucked right into the shells' path and they could have brought him down.

He buried the thought as Rivers scanned the sky and Phil carefully surveyed the airspace behind them for potential threats – there was nothing. It was a massive sky and they were two silver darts streaking and all alone. They swept the sky, but there was nothing to be seen and their precious fuel was now beginning to dip. Phil was thankful for his good luck as the pair of fighters turned for Kimpo.

Rivers led Phil into the traffic pattern at K-14 at 1,000 feet and 250 knots. Passing the runway, the leader broke off to port and seconds later his wingman followed. Banking at 45 degrees, Phil reduced power, extended his speed brakes and heaved his aircraft into a 4G turn. The Meteor washed off its speed to below 175 knots before he extended his landing gear and then his flaps. Rolling out on final approach he could see Wal landing on the left hand side of the runway and Phil followed suit by landing on the same line he had taken off from.

The two Meteors taxied back in formation, parked and shut their engines down. Phil completed his checks and unclipped his oxygen mask. His first combat mission was over and all he had done was fire a burst of 20mm rounds into space. The flight had been uneventful and incredibly benign yet, as the ground crew began to help unstrap Phil, he paused.

Hard Lessons

Bill Middlemiss with Phil. Bill had survived the dogfight of 1st December despite damage to his Meteor and his critical flight instruments reading zero. (Source: Susan Middlemiss)

A chill came over him, partially caused by the icy breeze but made worse by his sweat-soaked flying suit. He had only been flying for an hour and yet here he sat in a pool of nervous energy. As his adrenalin dumped, he pondered how he would respond to real aerial combat. Only time would tell.

The following days would see another patrol, or a scramble to intercept friendly fighters. On one occasion he flew cover for a downed American pilot. Phil felt that these flights offered an opportunity to gain experience on the Meteor and appreciate the lie of the land, but still there was none of the combat he had been trained for. However, there was always some form of challenge lurking.

With only a handful of sorties under his belt and a few more hours experience on the Meteor he was tasked to fly from Suwon to Kimpo as dusk approached. One delay followed another until Phil found himself flying north with the sun setting quickly on his left. It was only an hour flight, but the night was closing in and Phil had never flown the Meteor at night.

He wound up the cockpit lighting and made for K-14 as quickly as he could.

He had only ever landed a jet at night once and that was a Vampire. The truth was that he hadn't really consistently flown at night since his basic training at Point Cook more than a year before. Phil sped into the landing pattern and it became night almost as he began his approach to land, slipping further down into the darkness. As he looked at the runway ahead there was a dull glow of parallel flare paths but the perspective looked wrong as he pushed and pulled on the controls to change the picture. He was getting closer to the ground and still he was fighting the aircraft. Phil decided to put a stop to this, opening the throttles and raising the landing gear and flaps in turn.

He accelerated to 150 knots and then climbed back up into the circuit to make a second approach. This time the situation was more controlled although his heart was still beating in his chest from the first attempt. The runway now lay ahead, steady in the windscreen. He held the aim point in his line of sight and rigidly maintained his airspeed until the wheels touched down on the PSP of K-14's runway.

Back in his tent he contemplated his nighttime return and the near-miss with Wal River's shells. It was a sober reminder of just how little experience he had and that much of the training was on the job. A dozen hours on a jet was not much time and he could see where Steege's reservations were coming from about the limitations of the Meteor and the new pilots he was being sent. However, fighter pilots are meant to fight and it was an opinion shared not only by the pilots but a good many officers far higher on the food chain if one was to believe the rumours. The rumour was also that there was a new commanding officer on the way.

Hard Lessons

Phil flew his first operational sortie in Meteor A77-368. Today, that aircraft is on display at the Australian War Memorial.

The harsh winter posed operational challenges for 77 Squadron.

In the heat of combat, the profiles of the American F-86 Sabre (top) and the MiG-15 were very similar. (Source: Kevin Griffin via Alamy)

Chapter Twenty-Four

The Boss

Christmas Eve 1951 was celebrated at K-14 with officers and airmen of 77 Squadron and American guests bidding farewell to Wing Commander Steege and welcoming the new commanding officer, Squadron Leader Ron Susans DFC. A rare appearance of Australian beer was partnered with a steak and sausage supper and for a short time the war was replaced by revelry. Still, it was never far away.

When 1952 arrived a few days later, the New Year was announced by 'Bedcheck Charlie', an old Russian biplane. In the wee hours of January 1st, the enemy Polikarpov Po-2 made a low pass over K-14 dropping a number of small bombs and causing minimal damage on the flight line. For Phil, the main damage was to a good night's sleep and that became the main cause for complaint whenever 'Charlie' called at night. When the day dawned for Phil it was another scramble, another patrol and airborne intercept of friendly American Sabres.

The new CO was a big man in both reputation and stature. Atop Ron Susan's tall frame was a head of thick dark hair and a healthy moustache sat on his top lip. In appearance he was the fighter pilot's fighter pilot with a pedigree to match. He had flown fighters in World War Two out of North Africa, Sicily, Malta and Italy, accounting for a number of the enemy. He subsequently flew Spitfires in the Pacific theatre and most recently he had been on a course in the UK flying RAF Vampire and Meteor jets.

Without delay Susans set about seeing what he had to work with and found the squadron low on morale in its current role. He spoke with General Everest, who was in charge of the US 5th Air Force, about the way forward for 77 Squadron and envisioned the squadron operating in a ground attack role using the Meteor to deliver low-level rocket strikes on designated targets. He highlighted the Meteor's suitability to the role as a durable design and stable platform from which to deliver rockets and cannon fire. Furthermore, the Meteor's two engines offered a higher chance of survivability in the face of ground fire. Susans won his case and the concept was given the green light.

Within days the squadron was ready for its new role, however the bleak Korean winter had other ideas. Freezing temperatures, low cloud and a landscape blanketed in snow made flying and navigation a challenge. In spite of the conditions, the patrols continued with one taking Phil as far north as the Yalu River. This was 'MiG Alley' where dogfights between Sabres and MiGs frequently took place.

Beyond the combat in the 'Alley', a good deal of secrecy and politics surrounded the MiG fighters. Supposedly flown by Chinese and North Korean pilots, it became apparent to the United Nation's pilots that there were skillful Soviet veterans at the controls of some of these fighters. These pilots operated from Chinese airfields in Manchuria, which were not able to be attacked under the UN guidelines for fear of an escalation of the war, leading to frustration among their opponents. Following an engagement, the MiGs could head north over the Yalu River to the safety of their untouchable airfields.

Now Phil once again sat in Meteor '368' with Wal Rivers in the lead. The pair scanned the hostile skies for any hint of friend or foe, although, at a distance, the Sabre and the MiG painted a very similar silhouette. Then Phil saw them. Two swept wing fighters high above and tracking north. He called the 'bogeys' to Wal and the two pilots watched the MiGs, waiting for them to dive on the disadvantaged Meteors. The lower altitude of the Meteors did suit their operational performance and should the MiGs decide to dive there would be a high chance they would leave contrails in their wake as they passed down through the condensation level. This would make them slightly easier to sight. Phil fought the urge to become transfixed by the enemy aircraft above and continued to watch his 'six' for any other fighters attacking from the rear.

He knew that the diving MiG would have the better of the fight, but still he was ready and hoping for an opportunity to mix it with the enemy. He tightened his harness a little more than usual and wriggled down into the seat. His head was swiveling – left, right, behind and above. But the MiGs held their course and altitude, seemingly unaware of the two Meteors below them. Only when they

The Boss

Wing Commander Ron Susans DFC. (Source: Martin Susans)

were well out of sight did Wal and Phil turn south once more and head for Suwon.

The weather had cleared somewhat and the squadron's first ground attack rocket missions had commenced. Recently promoted Wing Commander Susans had called for a thousand sorties in January and the revitalised pilots wanted to meet their new CO's target.

Phil's first ground attack began the night before when US intelligence had identified targets for the next day and called the 'Frag Order' through to 77 Squadron. As the pilots gathered for briefing, the squadron's Intelligence Officer, Stan Bromhead, stood beside a map that reached nine feet to the ceiling of the Nissen hut and was just as large across. Like Susans, he sported a moustache, although slightly turned up at the ends.

The pilots settled into their seats. Ron Susans would lead the strike with Phil on his wing while the second pair would be Keith Martin with Phil's mate 'Vic' Oborn. Their names, aircraft numbers, radio frequencies and call signs were chalked on a large blackboard beside the map. They would operate as 'Godfrey Special'. Bromhead began by nominating the target, buildings near Chinnampo. The town lay to the south of the North Korean capital, Pyongyang, and on the northern shore of the Taedong River.

Bromhead detailed the target, expected anti-aircraft fire and the optimum direction of attack and the planned route of escape. The current bomb line and Main Supply Route (MSR) were highlighted as were emergency details, US-held islands and search and rescue bases. Phil busily made notes, marking the anti-aircraft sites directly on his chart. By the end of the briefing his head was full of the next day's details.

Phil walked back to his tent and was grateful that he was flying with Susans on this first attack. The 'Boss' was a born leader and instilled confidence in those around him. Even in the limited dealings Phil had had with Susans to date, the commanding officer had made the junior sergeant pilot genuinely feel that he was a vital squadron member. Phil was determined not to let him down and settled down for the night with a mix of anticipation and fear. It was not the fear of the enemy or even the fear of dying, for he had faced that in New Guinea. His fear was of making a mistake and letting his mates down. That would be the most difficult fate to live with. In a few hours he would be on his way to the target and he would have his answers. For now it was time to slow his breathing and sleep.

Chapter Twenty-Five

A Day of Firsts

By the time the jeep dropped Phil at his aircraft, the resilient ground crew had already removed the canvas shrouds that protected the engines and canopy from the blanket of snow. He climbed up and began to ready the aircraft through a ritual that was becoming more familiar but was still far from second nature. Susans signaled and the four Meteors stirred into life before moving off along the taxiway, one behind the other.

The icy PSP felt slippery beneath the Meteor's wheels especially when turning. Each aircraft tucked into the warm air flowing from the engines of the jet ahead in an attempt to keep ice from forming on the leading edges of their wings. Out in front, Susans had no such luxury and initially flying at a higher speed was his only defence against the lift-eroding ice.

Each aircraft carried eight 60lb rockets, four beneath each wing, adding to the four 20mm cannons in the nose. As the four Meteors of 'Godfrey Special' lined up on the runway, they did so in pairs with the wingmen sitting behind and to the right of their leaders. Stationary on the runway they throttled up to take off power before Susans and Phil released their brakes and roared off down the runway. As Susans lifted off, Phil followed suit, tucked in closely on his CO's wing. The pair climbed away steeply to avoid disturbing the air through which Martin and 'Vic' Oborn would climb through.

The second pair stayed on the runway until they were beyond the point where the first two Meteors had lifted off before climbing away, cleaning up their landing gear and flaps as they went. Soon the four aircraft joined up in a finger four battle formation with the lead pair sitting 200 yards from the others. With their engines spinning at 14,000 rpm, the Meteors rocketed up into the sky as Susans checked in with the ground controller.

Initially navigating along the main supply route, the path was barely discernible in a landscape covered in snow. The white coating softened the edges of the jagged inhospitable terrain, Phil thought, although there was no doubting the dangers that lay beneath. With the radios silent, the cockpit was a quiet place with the only sounds being the slight whistle of the passing airflow and the echo of Phil's breathing into the oxygen mask. All the while North Korea slid by below.

They had been briefed to remain clear of Haeju as they made their way to the target as the port city was a known hot spot for anti-aircraft fire. From 15,000 feet Phil could make out the ground features associated with the target from the briefing the night before. The Taedong River, its mouth opening into the Yellow Sea and Chinnampo sitting on the northern shore. The target was a large building on the edge of the frozen harbour and was easily identifiable from altitude.

The Meteors descended to 5,000 feet to commence the attack with the four aircraft slipping, one behind the other, into a line astern formation. Then it began.

Susans rolled into a 35-degree dive and the other Meteors followed close behind, although varying their direction to avoid the anti-aircraft guns that were now inevitably tracking them. The screaming jets plunged towards the target as tracers began to spit at them from the ground. Now came the critical task of targeting amid the fury of the defences. The dive angle had to be held steady for ten to twenty seconds to allow the gunsight computer to assess the correct graticule position. Steady, steady, steady. Passing through 1,500 feet the pilots depressed the button on the top of the control column.

Then all hell broke loose.

Susans' rockets tore from their rails on his command, whistling towards the target and trailing efflux. Within seconds Phil freed his rockets and the pair behind did the same. The lethal ordnance sped away from the Meteors as if the jets were standing still and moments later the rockets were exploding and devastating the building below.

As the air filled with smoke and rocket fragments, the Meteor pilots pulled their jets into a climbing turn with their throttles at full power. The heavier, faster Meteor did not pull out of a dive like the Mustang he had trained on. Phil fought the g-forces with his tensed guts and strained his neck looking towards his escape path. Blacking out was a real threat and both man and machine groaned under the

A Day of Firsts

The Meteors' 60lb rockets being assembled by South Korean workers.

increased load of gravity. Tracers flicked past his canopy as he flew through the flying debris of his own rockets hoping that he wasn't about to shoot himself down.

He spotted Susans also heaving his jet towards the heavens, with mist enveloping his wings and thin ribbons of vapour trailing from the tips. Amid the fury of the attack, Phil thought that his leader's aircraft looked quite spectacular, unaware that moisture was condensing and creating equally impressive patterns on his own wings.

He momentarily looked behind to see the other two silver jets emerging from the target before refocusing on his escape as black puffs began to pockmark the sky. They were the tell-tale signs of anti-aircraft fire endeavouring to create a sky of flying fragments through which the Meteors had to pass. Each did so and emerged unscathed, although all too often this was not to be the case.

Clear of the target and at a safe altitude, Susans called for each member of 'Godfrey Special' to check in on the radio. It was the standard means of taking a head count that took place after every mission. Sometimes there was a stony silence, but today every pilot checked in briskly. They reformed into the finger four and set course for Kimpo.

Back at K-14, the four jets taxied back in formation before parking and shutting

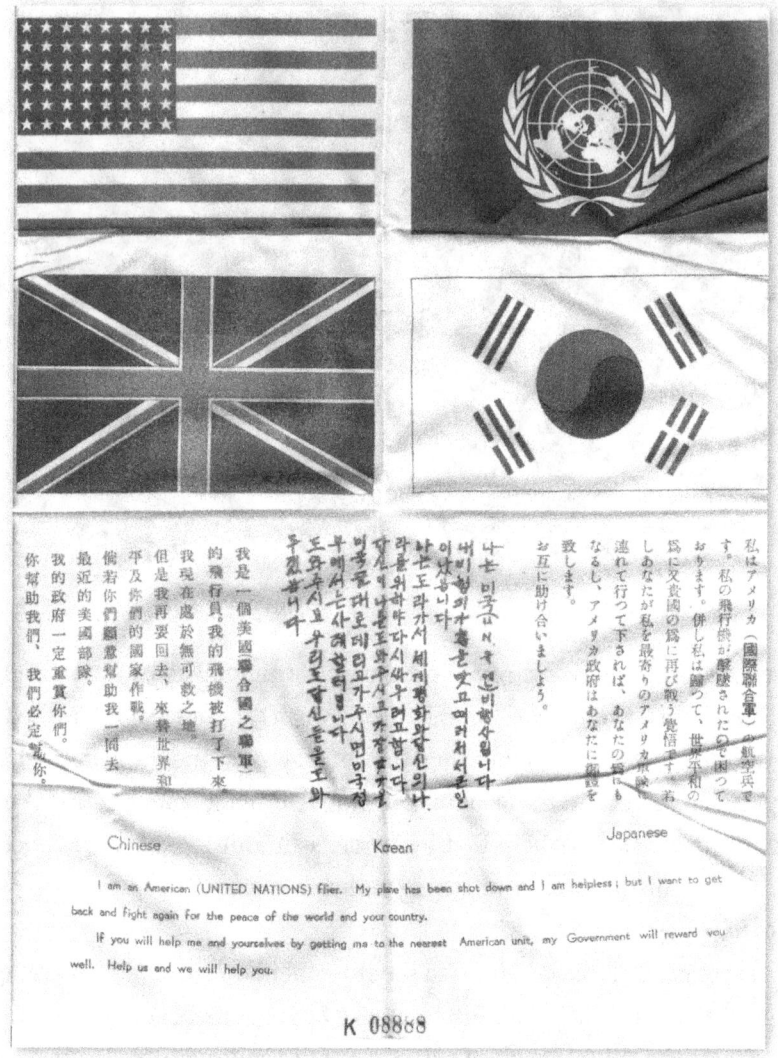

Phil's Blood Chit. This was carried by pilots and offered a reward for the safe return of a downed pilot.

down. Phil removed his gloves and placed them on top of the instrument panel next to the gunsight. As he loosened his helmet, he paused to process what the last hour had involved. It had not been an uneventful patrol or a training exercise. It had been an attack on a target. He had held steady when the tracers flicked by and delivered his rockets as he had been required. He looked down and the sweat was there, but not as much.

He climbed down from the Meteor and walked around it to check for any visible damage. Not finding any, he and 'Vic' exchanged a few words about how very different this was to Point Cook, or even Williamtown for that matter. Along with Susans and Martin, they were debriefed by Bromhead about the effectiveness of the strike and details about any ground fire they encountered. These words were recorded and used by the Intelligence Officer to build an updated picture of the enemy north of the bomb line.

As they left the Nissen hut, Susans pulled Phil aside and briefly told him that he had done well. It was just a few words but from a man that Phil held in the highest regard. Just as importantly, it let Phil know that today he hadn't messed up or let his mates down and he could sleep well in that knowledge. He couldn't sleep just yet, however, as he had to sign for Meteor A77-17 as there was another mission to be flown.

The second sortie was a patrol but the earlier strike and Susans' words had boosted Phil's confidence. By the time he returned from the second flight he felt a different man to the pilot that had walked to the flight line that morning – no better, just proven. That meant a great deal.

In some ways, though, Phil was still a raw boy from the bush. With his two sorties completed, Phil was approached to run an errand with Susans. As the commanding officer handed him the keys to the jeep, Phil froze where he stood, lost for words. With the CO already in the passenger seat and waiting, he finally revealed the truth, "I can't drive, Sir."

Susans looked back wide-eyed and two nearby ground crewman began to laugh.

"You're kidding."

"No, Sir. I can ride a motor-bike, but I've never driven a car."

Now it was Susans' turn to laugh. "Hop in. You're about to have your first lesson".

As the evening approached, Phil climbed aboard a truck with 'Vic', Ken, Bruce and Bob and headed to dinner. Meals were hosted by the American 67th Tactical Reconnaissance Wing at their Officers' Mess. Despite a good many Australian pilots being sergeants and not officers, the Americans recognised all aircrew as holding officer status. The Australian sergeant pilots refrained from wearing any rank insignia and were always made to feel welcome.

The meals were of a good standard and Phil could not help but compare the situation to eating rations in the jungle. As the night wore on, the pilots gathered at the bar for a drink and the chance to exchange tales tall and true. A non-drinker and rather quiet by nature, Phil slipped away unnoticed and retired to his tent. Once he was there he checked his flying gear, polished his boots and cleaned his .38 revolver.

He could hear the lads singing back at the Mess as he sat alone on his bunk. He pulled out a letter from Edith and read it for the hundredth time. He knew that in her job she would be watching for his name and he wanted her to be proud of anything that he might do. He'd never had a girlfriend before and it would be nice to have someone waiting at home, he thought. She had written a number of times and he hadn't wanted to write back. Writing was not his strong point.

However, he knew that she was a prolific letter writer, so he resolved to sit down to pen a few words. He sat there for a good while as he had no idea what to say. He tapped his pen and shuffled in his seat but the words would not come. He couldn't share the details of today's mission and he couldn't think of anything else to write. Then he sighted a photograph of a Sabre taking off among his things. He turned it over and wrote on the back. "Dear Edith. This is a Sabre. The drop tanks on these cost nearly as much as a car. Phillip. xx"

It had been a big day. His first rocket strike and his first letter home. He was a world away, but felt that he now truly belonged.

A Day of Firsts

Phil stands beside Meteor '163' with his trousers tucked into his boots. A 'trademark' that he carried over from his time in the army.

Covers provided rudimentary protection from the cold on the 77 Squadron flight line.

Chapter Twenty-Six

Frozen

Phil was suited to a military life. He relished the order and deeply appreciated the equality. A man was judged on his efforts and that's all he ever wanted. As he found in his years in the Army, if you do your job, where you came from did not matter. He was embarrassed by his lack of formal education, particularly among the other pilots, but not a single squadron mate ever passed judgement.

That is not to say that he didn't enjoy a joke or the company of his mates - he did. Some of those from his course at Point Cook had become like brothers. Bob Strawbridge, 'Vic' Oborn, Bruce Gillan and Ken Towner were all here and they lived, breathed and fought together. Phil just tended to avoid the crowded club, preferring the solitude of an empty tent or a distant corner of the airfield where he would set up targets and spend time shooting his revolver or a borrowed rifle.

He knew he wasn't the best pilot, but he was always ready to fly and do what was asked of him and that led to him beginning to accumulate missions at an ever-increasing rate. Ron Susans seemed to like the young Queenslander's rough edges and often had 'Zuppie' fly his wing. The 'Boss' certainly did more than his fair share of operational sorties for a commanding officer. In return, Phil held Susans in the highest regard as a pilot, leader and man. Such bonds can be forged quickly by men under fire, but can subsequently endure a lifetime.

Still, there was no single pilot Phil was paired with more than any other and there was not any particular Meteor that he preferred to fly. Some pilots favoured one aircraft or another and some even had personalised art painted on the nose. Phil figured that the CO was about the only bloke with enough influence to organise the same aircraft consistently so he never bothered to try. Scheduled maintenance, battle damage and limited resources meant that Phil rarely flew the same aircraft twice in succession but it didn't worry him in the slightest. He was just happy to fly.

However, there was one duty that Phil felt was less than desirable - the 'Baker Alert'. It called for two pilots to be strapped in and ready to take-off within two minutes. The alert ran from an hour before dawn until an hour after sunrise with a corresponding two hour alert again at sunset. The Meteors were generally only armed with their 20mm cannons and were at the ready to be scrambled to intercept any intruding aircraft or occasionally search for a downed pilot.

In winter, 'Baker Alert' was a miserable task. The long-suffering ground crew would be readying the snow-covered Meteors well before dawn, removing canvas covers, plugging in the battery carts and readying the cockpit for the pilot. The Martin Baker ejection seat in which the pilots sat was one of the major complaints on these mornings. The pilot actually sat on his dinghy pack which was strapped to him and would leave the aircraft with him in the case of an ejection. Atop the dinghy, and in immediate contact with the pilot's backside, was a rubber bladder that contained emergency drinking water. In sub-zero Korean temperatures, this bladder froze solid.

The pilot would then have to climb into the frozen cockpit and be strapped into a seat with a freezer brick for a cushion. There they would sit for two uncomfortable hours. A certain pilot with initiative did discover that sitting on a newspaper did provide a small degree of relief on the miserable pre-dawn 'Baker Alert'.

The winter permeated every aspect of life in Korea, cutting through tents and clothing no matter how many layers were worn. Jerry cans froze, beer bottles froze and even sweat-drenched flying suits could freeze if they weren't left near the tent's pot belly stove. Should anyone be lucky to obtain one of the American steaks from their comrades-in-arms, it could be left on a tent flap in a form of rudimentary refrigeration. Phil would never again complain about the cold winters on the Queensland Darling Downs.

The day after his first rocket attack, Phil sat in his frozen seat as the sun rose, but fortunately for a patrol and not a 'Baker Alert'. He and Flight Lieutenant John 'Butch' Hannan departed and patrolled the area between Haeju and Singye without event and high above the deadly anti-aircraft guns of Haeju.

Later that day, Phil and his mate Bruce Gillan flew together for the first time. The two sergeant pilots were tasked with flying an airborne patrol but had no

The belly-mounted ventral tank was a vulnerable aspect of the Meteor. Here Phil examines his ventral tank after it was damaged by ground fire.

sooner contacted the ground controller than they were diverted to search for a downed pilot near the mouth of the river. They swept the area without success before returning to K-14 where Phil discovered a bullet hole in the leading edge of his right wing. Someone had obviously objected to their presence in the area and now Phil had his first battle damage despite being unaware that anyone was shooting at him.

This minimal damage to his Meteor was added to the roster of scheduled maintenance for the aircraft and, much to his surprise, Phil was rostered to fly the aircraft back to Iwakuni in Japan. He had even been given leave in Japan. That evening he readied for the ferry flight and reminded Bruce of how much he would enjoy his time away from Kimpo. The two pilots sparred in good humour, as they had done since Point Cook, although Bruce had not been quite as jovial since the dogfight in December when Vance and Bruce Thomson were shot down. It was good to see him laughing, Phil thought.

The next day as he was set to depart, three of his mates were tasked to fly together. Bruce, 'Vic' and Bob were to fly a patrol with Wal Rivers and part of him wished he was going with them although, as he said goodbye, he made sure not to let them know. Deeper down, he wondered if he was going to miss anything while he was away. The squadron was now established in its ground attack role and Phil was keen to play his part.

As Kimpo, disappeared behind his tail, Phil tracked via Pohang across the Sea of Japan, making landfall at Ashiya before turning left for Iwakuni. The flight was enjoyable, his lone jet in friendly skies. The war was only an hour behind him but it seemed far more distant. Men on the ground were fighting in the bitter cold, pilots were dogfighting in MiG Alley while his own squadron was diving through flak to destroy targets on the ground. Still, here he sat, listening to his own breathing in clear skies and not a care in the world.

It was a feeling that pervaded him over the next week as he tried to relax in Japan. He took in the sights but continually wondered how the boys were going back at Kimpo. It was a strange sensation that bordered on guilt and detracted from really enjoying his leave. The week both flew by and dragged on but he was soon on board one of the RAAF's C-47 Dakotas and heading north to K-14. His return did not go as planned.

He wasn't back for long before he learned the squadron had suffered losses the day before on two separate missions. Throwing his gear on his bunk, Bruce's corner of the tent looked ominously vacant. Bob Strawbridge was there moments later and began to explain how the day had unravelled. Bob had been on an armed reconnaissance mission as one of six aircraft near Haeju. Ron Susans was paired with Ken 'Black' Murray, 'Harry' Browne-Gaylord with Bill Bennett and Bob with Wal Rivers.

Beneath a low cloud base with snow falling lightly, they had split into three pairs to attack any targets they could find. He heard 'Harry' call Bill on the radio to tell him that he'd been hit by ground fire and had lost his airspeed indicator and altimeter

Phil taking aim with his revolver by the Han River.

Between sorties. (L to R) Purssey, Martin, Middelton, Cadan and Zupp.

and that was the last anyone heard from him. Phil sat in silence for a moment and asked the question that he dreaded. "And Bruce?"

Bob confessed he was equally unsure of Bruce Gillan's fate. He related that Bruce had departed on the second mission to Haeju and was airborne before Bob returned to K-14. Apparently the weather near Haeju was even worse and again the six aircraft split into pairs. Bruce and Al Avery were attacking a water tower when Bruce called that he'd been hit and was heading for home. Al then said that Bruce's Meteor started to stream fuel and he thought he saw pieces fly from the cockpit as the aircraft began to trail smoke. Bruce appeared to level off and Al pulled up alongside, but the canopy and ejection seat was gone. There was no call over the radio and nothing has been heard of Bruce since despite numerous aircraft looking.

Phil pondered at the reality. 'Harry' Browne-Gaylord, the poster boy for fighter pilots that had mentored Phil on the Mustang, and his mate Bruce Gillan were both gone. A week before Phil and Bruce had been flying and laughing together and now there was another empty bunk. He could only hope that they would be found or perhaps be taken prisoner.

Neither pilot was ever heard from again. Decades later, Bruce's mother would still call Phil at his home clinging to hope that her son was alive.

Battle damage. The shattered remnants of Phil's canopy after being hit by ground fire on 6th February 1952.

Chapter Twenty-Seven

A Close Call

Phil saw out the rest of January 1952 flying strikes on Haeju. Flying Susans' wing on the 29th as one of a section of four Meteors, Phil and his mates blasted nearly thirty rockets into a building suspected of housing armaments. The building was left a smouldering wreck; a scene recreated days later when Phil, 'Vic' Oborn and Ken Murray followed Bill Bennett onto a similar target. The four jets fired their rockets at the target setting it ablaze before sweeping back around at low level for a second run. With their rockets gone they set their sights on a line of nearby huts and unleashed their 20mm cannons. Sixteen barrels spat their fury as tracers wove their path to the buildings, shredding walls and roofs alike. After two passes and expending a full load of ammunition, it was time to set course for Kimpo without time to survey the damage. Even so, each time he had cleared a target near Haeju, Phil would cast his eye over the white-blanketed Korean landscape hoping for some sign of Bruce or Harry. None was ever forthcoming.

New pilots continued to arrive at the squadron. Lionel Cowper, Ian Cranston, Col King, Jack Evans and John Parker were all mates at Point Cook on Number 4 Course. There were already a number of familiar faces at the squadron to greet them, including Phil and Ken Towner who took them on an impromptu tour. With the constant trickle of new pilots, Phil did not feel as if he was still the newest kid on the block and experience was everything in Korea. In many ways he found that it was on the job training where you could learn from your mistakes if they didn't kill you. The hostile terrain, the ground fire, target fascination, the g-forces and inertia of a pull-up, the debris thrown up by one's own rocket strikes; they were all threats that had to be seen to be appreciated and even with time, they were still lethal. Yes, experience and luck were critical elements of survival in Phil's world.

The simple act of returning to Kimpo was often fraught with chance. Generally low on fuel, the Meteors would thread their way home along roads and canals and any other feature they could readily identify, pinned down by the cloud cover. More than once they had let down over coastal waters and sped along the Han River to find their base. For Phil this low flying was almost a necessity as his time flying in cloud and on instruments amounted to only twenty hours and, of that, virtually zero was in the Meteor. Even so, he was comfortable flying in the nap of the earth. The sensation of speed at little more than treetop height was exhilarating as the world flashed by.

After one sortie, as number two to the leader, he screamed along a narrow waterway in trail behind the other Meteor as they sought out K-14. The silver jet ahead seemed to skim the surface and in the distance Phil could make out the solitary form of a North Korean crossing an arched bridge, a long plank over his shoulder. He wondered whether the leader would fire and seconds later the puffing of smoke from the Meteor's cannons gave him the answer. The plank flew skyward as the man dropped and seconds later Phil blasted over the scene.

Back at Kimpo, the leader asked Phil if he'd seen the man on the bridge. When Phil replied that he had, the leader burst into laughter. "I let a burst of cannon go just as I was over his head. He must have shit himself!"

In spite of the more serious challenges, so far Phil had survived nearly forty missions and, along with other 77 Squadron pilots, it was announced that he was to receive the American Air Medal. The Australians shared Kimpo and the skies with the Americans and their recent success in the ground attack role had not gone unnoticed. It would still be some weeks before a 'gong parade' would take place and Colonel Thyng would pin the medal on his chest, but Phil was honoured and even a little excited by the announcement. As was his way, though, he kept it to himself.

Despite the freezing temperatures, February was shaping to be a very hot month for the squadron. The goal of 1,000 missions for January had been interrupted, but Susans and his pilots were determined to reach the milestone in February. From the outset the strikes were flown hard and Haeju was again on the receiving end. Phil returned from his first sortie of the month and counted a number of holes in his aircraft, including a sizeable one in the ever-vulnerable ventral tank.

The pace was incessant with two or three missions flown by each pilot every

A Close Call

The buckled flying goggles Phil was wearing when he was struck in the face by shrapnel and Perspex.

day. As always, Phil could be found in his tent or on a homemade rifle range if needed and all the while his number of missions continued to grow. Next came an attack on rail sheds near Sariwon that yielded deadly results before Phil was back in the melee of Haeju on another attack, rocketing and strafing buildings, this time with 'Butch' Hannan. Little did either man know that in a few days' time, they would be thrown together in a way that neither foresaw.

It was Butch that had originally approached Ron Susans with the idea to attack a particularly hot spot to the north, near Sibyon-ni. Susans agreed and turned to Wal Rivers nearby and suggested that he join Hannan for the sortie. The two officers then paired up with Sergeant Ian Cranston and Warrant Officer Keith 'Bomber' Hill to complete the four.

Their initial rocket strike to the west on Sibyon-ni produced unknown results before the Meteors sped east towards an area of intense ground fire. Wal Rivers was well into his second tour over Korea and the flak bursts were as intense as anything he had witnessed. The filthy aftermath of the explosions filled the sky making sighting any targets very difficult, although Wal managed to catch a glimpse of two .50 calibre gun pits. He called it in to 'Butch' who instructed him he take the lead.

As was his technique, Rivers rolled in at an angle to the target, jinking left and right to make it difficult for the anti-aircraft gunners to both target him and anticipate where his final run in would be. With 'Bomber' on his wing, they pierced the hostile haze of flak and unleashed their cannons on the gun pits before heaving back on their control columns and making for the clear air above.

As Rivers climbed away he looked back to see 'Butch' making his run on the target, but there was no jinking left or right, just a straight run at the heavily fortified position. No sooner had he fired upon the target than flames began to pour from his ventral tank. Hannan peeled off towards the south and Kimpo but the aircraft was never going to make it. Surrounded by treacherous, hostile terrain, and his aircraft rapidly being consumed by fire, Hannan ejected from the Meteor to the south of Sibyon-ni.

The other aircraft saw his parachute open but then lost him against the snow and hills. Running low on fuel and ammunition and with 'Bomber' Hill calling in damage from ground fire, Rivers requested support for the downed pilot but was advised that the area was a no-go zone for the American helicopters due to the concentration of gun emplacements. Rivers couldn't blame them and wondered why any Allied aircraft were here at all.

Phil and Ray Taylor were overhead on patrol when they were called in to cover Hannan, who was now alone somewhere among the snow-covered hills, his aircraft a smouldering wreck. By the time the pair arrived, the flak had intensified even further as Rivers watched Taylor climb overhead and Phil depart to guide in other friendly aircraft. When Phil returned, he relayed that he'd sighted something red by the road and not far from yet another .50 calibre gun pit.

The silver Meteor below banked steeply, reversing its turn at treetop height and with flak bursts all around. The turn was not complete when Phil called that he'd been hit and Rivers dreaded that now two pilots were to be lost on the sortie. However, Phil's Meteor came into view once again, almost vertical and climbing away from the chaos below.

In the cockpit, the g-force of the pull-up had almost led to Phil blacking out, but now his thoughts and vision were returning to full clarity. He scanned his instruments – yes, he was climbing and the aircraft seemed intact. The noise was intense as Phil realised his canopy had been shattered. His oxygen mask had been wrenched away and his goggles had been blown crooked and one lens was missing. Still climbing, he straightened his gear and self-assessed his situation. He could taste blood in his mouth and feel barbs stinging and throbbing in his cheek and jaw. His flight suit and life jacket wore a spattering of red stains. In the heat of the moment, surrounded by blood and confusion he thought to himself, "If I'm dying, I actually don't feel that bad".

A Close Call

Phil squats beside the damaged canopy of Meteor A77-15. Some of the injuries to his face are evident.

His headset burst into life with the voice of Rivers asking where he'd been hit. "In the head", was Phil's reply. "My canopy's gone". As quick as a flash and tinged with relief, Rivers answered, "That's your hardest bit, 'Zuppie'. It must have bounced off your bald head."

Reality soon returned and the realisation that 'Butch' was somewhere down there. Low on fuel and battle-damaged, they had to depart. Phil limped his battered Meteor back to Kimpo, bringing her to a halt and shutting down on the apron. As he sat there surveying the scene he could see nicks in the metal all about the cockpit where the pieces of the projectile had carved a random path. A ground crewman climbed up to the cockpit. Initially a little confronted by the bloodied pilot, he then began to assess the battle damage and shattered canopy. As Phil pointed out the various nicks, the fitter focused on the radio-compass' face atop the instrument panel, beside the gunsight.

Embedded was the main projectile, the size of a man's thumb. He turned to Phil and commented, "Mate, that's big!" Phil looked back and replied, "Yeah, and it was bloody hot!" In his confusion, as he climbed away from the gun pits, Phil had reached up and tried to grab the errant slug to remove it from the radio-compass. The two laughed at the random nature of the act in the heat of battle.

Less humorous was the damage to Phil's goggles. The metal of the right frame was badly buckled and the lens gone where it had obviously taken a substantial hit. How he had not lost an eye, or worse, was a sobering thought. He was grazed and bruised about the eye but most of the blood had flowed from a series of lacerations to his cheek and jaw line. There was more blood than damage, he thought. Overall he felt fine, but was required to make his way to the American Base Hospital for assessment. There his wounds were tended to and small pieces of metal and Perspex removed from his face.

The American medical staff and officers from the Sabre squadron gathered around asking if he was the pilot that had just returned in the Meteor with the 'top down'. They seemed impressed but Phil played the incident down, keen to get out of the hospital and back to his tent. Little did he know that the Americans recommended him for a medal for the act and that it would be nearly forty years and the subject of international diplomacy before he ever heard of being the first Australian to be awarded the Purple Heart.

Chapter Twenty-Eight

The 1,000 Mission Month

The squadron sent patrol after patrol for the rest of the day looking for 'Butch' without success. During the search 'Bomber' Hill was hit again, this time the projectile passed through his seat but left him unscathed. The squadron had suffered yet another loss, but were fortunate not to have lost more Meteors and men. 'Butch' was ultimately found by North Korean soldiers. He was destined to spend the rest of the war in brutal confinement.

Phil spent the night in his tent, a little sore but knowing that he'd been extremely lucky. His thoughts turned to 'Butch' and, in turn, Vance, Bruce and 'Harry'. Were any of them alive or dead? Ejecting over North Korea was a concept he did not warm to and he hoped that if he was ever hit again, he'd be able to make it back to friendly territory. He often flew in an immersion suit, thinking that if he was hit he would be able to limp his Meteor out to sea and in the direction of the Navy. There he would eject and take his chances with the frigid waters in preference to the North Korean Army. After a while, he reassured himself as most fighter pilots do; it won't be him anyway, it'll be the other guy. With that thought he lay back on his bunk and fell asleep, despite the rousing music and song still emanating from the aircrew club.

The new day arrived and Phil once again flew on patrol high above the bomb line with Ray Taylor as he had done less than 24 hours earlier. On his second patrol of the day, he and Keith Martin routed their sortie to where Butch was last seen, but to no avail. They were two very routine flights but still counted towards the squadron's goal of 1,000 missions in February.

The next day Ron Susans led a rocket strike at the Chaeryong Iron Mine

Phil's gun camera captures the successful strike on locomotives near Sariwon.

The 1,000 Mission Month

Comments from Phil's log book regarding sorties flown in February 1952.

using napalm for the first time with success. Four days later it was Phil and 'Vic' Oborn's turn to hit the same target which they did, destroying three buildings, before turning to strafe the revetment that surrounded the complex. Phil revisited the same target again shortly after and together the Meteors set a further five buildings ablaze, leaving brown, black and white smoke billowing into the sky.

The Meteor was proving very effective in the ground attack role, although flight at such low altitudes came with sizeable risk from ground fire in all directions as well as other ingenious devices employed by the North Koreans. As they returned from this latest strike on Chaeryong the pilots noted steel cables mounted on pylons and stretched across the valleys at around 200 feet above the ground. Nearly invisible, they were set to bring down the low-flying jets. In a similar vein, there were reports that trucks were sometimes painted on the road to lure the Meteors down into a flak trap. By the time pilots realised the trucks were not real, they were well within range of the anti-aircraft positions.

By contrast the trains, boxcars and trucks Phil attacked next were very real.

Mid-month, four Meteors led by Wal Rivers and flown by Phil, 'Bomber' Hill and Phil Hamilton-Foster were called up by 'Hammer Able', a pair of American Mustang reconnaissance aircraft that were orbiting overhead. They had found a number of camouflaged vehicles caught in the open. Worsening the situation for the convoy was that the road was in a small ravine with nowhere to leave the road and take cover.

Wal dived on the target first with Phil behind him. Hamilton-Foster and 'Bomber' were the second pair as numbers three and four. Wal and Phil released their rockets and they sped towards the trucks, their ribbon-like trails in tow. Explosion after explosion erupted as the second pair made their strike, only to be interrupted by smoke beginning to stream from Hamilton-Foster's ventral tank. Knowing that fire was just a breath away, he jettisoned his tank and remaining rockets before rejoining the first pair and heading for home. When two American reconnaissance aircraft later surveyed the scene, it was carnage. In the short, sharp rocket attack, 28 vehicles had been totally destroyed and another seven severely damaged.

The squadron was hitting a range of ground targets hard, but not without further loss. Dick Robinson had graduated one course behind Phil at Point Cook and arrived in Korea early in January. Tragically, he became the fourth pilot lost in as many weeks when attacking a target near Haeju. Hit by ground fire, his ventral tank began streaming and Robinson called that he was getting out. That was his last transmission and within seconds the ventral tank caught fire and the tail separated from the rest of the Meteor before the aircraft plunged into the ground. The other fighters swept the scene, but there was no sign of life.

February continued its furious pace. With Bill Bennett, Phil scored direct hits on locomotives near Sariwon, an event dramatically captured on his gun camera and in a photo that he subsequently acquired from the Intelligence Officer. With the Meteor at low-level and in a left bank, the shot showed grain silos in the snow-covered foreground and mountains in the distance. The attack had been a blur but now he had a photograph of that instant frozen in time. That evening, Phil pondered the detail of the surroundings, the boxcars, the engines, the fences, all had felt the fury of his and Bennett's rockets and cannons. Then he carefully stowed the photograph in his kit bag, along with his shattered goggles and a fragment of

The 1,000 Mission Month

Colonel Harrison Thyng presents Phil with the American Air Medal.

his destroyed canopy – mementos that were destined to make the journey home.

Day after day he attacked buildings, bridges and anything that moved on the road. Haeju, Chongdan, Ongjin, Singye and so many other names on a map became the scenes of battle inked into his logbook with brief comments. Chodo, Sinwon-ni, Chorwon and their like had been located by little more than a map, a compass and an occasional road peeking through the snow. With each sortie his familiarity with the Meteor and the environment grew. Even the sound of ground fire striking the jet no longer drew his attention away from the target. He figured that he would never know anything about the bullet that would kill him so these thumps on his airframe were actually reassuring near misses. It was cock-eyed logic, but it allowed him to function and not fear the streams of tracer that sped towards him. If anything, the thought that they were trying to kill him just made him more aggressive.

By the time February drew to a close the squadron had met its goal of 1,000 missions with the last sortie flown by Flying Officer Hamilton-Foster and Sergeant Ian Cranston. Phil's personal tally was fifty missions for the month with his total sitting at 88. Ron Susans had brought a purpose to the squadron under his leadership and morale. The squadron had also introduced new weaponry and now their operations were to be filmed at close quarters for a newsreel back home although Phil doubted anyone other than Edith might get to see it.

Phil's efforts hadn't gone unnoticed by his CO. In his periodic assessment, Susans described Phil as being,

The rough diamond type who is keen to do a good job. He has flown 85 operational missions in Korea and has been wounded in action. Awarded the American Purple Heart and Air Medal.

It seemed as though the Americans at the base hospital had followed through on their desire to see the pilot of the damaged Meteor recognised with the award of the Purple Heart, but Phil still knew nothing of the decoration.

March began with the weather playing havoc with operations. Low cloud and poor visibility limited the number of strikes and the pace of operations was in stark contrast to the previous month. Only occasional strikes could be launched in the first weeks and patrols became the standard. Even so, Phil clocked up his 100th mission. He attacked buildings and trains at Ongjin, Chinnampo and Nuchon Ni when the weather permitted and came home holed in the left wing on one occasion and in the ventral tank on another. The latter was again the culprit when yet another graduate of No. 5 Course, Ian Cranston, was lost. As Wal Rivers called to him to jettison the tank, the Meteor followed the familiar pattern of streaming fuel and then a trail of flame before it rolled on to its back and flew into the ground.

Phil had the opportunity to leave the war behind when he was granted an unexpected pass for a week in Japan. The condition was that he also flew test flights out of Iwakuni to verify the serviceability of various Meteors and their guns before they were sent back to the battlefield. It was a small price to pay but, while he appreciated the reprieve, after a couple of days he was restless. Out of

The 1,000 Mission Month

character, one evening Phil took to drinking as he had only ever done a few times before. Taking it to excess, he got extremely drunk, or 'tight' as he called it. The next day he woke feeling ill and full of regret and convinced that he had seen enough of Japan. He couldn't wait to return to his squadron.

He had no sooner returned to Kimpo than he was flying again and back at Haeju. Led by Bill Purssey, Phil, Ken Smith and 'Vic' Oborn destroyed a number of buildings on a rocket strike but not before the enemy had thrown up substantial ground fire and landed hits on Phil and 'Smithy'. Back at Kimpo, he surveyed the damage to the Meteor which was primarily holes made by .50 calibre rounds in the wing and fuselage.

The month ended with Lionel Cowper failing to pull out of a dive while rocketing a target at Haeju. Phil and 'Smithy' had been attacking the same position a week earlier when they'd been hit by ground fire and Phil wondered if the same flak position had brought Lionel's aircraft down. Others considered that he may have suffered from target fascination and left his pull out too late. Perhaps small arms fire killed him before he ever reached the target. The truth was that nobody truly knew except Lionel. Even some of those on the mission that day only realised that he was gone when they checked in clear of the target. Lionel Cowper was yet another of the No. 5 Course group and his loss was deeply felt by his mates.

Hits by ground fire had become the norm. Destroying buildings and strafing troops had become the norm. Even losing fellow pilots had unfortunately lost any element of surprise. For Phil, he felt strangely at home in an environment that he knew many would find horrific. To him it was an honest world, black and white, with very little grey. Here, he trusted the men he fought beside and his only real fear was letting them down. Even this fear had subsided now that he had substantial combat experience under his belt.

The small kid from the bush who had been bullied and ignored had found the respect of men that mattered and he was not about to let that slide. He knew that he didn't drink and socialise like the majority, but nobody judged him for that and there were still times to share a joke away from the aircrew club. For Ron Susans and those under his command, Phil was determined to never let this band of brothers down.

Phil's log book, covered in a map of Korea.

Chapter Twenty-Nine

Words

The squadron had lost more than twenty pilots in Korea so far, making a pilot's chances about one in four of being killed or captured. So far Bruce Gillan, Doug Robertson, Bruce Thomson and Vance Drummond had been lost from Phil's pilot's course while he, Blackwell, Oborn, Myers, Strawbridge, Murray and Towner were still on active duty. These losses were high and back in Australia Edith was at RAAF Base Richmond processing the files of those that had been killed. She also met many of the boys returning home, keen to hear any firsthand words about Phillip. They would often entertain her with his efforts as the last jet over the target and how hard and low he flew his attacks, thinking that would impress the pretty corporal. It did not. Inside she feared for him and dreaded that he would meet the same fate as the only other man who had won her heart.

In spite of her fears, she wrote regularly to Phil and he managed some sporadic replies. On April 2nd he sat down to write home, although the letter took two weeks to finish. That day he had flown four missions, including two rocket attacks on Haeju.

Edith's letters were a highlight, although he could not match her rate of correspondence. Edith treasured every word from Phil as rare as they were. News of him losing his canopy and being wounded by intense ground fire had filtered back to Australia where Edith's commanding officer asked her what she knew of his close call. She was rather embarrassed to answer that she knew nothing and was sick inside that he'd been wounded. How badly? When? What happened?

Her mood changed quickly when her CO placed a newspaper on her desk, tapping a headline with a cheeky grin and offering, "He's in the news, too." Edith spun the paper around to face her expecting to see some announcement relating to the war or a medal ceremony, but none was forthcoming. As her fellow workers peered over her shoulder, she read the headline, "RAAF PILOTS HAVE BALDNESS CURE".

It explained that a senior officer had mentioned that in this new era of fast jets, the pilots' hair was turning grey prematurely. Somehow this myth escalated to the hair falling out altogether and someone had interviewed the 77 Squadron pilots. Phil's response was a little way down the column, but his sense of humour was unmistakable as 'Sgt. P. Zupp of Middle Ridge, Toowoomba' was quoted saying, "I used to be called Ping Pong because of my bald head. Now, I am called Gorilla!"

The staff in the office at Headquarters RAAF Base Richmond burst into laughter and Edith couldn't help but join in. That night her laughter had subsided and she went back to her barracks and began writing. The next day her letter to Korea was on its way.

For Phil, while he only wrote the occasional letter to Edith, he religiously completed his logbook at the end of the day. He would sit with his inkwell and nibbed pen and list the date, the aircraft type and a brief description of the duty on the left page. On the right he would tally the hours aloft and the progressive total of missions flown. At the end of the month he would summarise his month's flying operations in red ink, then stamp and sign it before having it countersigned by his flight commander and commanding officer.

Within the logbook he had also glued a citation that had arrived recently. Phil had been Mentioned-in-Despatches and, aside from the citation, it allowed him to wear an oak leaf cluster on his Korean medal ribbon. His logbook was an inconspicuous place to store the citation an award, but it was typical of Phil. Here it would be safe and secure. Treasured, but tucked away. Still, as he read the words quietly in his tent, it meant a great deal to him.

CITATION:

Sergeant Zupp has flown a total of 108 operational sorties in Meteor aircraft in support of the United Nations Forces in Korea.

During this period he has pressed home attacks with vigor and determination and on one occasion when his aircraft was hit and he himself wounded he displayed great skill and fortitude by bringing his aircraft safely to base.

His devotion to duty in no small way was responsible for the fine squadron effort during this period.

as you mentioned going to quite a few towns at different times in one of your earlier letters.

The tightening-up on leave and the "orderly V.A.A.F." idea seem to be just some more of those irksome things the R.A.A.F. gets up to every now and then.

By now you have no doubt heard of Lionel Cowper going-in, it upset a few of the chaps who were on his course at Point Cook, but they'll get used to it. Four of us made a rocket attack on the same target earlier in the day and Smithy and myself both got clobbered apparently by the same flak position.

Don't know what your ex-boss is referring to about my being in the news, perhaps it's the incident where my canopy was hit, think I sent you a photo of it. Speaking of photos I have put a few in with this as you can see, but am still waiting for some better ones. Hope they are of interest to you.

Since the airmen's bar got burnt down some time back they have been using a large tent right next to mine and every night if there isn't a movie on there is much guzzling of grog

An excerpt from Phil's letter home to Edith, mentioning the loss of Lionel Cowper.

As well as the formal entries and the citation, Phil entered his own comments into this treasured book that now sported a map of Korea for its cover. It was a practice that Steege had reprimanded him for, demanding that anything other than official requirements be deleted. He reluctantly did so but, with the arrival of Susans, he once again began to make his notes and the new CO didn't mind at all. They meant more to Phil than simply 'Scramble', 'Patrol' or 'R/P and Strafing'. He would comment that the target was a bridge, or buildings, or a search for a downed pilot and each comment would remind him of the sortie in far more detail.

Phil noted the different targets as they were not always buildings, airfields, trains and bridges. The cold reality was that sometimes soldiers were strafed and the lower he got to fire, the further his rounds penetrated into lines of men. That week, in searching for the crew of a downed American B-26 bomber, he had caught a group of North Koreans in the open and in the search area. He did not hesitate in firing upon them as otherwise those same men may have found the crew first.

Ox carts and food stores were all legitimate targets and more than once he was able to catch the enemy unaware in revetments, or taking cover in the tree line, and thread cannon fire along the length. It was bloody and brutal and far more personal than any building could ever be.

Jim Flemming had warned him of this side of the war before he left for Korea. Jim had seen rivers run red and knew that perfectly good pilots had genuine difficulty pulling the trigger when the target was made of flesh and bone and not steel and brick. For Phil, there was no philosophical contemplation. It was the task he was there to do. He had seen the savagery in New Guinea first hand and the devastation of Hiroshima. He was not naïve. He had always reasoned that the enemy was trying to kill him just as hard as he was trying to kill them.

On April 13th, Phil was paired with the likeable Max 'Bluey' Colebrook who was on his second tour of Korea with 77 Squadron. It was Phil's third mission for the day and again Haeju was the target, where they rocketed a supply tunnel, revetment and buildings.

Two hours later 'Bluey' was back in the air as 'Godfrey White 2' with Flight Lieutenant Pete Middleton flying as number one. They were strafing a number of motorcycles and a suspected gun position when Colebrook called that he'd been

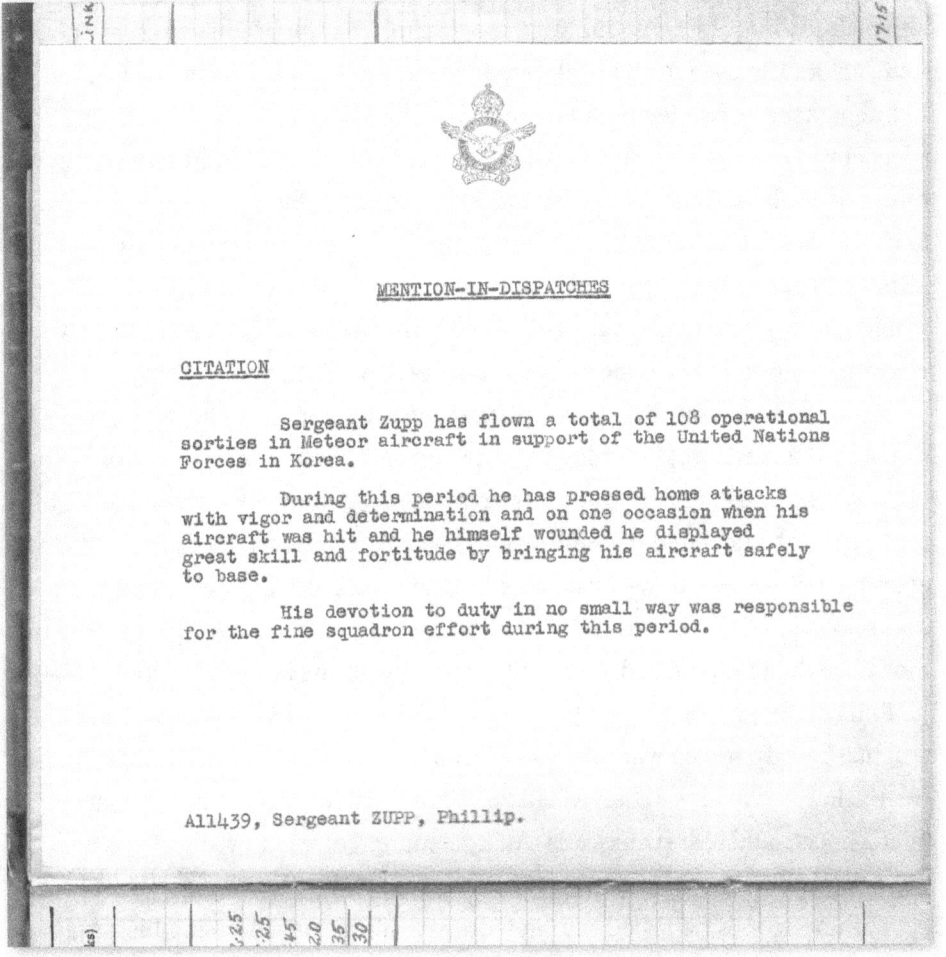

Phil's citation for being Mentioned-in-Despatches is discreetly glued into his log book.

hit. Middleton looked back to see his wingman pulling up, his ventral tank on fire. Middleton called this to Colebrook, who responded and jettisoned his ventral tank almost immediately. A few seconds later he reported that the tank was gone and he was heading back to base. Sergeant Max 'Bluey' Colebrook DFM was never heard from again.

As soon as the news of 'Bluey' reached Kimpo, the squadron immediately launched pairs to search the area and fly cover as needed. Two by two the Meteors departed with Phil flying beside Flight Lieutenant Lawrence 'Scotty' Cadan, another veteran pilot on his second tour. Phil and 'Scotty' thought that they sighted a parachute, but otherwise no trace was found. That night Phil inked in another four missions in a single day and noted, 'Searched for Sgt. Colebrook. Reckon we found parachute. Landed with no fuel.'

Fuel was a constant enemy with the Meteor limited to around ninety minutes on a patrol, although low-level combat consumed the fuel at a much higher rate. Some strikes were flown in only forty minutes if the target was nearby. On a number of occasions Phil would land at Kimpo with virtually no fuel or his engines would flame out as he taxied back in to park the Meteor. Again, these days would warrant mention in his logbook as did targets of opportunity.

'Targets of opportunity' was a phrase given to just about anything that was discovered inadvertently while the Meteors still had ammunition on board, often when returning from the main mission. Over the months Phil had strafed trucks, trains and buildings and even a Mustang abandoned on mud flats in enemy territory. Anything that moved on the road was a potential target, even a motorcycle as these were employed by the enemy as couriers. So it was one morning when Phil spotted a lone rider speeding to the north of the bomb line.

Phil had fought the ground war in New Guinea and here in Korea the soldiers fought a bloody, frozen war full of suffering. Who was to know what this dispatch rider below had in his satchel? Allied positions? Artillery installations? That sort of intelligence could cost Americans, Australians and other United Nations soldiers their lives. Phil did not hesitate.

Within seconds he rolled the Meteor over and down, reversing his turn back towards the rider. He bottomed out level, fast, low and head on with the rider. It was only at this point that he sensed his target was even aware of his presence and at that same moment he squeezed the trigger. The surface of the road erupted in a rapid fire trail with Phil reaching the motor bike just after his bullets did. The scene had settled by the time he was pulling up and looking back over his shoulder. There was no movement from the man or his machine. Phil did not feel proud or sorry. He felt nothing as he turned for Kimpo. This was war. Still, it would be many years before he spoke of the incident to anyone.

Later in April, Phil and Flight Lieutenant Bill Purssey destroyed a number of trucks in a ravine, leaving the scene on fire and belching black smoke high into the sky. Only days later Purssey was flying with Bill Bennett and Ken Towner and attacking trucks once again. This time the ground fire was intense, striking Bennett's Meteor in the ventral tank and shooting off his elevator trim control. Bennett jettisoned his belly tank as Towner called Purssey to say that he was on fire and to get out.

That night Ken Towner told Phil how he saw Purssey head out over water only to witness in horror as the wing separated from the airframe. Towner saw the canopy released and then at about 600 feet above the water the ejection seat shot from the Meteor. But Towner never saw a parachute before Purssey hit the water. Bill Purssey, a veteran fighter pilot of World War Two, would receive the Distinguished Flying Cross, but it would be much later when his mother accepted the decoration from Her Majesty Queen Elizabeth II.

Another pilot had gone and yet again the ventral tank had played its part in his demise. The squadron was now consistently losing pilots and this was a reflection of the dangerous nature of ground attack. At such low level the hazards were many and the time to react minimal. Phil had taken hits in the ventral tank, but only discovered the damage after landing. Again he appreciated the value of luck in the equation as so many had seen the tank end their life in seconds. Every pilot dreaded the call that they were hit in the ventral tank and streaming flames or fuel. So far, so good, Phil thought.

He finally finished the letter to Edith and its tone was mixed. He spoke of his restlessness in Japan and light-heartedly told her that "there is hope for me yet!" replying to Edith's letter listing the number of WAAFs that were getting married. He knew that she was worried, though she would never say so. He also knew that, by virtue of her job, she would be one of the first to know if he was killed. Even so, he wrote, "By now you have no doubt heard of Lionel Cowper going in. It upset a few of the chaps who were on his course at Point Cook, but they'll get used to it."

Phil was more than midway through his tour of Korea and he had been used to it for some time now.

Phil stands with ground crew in front of a Meteor armed with rockets.

Chapter Thirty

"There's no bloody MiGs in Korea"

More new faces continued to arrive at the squadron. Sergeants Geoff Lushey and Tony Armstrong were first to arrive in Korea from Course No. 6, while Don Robertson, Bill Simmonds and John Surman arriving as commissioned officers from the RAAF College at Point Cook. Don had actually graduated as dux of the course, winning the Sword of Honour. It was indicative of the new Air Force on the rise, compared to Phil and his like who were still non-commissioned sergeant pilots. Even so, the Australian egalitarian approach filtered down into 77 Squadron operations.

Every pilot at Kimpo recognised the value of experience. Phil considered that if a pilot wasn't killed in the first six weeks of operations, their life expectancy went up steeply. Consequently, new pilots arriving in Korea often flew the wing of a sergeant pilot regardless of rank. In turn, sergeant pilots would undertake sorties in pairs without an officer in sight.

Phil had taken a preference to a position in the section that wasn't popular – 'Tail End Charlie'. In a section of four Meteors, this was position number four and the last jet to attack. The element of surprise was an advantage of the speeding Meteors attacking their targets, but often by the time the final aircraft approached, the ground fire had found its range too. The method in Phil's madness was that he had the ability to see where the preceding aircraft's rockets or tracers were striking the ground and this could be an indication of a tailwind if the shots were going long.

His other preferred technique was also potentially hazardous. Many pilots adopted the sound practice of jinking and weaving as they approached the target.

Phil's preference was to line up his aiming point well in advance and fly a relatively long, straight approach and fire from a very stable platform. In combination, with his position at 'Tail End Charlie', Phil took his fair share of hits from the bullets and flak being hurled in to the air. However, as Geoff Lushey would relate, it was effective and Phil never left anyone in any doubt what he was about to do.

While ground attack remained the stable diet of 77 squadron operations, there was also a subtle shift in focus taking place. More and more the Meteors were tasked to fly over the North Korean capital of Pyongyang. Heavily defended and a hot-spot for MiGs, it exposed the Meteors to the potential for air-to-air combat for the first time since Phil had arrived in Korea when Vance and Bruce had been shot down.

In this new environment, Phil was tasked with Ken Towner to fly a patrol to the north. They had no sooner levelled off than the controller gave them an intercept to escort an American B-29 Superfortress bomber. The B-29 was a common sight over Korea, but was most famous for being the same type as the 'Enola Gay' that had dropped the atomic bomb on Hiroshima in 1945.

As Phil and Ken came on station near the silver bomber, Phil marveled at its size and power. It glinted in the sun as the two Meteors weaved and scanned the sky for MiGs, which were inevitably drawn to the sight of a bomber. Its wingspan was massive and you could nearly place four Meteors side-by-side from wingtip to wingtip, Phil thought. Four massive propellers pulled the bomber through the sky while its nose was all glass, like a futuristic greenhouse. It had machine guns, top and bottom, fore and aft, protruding from remotely controlled turrets. Phil figured that as bombers go, this is about as good as it gets.

There was nothing else in the sky above, not even a contrail or cloud. Phil looked across at Ken and was struck by the situation. Only a year ago he, Ken and 'Vic' Oborn were new 'bog rat' pilots making their first flights in the Mustang at Canberra. Now here he sat with Ken, each a decorated fighter pilot with well over 100 combat missions under his belt, escorting a Superfortress over Korea and with the chance of encountering a MiG at any moment. It had been a whirlwind twelve months. As quickly as the thought had entered his head, it was gone. His eyes continued to scan the skies looking for the enemy. Nothing. Soon after, they both left the massive bomber and turned for home.

"There's no bloody MiGs in Korea"

Phil climbs from his Meteor after another sortie.

Korea's blanket of snow was now gone and navigation was a different ball game for the pilots as landmarks and features had magically emerged. The bitter cold had been replaced by heat, downpours and mosquitoes. The heat was on the pilots too as the MiG presence again became very real.

Ken Murray and John Surman had been on patrol west of Pyongyang when they first spotted nine MiGs. First, two had swept by without firing before Surman called Murray to tell him there was a MiG on his tail. Murray broke away immediately and Surman fired two bursts from his cannons at the enemy jet. Pieces flew from the MiG's tail and flame burst from the rear fuselage. The fight was over in seconds and the young graduate from the RAAF College had claimed the squadron's first air-to-air kill since 1951.

Despite the odds, part of Phil wanted to take on a MiG. Part of him wanted to pit his skill against the enemy, but the situation had not yet eventuated. He had chatted at length with Ken Murray about the enemy fighter and the next day Ken Towner and Don Robertson also had an encounter. Soon after that, Surman's fellow graduate, Bill Simmonds, also shot down a MiG. Covering an American bombing raid on Sunan, the four Meteors were set upon when Simmonds latched onto the tail of one of the aggressors. He fired a long burst at very close range and soon after the enemy pilot was seen to eject while his aircraft was seen to spin down and crash. It seemed as though the war in the air was returning, but Phil was yet to sight the swept wing fighter except for his very distant meeting months earlier. His war remained down among the weeds.

On May 6th Phil was paired with his good mate from Point Cook, 'Vic' Oborn. As usual, 'Vic' took the lead and Phil sat as number two on his wing. The sortie was to be operated under naval control, whose callsign was 'Sitting Duck', and the fighters were tasked to attack a railway siding. Armed with eight rockets each and full loads of 20mm ammunition, 'Vic' led the two Meteors in to the dive on the target with Phil falling in behind as he preferred.

Tracers whizzed past their canopies as the ground defences opened fire. 'Vic' and Phil's rockets sped from beneath their wings and ripped into three box-cars, obliterating them where they sat. Pulling up clear of the target they could see smoke rising from the wreckage. Then, against his leader's better judgement, Phil hooked the Meteor around in a tight turn and dived to make a second pass against the gun position. Second passes were always fraught with risk as they lacked the element of surprise and gave the now very alert enemy another opportunity.

'Vic' descended to cover his wingman who was flying ever lower and skipping around the horizon to line up for the second run on the target. By now the pair were so low that 'Vic' could clearly make out the North Korean soldiers firing their rifles from beneath nearby trees but, even so, he was still looking at the top of Phil's Meteor.

Inside the cockpit, Phil gritted his teeth behind the oxygen mask absolutely focused through the line of tracers and on the spitting weaponry that lay dead ahead. Flexing his left wrist, he closed the ring of dots on his gunsight, encircling the approaching gun pits. Squinting, he could see the crew frantically firing their weapons. Phil steadied, squeezed and hurled forth a barrage of 20mm cannon fire that tracked a destructive path straight through the two gun positions. Bodies flew as their tracers' path now wheeled crazily away from the attacking aircraft and spat harmlessly into the open sky before ceasing to fire at all.

The pair flew with Ron Susans and Don Robertson the next day to claim ten buildings. On this occasion, Phil's position as 'Tail End Charlie' left him with a

"There's no bloody MiGs in Korea"

Battle damage to the rudder of Phil's Meteor. (Source: Arnold Jordan)

sizeable hole in his left engine nacelle. But still no MiGs.

Phil's mate, Col King, lost track how many times Phil had lamented the absence of enemy fighters in the skies over Korea. It was becoming a running joke among the boys of 77 Squadron. Every time the canopy slid back after an uneventful combat air patrol or bomber escort, Phil would pull his oxygen mask away from his face and utter the words, "There's no bloody MiGs in Korea".

The humour stemmed from the fact that no one particularly wanted to encounter a MiG-15 in their aging Meteor and, despite Surman's and Simmond's success, the odds of being on the winning side were rather low. Yet, tongue-in-cheek, Phil would continually exaggerate his disappointment at the absence of air-to-air combat.

The routine of ground strikes and combat air patrols continued in May. One morning he had flown on Pete Middleton's wing during a rocket strike near Ongjin. The four aircraft had destroyed eight buildings before making their way uneventfully home. Now, five hours later, Phil sat in behind the leader as the two Meteors again made their way north-west of Seoul as part of a concentrated series of strikes. The controller, 'Shirley', cleared the Meteors, armed with rockets, and they prepared to make their strike on a cluster of buildings on the coast as part of a co-operative naval exercise. Phil checked his 'GUNS/R.P.' switch was flicked across to 'Rocket Projectiles' and re-affirmed the location of the firing button atop his control column. He was ready to go.

The first Meteor dived and released a salvo of rockets that snaked towards the target in a loose formation before detonating as they struck the earth below. Far enough behind to avoid the efflux and flying debris, Phil dived on the target as his leader now heaved his Meteor almost vertically away from the chaos below. The pitched roofs ahead began to consume his focus as he stared through the gunsight. Finger on the firing button. Steady. Steady. Fire! The Meteor bucked slightly as the rockets sped away and Phil pulled back as the Meteor set course for the heavens, his leader a speck in the distance above him.

Shit!

He never got to see the result of his efforts as something flashed past, hurtling in the opposite direction. The silver form had whizzed by in a blink and Phil's already elevated heart rate now thumped in his chest as the realisation struck him. It was a MiG!

There had been no tracers to warn him of the MiG's attack out of the west, just the rush of two aircraft passing at around 600 knots. Phil called a break and instinctively pulled back and rolled to the right, his body and the Meteor seeming to groan under the rapid onset of the g-forces. Ribbons of water vapour trailed from his wingtips as he wheeled around the horizon, his eyes searching for the MiG who now seemed to be flying his own ever-tightening arc out to the east. His eyes then locked on the tiny dot speeding in the distance. Phil pushed the throttles so far forward they almost went off their rails.

The Meteor accelerated and Phil would not let his eyes slip away from the silver dart in the distance. This was it. Like two jousting knights, the fighter pilots were rounding the top of the marks to face off and charge at each other head-on. It was a manoeuvre as old as aerial dogfighting and as old as combat itself.

His heart was now racing and the sound of breathing in his oxygen mask seemed to drown out all other sounds. He flicked the switch back to guns and rested his finger on the trigger. The MiG again had the advantages of speed, altitude and manoeuvrability. This bloke was out to kill him, but Phil was equally determined to win this fight. In a matter of a minute the rocket attack had become a dogfight and he was hurtling towards the MiG.

"There's no bloody MiGs in Korea"

Then the MiG reversed his turn away from the fight and up into the sun. Phil was confused. Was the fight over before it started? Surely not. This bloke has the upper hand and he's bugging out? With throttles still wide open and the engines gulping fuel, Phil kept heading towards the sun, chasing an unseen target. The stupidity of the pursuit began to dawn on him at the same time as his leader's calls started to break through his concentration and his earphones.

His tone was not pleasant, reigning in his wayward number two, not entirely sure what had transpired to send him disappearing in the opposite direction. Reality started to return and Phil looked to form up with his leader once again when his racing heartbeat was replaced by a rush of cold through his veins. His fuel gauges were rapidly closing in on zero.

The full-throttle chase had left the Meteor with very little fuel, a fact he relayed to his increasingly disgruntled leader. They quickly set course for Kimpo by the most direct route. It was a relatively short flight, and now his air base was only minutes away, but the gauges did not tell a very heartening story. They were now sitting on zero and he ran through the ejection procedure in his head. At any moment Phil expected to hear the sound of one, if not both, of the Derwent engines winding down. The situation was becoming more intense than his MiG encounter and he now had nothing but time to focus on his fuel-starved Meteor.

He maintained his altitude as Kimpo loomed ahead, fully prepared to glide the Meteor to the airfield if he could. He held a 'High Key' position overhead and to his relief, both engines were still running even though the gauges suggested they should have gone silent some time back. He wheeled into the landing pattern and judiciously extended his wheels and flaps at the last possible moment. With all of this drag hanging out in the airflow he knew the Meteor would glide like a brick and he sweated on the engines being kind to him for just a little longer.

Fortunately, the gods shone upon him until his wheels touched down on Kimpo's metal-topped runway. As he turned off the runway, he finally started to breathe again until one of his engines spooled down followed, moments later, by the other. He now sat relieved but embarrassed, stationary on the taxiway. The Meteor was silent. He flicked the necessary switches to 'off', unclipped his oxygen mask, slid the canopy open and let his head fall back against the seat. He was safe, but his mind was still racing.

Why hadn't the MiG fired on the first pass? Or had he? Had Phil not noticed the tracers? Perhaps he was out of ammunition and that's why he broke off the fight? Why then chase an invisible target into the sun? Dumb! And then almost flame out both engines in the air and have to eject!

His self-recriminations were well underway when the vehicle arrived to tow the Meteor back to the flight line. His boots had hardly hit the ground when his flight leader launched into him and highlighted the folly of his fuel-guzzling chase of an unidentified swept-wing jet that seemed quite happy to leave them alone after the initial pass.

After debrief, Phil went off on his own as he was prone to do. He laid down on his bunk even though it was only late afternoon and began to chew over the rocket attacks, the MiG and his near flame-out. The adrenaline was washing out of his system and now all he felt was fatigue as his thoughts became muddled and his eyes heavy. In the morning he would be airborne again. Another patrol and another rocket strike, but for now all he wanted to do was sleep.

Chapter Thirty-One

Towards 200

Phil was even more frustrated after his near miss with the MiG but kept pressing home his ground attacks with the same vigour as always. He had 170 missions to his name and knew that the end of his tour must be drawing near. It was not a thought he particularly entertained as he had found a home here in Korea.

There was no grey, no ambiguity, and after surviving his first missions he had gone on to gain valuable experience. He knew his place in the squadron and knew his job, but he also knew that 200 sorties were about as many as they would let him fly. Edith had told him that there were already rumblings in the newspapers back home and in the corridors of the RAAF that the pilots in Korea were being overworked.

Phil wasn't superstitious or nervous about being killed in his final weeks. He was more worried about missing out, about not being there. He also had no idea when his last mission would be as the CO generally didn't tell a pilot until it was

A Meteor climbs out of K-14 Kimpo. The ventral tank can be clearly seen on its belly.

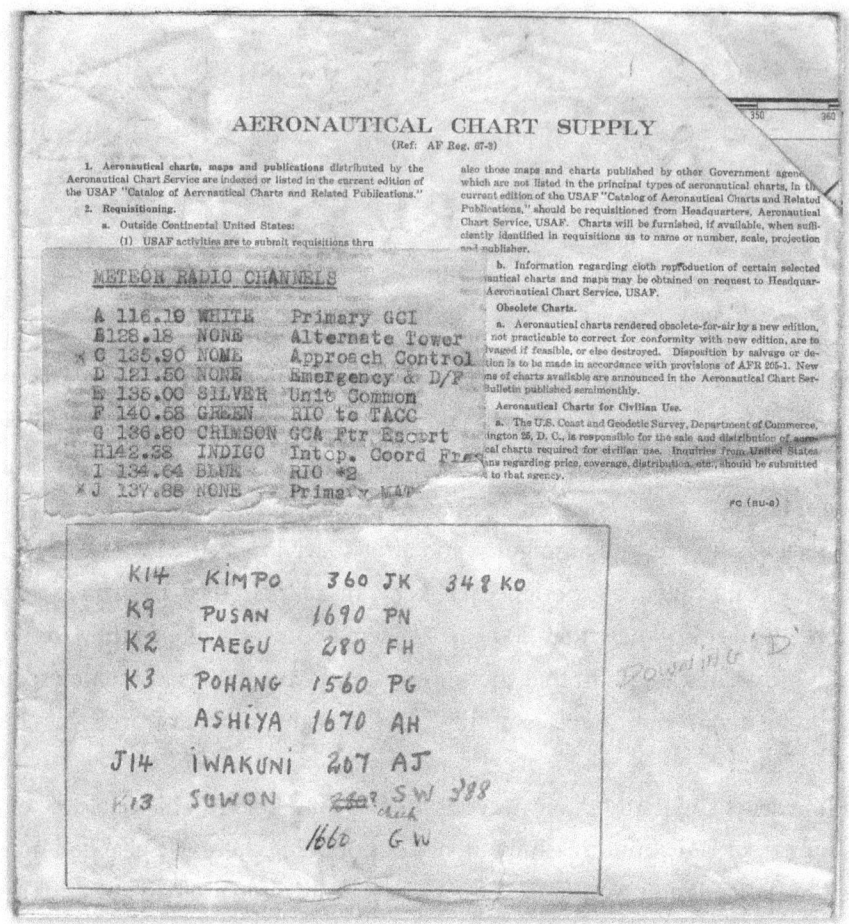

The reverse side of Phil's chart showing radio frequencies, Meteor data and a completed flight plan (above and right).

over to guard against any added pressure or nerves. It seemed a fair enough theory, but Phil reluctantly acknowledged that the day was lurking in his near future.

The fact was that death was a reality in operations and the chances still sat at about one in four. These odds were reinforced when Don Robertson was killed. After releasing his rockets, the Sword of Honour winner's Meteor had veered to the right before hitting the ground at a shallow angle and bursting into flames. That same day, as Phil sat in briefing, any such thoughts of death or going home were pushed to the back of his mind. The target the next day was buildings across the river from Chinnampo. He would be slotting in behind Bill Bennett, Geoff Lushey and Pete Middleton. The briefing was standard, watches were synchronised and

	Tr	Dist	HT W/V	T.A.S.	G/S	Co.T.	Co.M.	Time	I.A.S.		ETA
KIMPO → PUSAN	141	182	3000	345	350	149	155	31	210	1302	1306
PUSAN → ASHIYA	135	108	240/60	"	354	143	149	17½	"	"	1222
ASHIYA → IWAKUNI	077	80	"	"	392	080	086	12	"	"	1234
								60½			
J		314	340 250/45	350	335	308	314	61	240		
IWAKUNI → ASHIYA	257	80									
ASHIYA → PUSAN	315	108									
PUSAN → KIMPO	321	182									

CLIMB 14100			CRUISE MAX RANGE			DESCENT .7 MIN.	
To HEIGHT	TIME	DIST	R.P.M.	I.A.S.	T.A.S.	DIST	TIME
20000	6	40	12200	230	315	7	1
25000	8	45	12600	220	330		
30000	10	55	13000	210	345	12	1½
35000	13½	80	13500	205	370		
40000	18	110	13800	197	400	15	2

there was a final reminder about no unnecessary radio chatter.

As Phil walked to his Meteor, with '65' boldly painted on its nose, he thought how so much had become standard over the preceding six months. On those first missions everything from securing harnesses and helmets seemed to take concentration and now so many tasks had become second nature. Almost automatically, he climbed in, stowed his map, secured himself and waited for Bill Bennett's signal to start engines. It came and then eight Derwent engines roared into life.

Geoff sat on Bill's wing while Phil flew off Pete's. In twenty minutes they were approaching the target near the North Korean coastline. On Bennett's lead they rolled in on the buildings below as they had done so many times before: a thirty degree dive, rocket release at 1,500 feet to avoid debris, and then the gut-wrenching pull-up.

After 201 sorties, it was time for Phil to return to Australia.

Bennett was well ahead, then Geoff and then Pete. Phil picked his mark and began his long, straight dive. He held the roofline steady in his graticule, his fingers at the ready to set the rockets free as explosions were already beginning to erupt on the ground. Wait. Wait. Now!

The rockets were away and snaking towards the complex. Phil gritted his teeth and braced his guts, heaving back on the control column to pull his jet skyward and away from the chaos. As he did so, there was an innocuous thump' and his Meteor bucked beneath him. He hadn't a second to assess the hit when the dreaded words came through his helmet.

"Zuppie, you're streaming fuel."

It was his turn. His ventral tank had been hit again and this time he knew about it. Still holding in the g-forces, his right arm seemed to weigh a ton as he reached up to jettison the deadly fuel tank beneath him. The seconds lasted days as he finally grabbed the lever and pulled, knowing that it still wasn't over. The tank was gone but had fire already taken hold?

He was still climbing and there were no further calls forthcoming. He looked back to see if he was leaving a trail of vapour or flames but there was nothing, only the destruction below where the buildings had sat in his gunsight less than a minute before. The Meteors formed up, checked in and headed for Kimpo.

That night Ken Towner made light of Phil's near misadventure and Phil couldn't help but laugh. Still, in the back of his mind he knew how close he'd come and that Robinson, Purssey, Cranston, Colebrook and more hadn't been so fortunate when their ventral tanks were holed.

While the patrols continued, the squadron also made a maximum effort against an ordnance depot and factory buildings ten miles to the south-west of heavily defended Pyongyang. Each day, over two days, three sorties of eight Meteors took off from Kimpo and demolished the target. On the second day, the buildings were obscured by the weather so Phil's section broke off and proceeded at low level to Chongdan where they rocketed another target.

As May drew to a close, Ron Susans' tour of duty also came to an end. One of Phil's preferred duties had always been flying on the wing of his CO. For a commanding officer, Ron had flown a high number of operational sorties and earned the respect of his men as a consequence. He had always led from the front and his sorties generally ended up in the thick of the fighting. Now the boss that had made Phil feel a valued part of the squadron was heading home. Phil would hold Susans in the highest regard for the rest of his life and never met another leader of his calibre.

Susans was replaced by Bill Bennett as acting commanding officer until the arrival of Wing Commander Jack Kinninmont, a recipient of two Distinguished Flying Crosses in World War Two. Phil knew his time was approaching and wondered if he would ever meet the new boss.

The next week, Phil was the last Meteor taking aim on an electrical sub-station at Chaeryong. Lining up, he watched the first three Meteors release their rockets in rapid succession and 24 high explosive heads go to work on the generators and surrounding buildings. Today he held steady just a little longer and then fired. His eight rockets were on their way, landing direct hits on a transformer and starting a fire. As Phil looked back flames and smoke leapt into the air and his job was done. Sortie number 191 was completed.

On the last day of the month he was over Pyongyang when a fighter passed overhead at speed heading north. It must have been a MiG and he was ready to fight, but the jet just continued on, disappearing as quickly as it had arrived. Yes, there were MiGs in Korea, but none for Phil to fight.

When June arrived, Phil flew in an eight aircraft attack, led by Bill Bennett, on a factory at Haeju. On this sortie the two-seat T.7 Meteor flew in company with the fighters with a war correspondent, Charles Madden, on board. He bore witness to the nature of the pilots' work as they damaged the factory and destroyed another eight buildings. The surprise attack also caught a number of personnel in the open who suffered at the hands of the Meteors' barrage.

Madden's newspaper article subsequently rebutted the general belief that 77 Squadron pilots were only flying 100 missions before returning home. While the average was around 130, he referred to some pilots flying 200 missions. Phil was sitting on 196 when Madden flew with them to Haeju.

Two days later, John Surman was dead. The Meteors were attacking a pair of trucks as part of an armed reconnaissance mission. Flying as Col King's wingman, and number four in the section, Surman's Meteor was seen to mush into the ground at high speed, leaving flame in its wake, after apparently not pulling out in time. A graduate of the RAAF College with a confirmed MiG kill, the fair-headed pilot with a promising future had just turned 23. Now he was gone. After six weeks on operations, John Surman had become the thirtieth pilot to go down over Korea.

Phil's 200th mission was a non-event. He was scrambled as a section of four to cover the return of fellow Meteors after 'Val' Turner's engine had thrown a turbine blade through the engine nacelle. Despite being vectored by the controller, the section was unable to rendezvous and Phil and his compatriots returned to base.

That night the rain fell heavily on the roof as Phil sat down alone in his tent and penned '200' in to the special column he had created. It was a number he was proud of and he wondered how many more times they would let him fly. Bob

Towards 200

Strawbridge had already headed home.

The rain continued and thwarted Phil's attempts to build upon his 200. On June 11th he strapped into his Meteor '134' once again with Pete Middleton leading, Geoff Lushey as number two and his good mate, Ken Towner, at number three. Phil, as always, slotted in at number four as the section taxied out for an armed reconnaissance along the main supply route.

His hands moved through their checks as they had done so many times before. He sat off Ken's wing from take-off to target, comfortable and confident in the company of a good friend. Soon they were over the target and streaming in, one after the other with the Meteor's creating their telltale howl as the airflow rushed past and before their cannons erupted with fire. Lining up, long and last, the rockets and cannons roared beneath Phil's trigger finger. Down as low as always, the world flew by in a blur as small arms fire peppered the jets from below. Pull up, into the climbing turn away and sinking into the seat under the reassuring g-force. Minutes later, five buildings and two trucks had been reduced to rubble and scrap, the target on fire.

The attack had been quick and effective and now they sped across the countryside back to Kimpo where they landed and taxied to their respective bays. Phil shut down the engines, slid back the canopy and threw his gloves on the panel beside the gunsight in a habit that had become a ritual. Mission number 201.

As he began to unstrap his helmet, he saw Bill Bennett walking towards his Meteor with a smile on his face. Phil had his helmet off, but was still strapped in his seat, as Bill climbed up the side of the Meteor and leaned into the cockpit. He placed his hand on Phil's shoulder and said, "Good job, Zuppie. You're going home."

Welcome home. Phil reunited with Edith soon after his return from Korea.

Chapter Thirty-Two

Coming Home

In Korea, Phil had flown 270 hours and 201 combat missions, but now it was time to return to a nation at peace. Little did he know, his personnel file had raced him back to Australia and as his Qantas aircraft approached Sydney the remarks within were already being assessed to decide his future path.

Despite only knowing him a short time, Steege had described him as "an exceptionally keen N.C.O. pilot" and "unpolished socially, but has a cheery, pleasant manner". Susans wrote well of his "Rough Diamond" while Keith Martin, the squadron's executive officer, recommended that Phil should "undergo a Flying Instructors' Course on his return to Australia. He would be well suited due to his keenness". On his final assessment, by Bill Bennett, he had been described as "Average +" and would be suitable for "Further employment as a squadron pilot".

At every turn, Phil did not fit the traditional pilot mould. He was quiet and keen but rough around the edges. Martin's comments probably best painted the picture for those deciding Phil's fate. "A dogged and enthusiastic pilot rather than a brilliant one, Sgt. Zupp's strength lies in the fact that he will eagerly carry out any flying assignment that he is given."

Within his file were citations that spoke glowingly of his coolness under fire. For his Air Medal the Americans had written how his "rocketing and strafing runs were made from dangerously low altitudes and damaging enemy installations and equipment". It was not the first time his low flying had been singled out. Another citation mentioned "coming down to a dangerously low altitude" and "outstanding courage and superior airmanship". It was the citation for the American Purple Heart.

In so many ways, Phil was 'Tail End Charlie'. The under-educated kid had fought his way into the pack rather than leading it. He had found that he had the most to offer his squadron by being the last Meteor in on a long direct firing run to the target. It compromised his personal safety but it was effective. He was a draught horse in a paddock of stallions and he was fine with that.

When he arrived at RAAF Base Richmond, his orders were there. Within weeks he was to commence a Flying Instructor's Course at the Central Flying School at East Sale. His emotions were slightly mixed on receiving the news of the appointment as he was already considering a return to Korea for a second tour of duty. In contrast, Edith was thrilled by the news when they met for only the third time.

Far from being strangers, their conversation picked up where it had left off from Edith's last letter. She had so many questions but Phil had relatively few answers. Still, he was excited by the concept of having a girlfriend and possibly even something more at some point. He gave her a small, finely made trinket box from Japan that he had picked up on his way through and she was thrilled. They chatted well into the night that first evening before Edith had to return to her barracks.

She had been worried about his return as she had known so many boys from the last war that came home scarred and changed. She knew some of what he had been called to do in Korea, but never raised it with him, nor did he discuss it. They spoke about everything else. Phillip, as she had taken to calling him, seemed unaffected by combat. Still, he wasn't like the other pilots that came through her office. They were dashing and confident and quick with a smile. Vance Drummond and 'Harry' Browne-Gaylord were two that all of the girls swooned over, but they were lost somewhere over North Korea.

As word of his return spread, the newspapers started to seek out the pilot with "201 Missions Against the Reds!" as one headline described him. On one occasion he was even intercepted in a grocery store and asked about his time in Korea. The subject was topical as the defence minister, William McMahon, had spoken of the pilots being rotated out of service after 100 missions. War correspondent Charles Madden had countered that claim and Phil was one of the 200 mission men. When asked if 200 missions were too many for a single pilot, Phil went to great lengths to explain that these weren't long missions as flown by the bomber crews in the last war. He also added that, "The pilots would probably growl if they weren't kept busy."

Coming Home

FLEW 201 TIMES AGAINST REDS

SYDNEY: A Queensland pilot who flew 201 missions with the R.A.A.F. Meteor jet fighter squadron in Korea returned from Japan by Qantas Skymaster today.

He is Sergeant Phillip Zupp, of Middle Ridge, Toowoomba. Sergeant Zupp has completed his operational tour with No. 77 Squadron.

"PILOTS OVERWORKED" CLAIM DENIED

SYDNEY, Wednesday. — A report that Australian fighter pilots in No. 77 Squadron in Korea were being overworked was totally inaccurate, the Air Minister (Mr. McMahon) said tonight. Pilots of No. 77 Squadron completed only 100 missions or nine months on duty, whichever was the shortest. There was a substantial reserve of trained jet pilots at Williamtown, and replacements were sent as soon as men completed their tour of duty. "In the last two weeks I have been in close contact with pilots just returned from Korea, and I have not heard one complaint," said Mr. McMahon. He was commenting on reports that unless replacements were doubled Australia would not be giving a fair deal to the pilots of No. 77 Squadron.

Mentioned in Dispatches were Warrant Officer Keith Godden Hill, of Ipswich; Sergeant Phillip Zupp, of Toowoomba; Corporal Kevin Patrick Melican, of Hendra, Brisbane; and Corporal Malcolm Charles Tucker, of Brisbane.

TOOWOOMBA AIRMAN BACK FROM KOREA

SYDNEY, Wednesday.—Sergeant Phillip Zupp, of Toowoomba, who has flown 201 missions with No. 77 Squadron in Korea, returned from his operational tour to-day by air from Japan.

"R.A.A.F. KOREAN MISSIONS DEPEND UPON PILOT"

SYDNEY, Sunday.—Members of No. 77 Squadron R.A.A.F. would fly about 120 missions in their six months' service in Korea, said Squadron-Leader W. R. Bennett, the former Commanding Officer of the squadron, to-night. Squadron-Leader Bennett returned to Australia after eight months' service as deputy commanding officer and later as commanding officer of the squadron.

He said that the number of missions a pilot did depended on the pilot himself and the commanding officer. It was left entirely to the commanding officer to decide if the man was operationally tired.

"The morale is high and they love the Meteor," said the Squadron-Leader. "It is ideally suited to ground attack."

Squadron - Leader Bennett will fly home to Brisbane tomorrow morning.

In the news. Phil's mother collected clippings of her son's efforts on his return from Korea.

Edith was happy to see her new sweetheart in the papers but absolutely thrilled when he asked her to travel to Queensland to meet his parents and attend a civic reception for him in Toowoomba. As Edith set about shopping for the trip, Phil went ahead to see his family.

It was nighttime as he walked up the road to his brother's house. Fred had allowed his sons to stay up to greet their uncle. The boys sat wide-eyed as he spoke of flying the Meteor, the snowbound hills of Korea and other tales that skimmed the surface. Then he reached into the kit bag and pulled out some items wrapped in brown paper. One by one he showed them his maps, the photo from his gun camera, a piece of his shattered canopy and then his goggles from that eventful day. The lens buckled, the padding still carried bloodstains and indicated how close Phil had come to not making it home.

Phil stayed at Fred's that night and met his parents the next day. Their home was very humble, positioned at the top of a steep hill where his father still ploughed the soil behind his horse. His mother was relieved and proud to see him, resplendent in his navy blue uniform. His father welcomed him home too and mumbled something that Phil couldn't decipher.

Recalling his awkward moment in Korea when he couldn't drive the Jeep, Phil went to the local police station to request a learner's permit. As he walked into the station, the sergeant looked up at the young pilot, straight-backed and with wings and rows of ribbons above the left breast pocket of his uniform. When Phil asked for the permit, the police sergeant smiled, shook his head and began writing. The two chatted a little about flying fighter jets before the permit was signed and handed to Phil. Turning away, he looked down at the piece of paper to find that the man had written out a full driver's licence. When Phil endeavoured to correct him, the sergeant simply replied, "Get out. You'll only be back here next week pestering me for a driving test."

When Edith arrived days later, he took her to Fred's, embarrassed by his parent's tiny shack. Edith had grown up as the daughter of moderately wealthy land owners and had even had paid help to run the household. It was a world away from Phil's reality and he felt that she had fallen for the Air Force pilot, rather than the country boy. The truth was that Edith loved both. She was bursting with pride when he was presented with an award at the reception and felt for him as he stumbled to put a few words together to say thank you. However, she also had cause to laugh with Phil as his parents made a couple of faux-pas. First, his mother tried to wipe his oak leaf cluster from his medals, believing it was a chocolate stain. Then his father could be heard expressing his pride in his son on winning the "United Mason's Medal"! Truth be known, old 'Bill' Zupp had never heard of the United Nations and probably had no idea where Korea was.

The happy young couple spent the next few days relaxing as Edith sized up her potential husband. Firstly, the dreadful haircut had to go and, secondly, he needed pyjamas. If she was ever to share a bed with him he just simply must have pyjamas. As they set out on a day trip to the big city, Edith had dressed with a new hat and gloves while Phil was dressed in full uniform. She realised she'd never seen him in civilian clothes and the reason was simple. He didn't own any. Edith made another mental note.

Even so, she was proud to be seen, arms linked, with her decorated pilot who tried to grab a kiss whenever they went through a tunnel. As they walked along the railway platform Edith felt on top of the world until a less than desirable and disheveled man made a suggestive remark in Edith's direction. She had hardly processed the vulgar comment when Phil unlinked his arm and grabbed the taller man by the throat, slamming him against the wall. A second later Phil delivered a blow that had blood spraying from the man's nose. Another blow and the man slumped to the ground. It was over in an instant.

Phil linked his arm in Edith's once again and carried on as if nothing had happened. Her heart was racing, she had never seen anything so brutal in her life and was in a state of shock. Yet Phil seemed totally unaffected, even disconnected. His breathing wasn't elevated and his stride didn't change.

Perhaps, somewhere deep inside, the war had affected him after all, she thought.

Looking less than happy, Phil on the Flight Instructor Course at East Sale.
(Phil is standing at far right)

Chapter Thirty-Three

Flight Instructor

Little did Edith know, but since his return Phil's feelings had grown greatly and he had decided to propose. At the civic reception in Toowoomba he had been given a wallet with some cash that he now resolved to spend on an engagement ring. He awkwardly shopped for the diamond-dressed golden band and chose to ask the question before he left for Flight Instructor Training.

Caught off guard but exuberant, Edith said yes to the proposal having only ever spent a matter of days with her new fiancé. However, she knew that it was right. She even felt that her first fiancé, Frank, had somehow steered Phil into her life from the heavens. She knew it seemed silly, but it helped her say goodbye to her lost love and welcome this new man into her life with all of her heart. Phil had come home safely from Korea and no war was going to destroy her life ever again. As he left for East Sale, she set about organising a white wedding in November.

For Phil, his life still seemed polarised. His romantic excitement was tempered by a sense of agitation and a desire to return to Korea. The situation had only worsened when he learned that 'Smithy' had been killed in action and by the time he arrived at the Central Flying School, the agitation was constant.

Having settled in, his first order of business was to seek out a sympathetic senior officer at CFS and informally request a return to Korea. He knew that others had preceded him and that Ken Murray was also looking at going back for a second tour. However, instead of encouragement, or even consideration, he was told "no". Full stop. Phil was gutted and left in a state of confusion as he knew they needed pilots and he was volunteering.

He let the dust settle over a few days and again approached the officer and again the same answer was forthcoming. This time however, the officer explained to Phil that he had been recognised as instructor material and that he could best serve the RAAF by passing on his experience, rather than risk being killed on mission number 202. The Air Force had decided and that was all there was to it.

Accepting, but unhappy, he began reacquainting himself with the Tiger Moth. After the Meteor he found the Tiger very light and at times he felt ham-fisted and harsh on the little trainer. The biplane had to be finessed and kept in balance with subtle pressure on the rudder pedals. In Korea, the pedals were only ever used to kick the Meteor straight to aim at a target and taxi the jet on the ground. Slowly, he reacclimatised, but it wasn't easy. The study seemed unending and the preparation to give lectures and briefings was something he had never encountered before. Night after night he pored over the books and day after day he fought his shyness to present lessons to the class. All the while, he was unsettled and even missed the feelings that combat stirred in him.

He flew to Richmond to spend two days with Edith who was more than a little excited about the wedding. He sat opposite her the first evening, somewhat despondent, drawing the obvious query from his fiancé. He explained his desire to return to Korea and the Air Force's point blank rejection. Edith was furious.

She launched into a tirade that began with his lack of regard for her on the subject and closed with her revisiting her loss in World War Two. Phil had not seen this coming and sat speechless. The air was then sucked from the room when Edith offered up an ultimatum. "If you go back to Korea, I won't be here when you get back. I cannot and will not go through that again."

In her few words, more than those of the Air Force, he realised that he would never return to his squadron. She saw the look of loss on his face and did her best to comfort him and soften her previous assault. In response, Phil paced the room, not raising his eyes from the floor. He then stopped, his head still lowered. Edith waited for words or a blow from his fist to the wall, but there was nothing. Finally, he offered, "Okay" and "Goodnight", before kissing her on the cheek and leaving. She felt dreadful but knew that she just couldn't survive losing him.

Back at East Sale he studied hard, although his results were only ever rated as 'average'. The instructors appreciated his work ethic and integrity and although he was never the star of the course, they recognised he was an exceptionally keen and conscientious instructor in the making. They could also see that he not only kept to himself, but he was brooding and at times aggressive. They suspected that he

Flight Instructor

*Phil performing an engine run in his favourite aircraft, the Mustang.
(Source: RAAF Museum)*

was suffering from 'Battle Fatigue' or some such phenomena and sent him to the base hospital for review.

Phil had not been seated very long before he realised that he was being ambushed by a psychiatrist with a special interest in returning veterans. The man in the white coat began to tell Phil what he may well be feeling and why. He elaborated on the 'illness' and how understandable it was, pausing momentarily to jot down Phil's total lack of response. If he'd been agitated before, he was absolutely seething now. Inside he knew that he may be fatigued, he may be frustrated and he may be pissed off, but he wasn't bloody shell-shocked. He sat there trying to maintain a calm exterior as he imploded. He had been through two wars and an atomic bomb site and no university educated white coat was going to tell him what he felt.

Back in his room he paced the floor and slept even less that night. Days passed and there was still no further word from the medical department and it was eating him alive. What had they written on his file? Was he going to be discharged? Would he be barred from fighters or active service? His head was spinning.

In desperation, he called Edith, but not to discuss his situation. He started querying her regarding the how and where of personnel files in the Air Force, particularly medical files. Edith offered up her thoughts on where they may be and asked why he wanted to know, but he was only forthcoming with a thank you and nothing more.

That night Phil set about breaking the rules for the first time in his life. Armed with the information that Edith had provided, he clambered through a window in the far from secure administration building. Ferreting through the filing cabinets, it was easy to locate 'Zupp' at the very rear of the bottom drawer. Flicking through the pages he came to the psychiatrist's assessment. It suggested that Phil was possibly suffering from the after-effects of combat and should be monitored further. "Bullshit!", he thought as he removed the pages and folded them into his pocket before making his escape.

He knew that what he had done was wrong, but who were these so-called experts to control his career? They weren't pilots and they didn't understand. He knew now that he had to avoid attention of any kind and resolved to smile and wave as they believed a balanced individual would. He couldn't afford any slip up that would send them delving back into the file.

So he studied and he flew, the Tiger Moth and Wirraway mainly, but there were also hops in Lincolns, Dakotas and his beloved Mustang. His efforts continued to be solid rather than exemplary and it seemed that the psychiatric evaluation had been forgotten. As their wedding day approached, Edith could see that his demeanour had genuinely improved. He seemed to have accepted his fate professionally and shared in Edith's excitement. When the day arrived, Edith wore white and Phillip his navy blue uniform with a new crown above his chevrons indicating his promotion to flight sergeant. Ken Towner served as his best man to make the wedding an Air Force affair. Family, friends and newspaper photographers joined the happy couple, although Phil's father was nowhere to be seen. He rarely ventured far from the farm and never aloft in an aircraft. His mother had no such reluctance and had been determined to see her youngest child wed.

The honeymoon consisted of two days at East Sale before Phil put Edith on an aircraft home and returned to his books. Other than an occasional rendezvous with his new bride, the weeks continued much the same as they had until graduation

Flight Instructor

loomed within reach. After seventeen weeks, more than 100 hours of flight time and too many briefings to recall, Phil graduated as an Air Force instructor

When 1953 arrived, he was posted to RAAF Base Archerfield, not far from his family home in Queensland. The Korean War was still raging, but for Phil a new life beckoned, one of family and stability. Even so, his role as a flight instructor in peaceful Australia very nearly cost him his life.

Phil and Edith's wedding was covered in the newspapers as an 'all air force affair' with Ken Towner as Best Man.

Phil and his student in flight near the Queensland Darling Downs.

Chapter Thirty-Four

Peacetime

As the rules dictated, Edith resigned from the Air Force on becoming married and set about making a home in Queensland. Phil set about his new role as a flight instructor, at No. 1 FTS RAAF Archerfield, training new Air Force pilots in their basic stages on the Tiger Moth and Wirraway. He was now working alongside Jim Flemming, one of the instructors that had schooled him in Canberra on Mustangs prior to his departure for Korea. From very early on, Jim could recognise the ability in his protégé, despite somewhat differing styles.

Each day at the end of operations, Jim would regularly make his way to the Mess, only to see Phil working back with a handful of students offering extra tuition in one of the many classrooms. The first hours were critical for new cadets as they were screened for potential and, with as little as ten hours flight time, may be deemed as unsuitable and scrubbed from pilot training. Phil felt for them and remembered how much he wanted to learn to fly and how Squadron Leader McMahon had given him his break back at Rathmines. If it was at all in his power, these young men would make it too.

One such cadet was Colin Peck. Col had been flying with a less than merciful instructor known as 'The Screamer'. Col's first hours had been hell, paired with the volatile instructor yelling down the Gosport Tube and criticising him at every turn. Col felt that he was on the verge of being scrubbed and his confidence was at its lowest ebb. With only a handful of flights remaining before his make or break assessment, Col was paired with Phil and things were very different.

Phil was quiet and unassuming by comparison and encouraged his young student, pointing out an area here or there that he could refine, but never coming down on him like a bag of bricks. Col responded to Phil's style and after three hours together was sent solo in the Tiger Moth and, more importantly, survived the critical check flight. It was a pivotal moment for Col and a fork in the road that saw him become a respected fighter pilot and ultimately a senior check and training captain with Qantas.

Word spread of Phil's instructional technique and those rostered to fly with him considered themselves fortunate. To many, it was a surprise that the stocky fighter pilot with so many combat missions in Korea was actually so reserved and even gentle in the cockpit when it came to students. His patience seemed unlimited, but still waters can run deep. Korea was constantly in his thoughts and were rammed home when word of John Halley and Don Hillier being lost on operations reached him.

The loss was compounded only weeks later when another 4 Course graduate, and one of his closest friends, was killed. Bob Strawbridge was not in Korea, but back at home and flying his Mustang off the coast of Williamtown when it apparently collided with a Vampire doing the same thing. Other than some aircraft pieces washing up or found in a trawler's fishing net, no trace of Bob was ever found. It was a loss Phil felt for many years to come.

By night Phil attended classes at the University of Queensland to gain his Leaving Certificate. Having not completed his formal education had haunted him both personally and professionally. He knew that without this formal qualification, his chances of gaining a commission and becoming an officer were very slim. Edith encouraged him at every turn as he taught by day and became the student by night.

The nature of flight instruction meant that Phil often looked for ways to break the routine. Whether it was low flying off the coast or impromptu formation aerobatics with Jim Flemming there was always something brewing in his cockpit. On occasions he would take to chasing vast groups of pelicans in the Tiger Moth. Once Jim witnessed a huge pelican pass between the wings of Phil's Tiger Moth without impacting a single strut or bracing wire, each of which could have brought the aircraft down. More humorous was when the pelicans activated their defence mechanism and crapped in formation, covering the open cockpit biplane with guano.

At other times air displays would be held at Archerfield with the instructors showing off the Tiger Moth to the public by spinning down in formation and crossing over at the bottom, recovering a few hundred feet above the ground.

Peacetime

Not all sorties in the Tiger Moth went to plan for the young trainee pilots.

Unfortunately, during one practice session Phil lost count of the rotations he had spun the Tiger Moth through and glanced at his altimeter instead to time his recovery. Sickeningly, he suddenly realised that it would be misreading due to the irregular airflow of the spin and hurriedly recovered.

Jim had pulled out only to see Phil's Tiger disappear beyond a row of trees. He clenched his teeth and waited for the pall of smoke to rise. It never did. Seconds later the Tiger Moth emerged although, as Phil climbed from the cockpit back at Archerfield, he was still pale from the close call. The excitement wasn't limited to practice either.

In front of a gathered crowd one sunny afternoon, Phil was to play the enemy in a mock dogfight with Jim playing the heroic Allied pilot. The plan was for the two Tigers to dual before, ultimately, Jim would 'shoot' Phil down with his demise signaled by two red smoke canisters being fired by Phil through cables stemming from his cockpit.

The crowd was enthralled as the two biplanes twisted, turned, banked and roared low overhead but, when the time came, Phil refused to die. He simply

In 1954 Phil, Jim Flemming and other instructors flew the 1FTS Tiger Moths to their new home at Uranquinty.

kept leading Jim on, occasionally looking back and grinning. Finally, after some vigorous hand signals from Jim, Phil set the Tiger Moth up for the most dramatic of finales. Pitching up vertically, he all but stood the Tiger stationary in mid-air on its tail before kicking in the rudder and flicking it into a spin. Simultaneously he released the red smoke canisters for maximum effect.

Unfortunately, he had virtually no forward speed and the Tiger was soon engulfed in a cloud of scarlet with Jim once again watching on. A wingtip or a tail fin could be sighted as the aircraft spun down towards the earth. Phil's goggles were now opaque with the dye and he hurriedly wiped them and set about recovering the aircraft from the spin using his instruments.

Soon the Tiger was under control and Phil brought the machine back to earth, caked in dye. As he emerged from the cockpit, the upper half of his body was also coated in red until he raised the goggles atop his helmet to reveal a clean band about his eyes. Jim was in fits of laughter which were only worsened by the announcement that the enemy had landed and that he was actually the 'Red Baron'.

Surprisingly, for all of the antics, Phil drew the line at swapping aircraft with Navy pilots. At times, certain individuals would trade their Mustangs for Navy Hawker Sea Furies but Phil could see it going horribly wrong with a Court Martial not far behind for the unauthorised flights. It was painful for him as he thought that the Sea Fury was a thing of sheer beauty. Still, he was free to fly the Mustang.

At every opportunity he would climb into one of the resident Mustangs.

Peacetime

Occasionally he was tasked to tow banners or perform an aerobatics display, but at other times it was just the sheer pleasure of flying his favourite aircraft with its V12 engine and single seat. With his family's various farms not far away, he had often flown over in Tiger Moths, and even dropped messages from the open cockpit, but he also made his presence known in the Mustang.

Sighting the road leading up to one property he also caught sight of a group of children walking towards the front gate. He let down low along the dirt road with the kids spotting his fighter at a distance, its propeller forming a silver disc and curling up a trail of dust. They recognised it as their uncle and leapt clear of the road before he pulled up and barrel-rolled over the house, disappearing as quickly as he had arrived. Unfortunately, they had all leapt into barbed weeds on the roadside in search of safety.

Edith saw her husband slowly adapt to peacetime life over the months and enjoyed the regular nature of his work. They would visit family, picnic and make trips into the city together like any newly married couple. Phil had completed his studies at night school and been granted his commission. He was no longer among the dying breed of sergeant pilots. Now he was a pilot officer. In time, they welcomed a daughter, Pamela, and Phil's commando mate, Bill Elliott, was made the godfather. However, Edith was blissfully unaware of some the hair-raising flying Phil was performing at Archerfield until one day when she looked out of her train bound for Brisbane to see him in formation and waving to her.

Over two years, he had proven himself to be a valuable instructor and Edith loved their life in Queensland, but Phil still longed to fly fighters once more. The Korean War had ended in a ceasefire and no more pilots were being deployed to the 38th Parallel. This too spelt the end for 1FTS with it being merged with another flight training facility at Uranquinty in New South Wales. Led by Jim Flemming, Phil flew Tiger Moth A17-657 to its new home south of the border as one of five aircraft. After nearly 800 hours of training, Phil was now transferred from instructional duties and forced to move home.

Edith packed up their belongings as they readied for his next posting. He could not hide his excitement, nor Edith her reservations. He was returning to RAAF Williamtown, to 77 Squadron and the Gloster Meteor.

Meteors in formation near Williamtown, NSW.

Chapter Thirty-Five

Fighters, Failure and Farewell

It only took a single one-hour flight in the two-seat Meteor for Phil to be deemed safe to take to the skies again in the familiar F.8 fighter. Days later, he was called to fly in the 'Welcome Home' operation to mark 77 Squadron's return from more than a decade overseas, culminating with its time in Korea. In February 1955, a series of flypasts would take place over the capital cities and Phil would be one of the Meteor pilots to form a double-7 on the Brisbane leg.

Beyond the flypast, he was back flying fast jets in the environment he loved. Mock dogfights, air-to-air intercepts, close formation and aerobatics. There were simulated rocket strikes, which seemed very tame after executing real strikes in Korea, and air-to-ground gunnery. However, by comparison to combat, the flying hours were lean – only ten to fifteen hours a month. In April, Phil moved to 75 Squadron, which was also based at Williamtown, where the commanding officer was one of his instructors from Point Cook, Max Holdsworth. The squadron consisted of pilots old and new, from fellow Korean veterans like his old friend Jim Flemming, to students from Archerfield such as Wal Bowles and Col Peck.

Wal had admired Phil greatly since 1FTS and now found himself flying formation aerobatics with the experienced fighter pilot. Other times he would fly Phil's wingtip as Phil led a gaggle of four Meteors in and out of cloud. From his nearby vantage point, Wal could see a map spread all over the leader's cockpit, and Phil flying the Meteor with his knees holding the control column. He was in awe at times. On the ground, Phil would still seek to nurture the junior pilots as he had when he was instructing, helping them out with one of his endless series of rules of thumb or some other piece of guiding advice. To the junior pilot he was a quiet blend of confidence and capability – always safe and always reliable.

Ground staff also admired the quiet young pilot officer. After hours, the orderly officers could often be seen whizzing by the front of hangars on their yellow bicycles, whereas Phil would walk the flight line and stop at each and every hangar to check on the men. As a former mechanic, he understood their role and spoke their language and they appreciated the time he spent listening to their issues.

At this time, a peculiar and somewhat embarrassing event took place over the skies of Sydney, drawing 77 Squadron back into the fight. At the nearby Bankstown Airport, a light aircraft had taken off without the pilot after it had been hand-swung to start the engine. The errant Auster aeroplane drifted over the city towards the ocean, but the race was on to shoot the aircraft down before it crashed in a suburban area.

At first a Wirraway trainer from RAAF Richmond tried to shoot the aircraft down, using a hand-held Bren gun from the rear cockpit, but failed. Next, a Meteor from Williamtown flown by the 77 Squadron CO, Max Holdsworth, lined up for the kill but his cannons jammed. More Meteors were then called to the 'fight' but, embarrassingly, the Navy won the day when a pair of Sea Furies from Nowra shot the aircraft down. The Air Force's capability was called in to question by some, but the immediate fall-out was the establishment of a roster ensuring that a Meteor and pilot was always at a state of readiness. The unpopular duty spanned weekends and became affectionately known as the 'Auster Roster'.

On the home front, things weren't working out quite as well and the 'Auster Roster' was just another burden that Edith didn't appreciate. Aside from flying, her husband had his duties as orderly officer and, as a non-drinker, he was routinely voted to manage the money at the officer's bar when there were functions. Otherwise, Phil was rarely seen socially on the base and this was noted by certain officers.

Edith had set up home in a little cabin at Nelson's Bay, but there were little in the way of services nearby. She would have to boil water to wash nappies and the power supply was anything but reliable. Phillip would occasionally blast over the roof at low level, but otherwise the young Air Force wife and mother was starting to feel isolated. Despite repeated requests, there were no married quarters available on the base. Phil was an active and caring father to their daughter, despite never having had a paternal role model other than the stern rule of 'Old Bill'.

Operation 'Welcome Home'. Phil flew one leg of the tour in early 1955 that marked the return of 77 Squadron to Australia.

Even so, Edith's patience was getting short and the situation worsened when Phil told her that he was to be deployed with the squadron to the other side of the country for a month to take part in an exercise. Furthermore, he had been granted a position on the newly developed and coveted Fighter Combat Instructor (FCI) course on his return and she knew that she would see very little of him, as had been the case when he was studying at CFS at East Sale. Phil's excitement at being selected was tempered by his wife's reservations and also the news that Bruce Thomson had been killed. His tent mate from Korea that had survived being shot down and a lengthy term as a prisoner of war was gone, tragically lost off Point Cook as he instructed a student pilot in a Wirraway.

For Edith, enough was enough. Her childhood friend from Kempsey had written to tell her that the house next door to her was for sale. It was in Sydney's western suburbs at Guildford and Edith convinced Phil they should buy the house as soon as possible and move from the isolation of Nelson Bay. He agreed for her sake and set the wheels in motion to purchase the house using a War Service Loan. Edith seemed appeased and in a far better state by the time he had to set out on the deployment.

The Meteors left Williamtown, led by Squadron Leader Max Holdsworth, and stepped their way across the remote inland of central Australia. Laden with additional wing drop tanks and the infamous ventral tank, the Meteors staggered into the air at Forrest in incredible heat before finally arriving at RAAF Pearce later that day.

Central to their stint in Western Australia was an air defence exercise that simulated two atom bomb attacks with RAAF Canberra bombers playing the role of the enemy. In the heightened tension of the Cold War, the exercise had a high media profile with the pilots and jets being shadowed by reporters and cameras at every turn. After the Auster incident, the Meteors needed to provide a much better display.

RAAF Pearce resembled a wartime airfield as the Meteors sat at the ready knowing that the two bombers were inbound. At intervals they were scrambled, the ground crews shielding themselves as the Meteors threw up gravel in their wake. The first Canberra had been 'shot down' successfully and soon it was Phil's section's turn. He was the most experienced of the four pilots and Wal Bowles the most junior.

The four Meteors screamed to 25,000 feet, guided towards their target by the ground control radar. Still well out to sea and miles from their target, the Meteors manoeuvred for the attack. Positioning with the sun at their backs in the age-old fighter technique, they rolled down onto the twin-engine jet bomber before securing it in their sights and squeezing the trigger to capture the 'kill' on film. The victories that day were met with headlines that reassured the public at the height of the Cold War, but Phil felt hollow. There had been nobody shooting back and he was only firing film. He wondered whether the rest of his career would be mock attacks and pretending. Over the next few days, the exercise was repeated but the newspapers already had their headlines.

The day before the squadron was to return to the east coast, Phil had to air test the Meteor he would be flying home. The sun was just touching the horizon as he completed the last exercise off the coast when he dove the Meteor towards the water before heaving back on the stick and bringing the jet to fly vertically at an

Fighters, Failure and Farewell

A staged media shot of the briefing prior to the mock attack over Perth. Max Holdsworth is at far right.

incredible rate of climb. He looked towards the horizon and a wry smiled curled at the corner of his mouth beneath the oxygen mask. He was making the sun rise. He set course for Pearce but it was night by the time he landed. That simple moment was to become a cherished memory.

When he arrived home he had seven days to move house and start his FCI Course. Edith had researched that there was a reserve fighter squadron at RAAF Richmond, much closer to Sydney and told Phillip to apply as soon as possible. In the meantime, he would drive their small Austin A30 over the rough single lane highway back and forth between Sydney and RAAF Williamtown. His plan was to stay in the Mess during the week and drive home for weekends. It was a tall order, but he hoped that he could make it work.

Phil was now promoted to flying officer and about to embark on only the second FCI Course ever held and it was being carefully monitored for its performance. Also on course was his best man Ken Towner, Jim Flemming and, from Korea, John Parker, Jim Kichenside and Keith Martin. The familiar faces were a welcome sight, but the reality soon came crashing down. The study was intensive and he was having to relearn flying the Vampire, of which the two-seater model was a totally new experience. He was struggling to keep pace and his situation was being worsened by the long drive to Sydney and back each weekend. Making matters worse, his two written applications to be posted to Richmond on completion of the course were met with a negative response. Richmond's 22 Squadron operated Mustangs and the Air Force wanted Phil in a Meteor squadron.

He could feel the walls closing in around him and his flying was suffering. In just four weeks he fell from the excitement of starting the FCI Course to being on the threshold of failure. He had always been able to grind through adversity, but this was seemingly a bridge too far, even for Phil. After a poor assessment flight and less than flattering results in theory examinations, Phil was suspended on course, pending his ability to make up ground academically. It was the single greatest blow he had ever felt.

That night Ken Towner sat with Phil and the two mulled over options, but Phil knew what lay ahead. He told Ken that he could pass muster in the cockpit, but with a nervous wife, a young daughter and a long commute, he was never going to conquer the demanding theoretical aspects. In fact, he knew his days in the RAAF were numbered. His recent personal assessments had rated him well but always commented that his poor career prospects were due to his limited education and a reluctance to attend Mess functions or socialise. Ken tried to change his mind, but only days later he was back at 75 Squadron as a rank and file fighter pilot.

Phil still enjoyed the sheer joy and challenge of flying fighters, but the embarrassment of failure weighed heavily upon him. For three more months he flew the Meteor each day as if it were his last. He cherished the sights, the sounds and the smells but, when a letter arrived from The Royal Aero Club at Bankstown advising him that there was a flight instructor job if he wanted it, he knew the time had come to resign from the Air Force. Edith had not issued an ultimatum this time, but he knew that she was sick of his absences and weekend visits. This civilian job would mean that he would be home every night and that's what she wanted.

The Air Force interviewed him to ensure that his resignation wasn't on a whim. It wasn't. Even though his record as a fighter pilot was impressive, the powers that be saw little prospects, beyond being a squadron pilot, for the quiet kid from the bush or, as Ron Susan's called him, the rough diamond.

As Phil walked out to his Meteor on April 11th 1956, he knew that he was

Fighters, Failure and Farewell

On the right, Phil walks back after the successful 'attack' against the Canberra bomber.

closing a significant chapter of his life. The Air Force had taken him from a fight in the cane fields to a fighter pilot. He had seen combat and survived and watched friends die in flames on a frozen foreign landscape. The Air Force had given him self-respect and so much more. Now it was time to walk away.

He strapped in to the Meteor and started the engines as he had done so many times before. After 400 hours in the fighter's cockpit his hands moved from switch to lever with ease. A hard helmet now sat over his head, where a leather helmet had once been, almost as a symbol of how far flying had come in his years of service. His breathing echoed in the oxygen mask and his nasal voice responded to the take-off clearance. Then he soared.

He swept the Meteor about the sky, pushing it to every limit it possessed. The airflow rushed passed the canopy and the Machmeter threatened to burst from the scale in a dive before soaring once again into the heavens. He looped and rolled with the freedom that only the breadth of the skies and the power of jet engines could offer. Then, one last time, with the Meteor sitting as high as she would go, he pulled back the stick and kicked in the rudder. Around and around and around through thousands of feet the jet spun about its axis, falling to earth. In the cockpit the altimeter wound off altitude like a crazed clock while the airspeed lay low and dormant. Outside the world was a spinning blur and all the while his breathing was the only sound. As 10,000 feet approached he eased the Meteor out of its stalled state, allowing the air to give lift and life to the wings. One last low pass and one last landing. Then it was done. He was no longer an Air Force pilot – no longer a fighter pilot.

That night he sat and drew the nib from the ink well to his logbook. "11 April. Meteor Mk. 8. A77-855. Self. Solo. General Flying. Spinning. 1:00 hour".

A QANTAS Super Constellation in flight. (Source: Qantas Heritage Collection)

Chapter Thirty-Six

A Brave New World

With the exception of his time cutting cane, Phil had not been a civilian since 1944. His adult life had been spent in the military and now he was set to leave his regimented existence. He still wore a flying suit and boots and his yellow scarf that could double as a signaling device if forced down, but everything else felt different.

The Royal Aero Club of NSW was a hive of activity with students and instructors scurrying between lessons. Outside, the flight line of Tiger Moths, Austers and Chipmunks sat waiting. Without delay Phil was thrust into the world of civil flight instruction. Nobody even checked his competency on the Tiger Moth given that he had nearly one thousand hours in the biplane, although his most recent flight was more than a year before. His first civilian flight was an instructional flight with a young student flying circuits and bumps. It was to be the first of more than one hundred lessons Phil would fly during that first month.

The pace was hectic and not as measured as the military, but he refused to compromise on briefings and, consequently, his days were long. The Chipmunk, comparative luxury to the Tiger Moth with its enclosed cockpit and single low wing, still it had to be hand swung into life. This was a practice that also had to be taught to the students and was generally accompanied by Phil's account of the runaway Auster as a warning.

He was a popular instructor who was only counselled by the senior staff on one occasion. He had just completed a session of circuits with his student occupying the rear seat when he decided it was time for the student's first solo. Pulling clear of the runway and coming to a halt, Phil began to unstrap from the Tiger Moth and yelled to the student down the Gosport tube that they should fly one circuit, land and then come back to pick him up before returning to the aero club.

To his dismay the student replied, "I don't think I'm ready".

Without changing his tone, Phil advised the student that, "I do and it's my job to assess you. Fly one circuit, land and then come back to pick me up." He then climbed down from the Tiger, stood clear and gave the apprehensive student a smile and a thumbs up.

The student safely managed the take-off and landing, but later advised the Chief Flying Instructor that they would have liked to have had more dual instruction. The CFI pulled Phil aside and explained that this wasn't the make or break of the military and if a student wanted to pay for a few more lessons, then it was best to go along with their wishes.

Phil flew a hundred lessons month after month, although he had also applied to the national airline, QANTAS Empire Airways. A number of RAAF pilots were already there, including Col King and 'Blue' Waugh, and the pay and conditions far outshone those of the aero club. With a mortgage to repay, Phil was keen to unburden himself of the debt. They had lost the farm when he was a boy and he wasn't ever going to lose his home again. He hated debt with a passion and lived by the motto, 'My back is wet with honest sweat for I owe not any man'.

Flying by day, Phil had also studied navigation at night as his selected skill for a funded program to resettle ex-servicemen into a civilian life. In less than a year he had both his newest qualification and a call from Qantas offering him a position. On January 1st 1957 he stepped out of the Tiger Moth and two days later stepped into a Douglas DC-3 for his assessment flight. Successfully completed, it was back to the classroom for two months to learn every possible aspect of his new aircraft, the Lockheed L-1049 Super Constellation. The engineering side of Phil's brain enjoyed the complex systems and engines of the four-engine Lockheed, despite its reputation as the best three-engine airliner in the world!

When the book-work was completed and the exams passed, Phil took to the air for the first time in the Super Constellation, flying circuits and practising engine failures just as if it were any other aeroplane. For the first time in his career, Phil was not alone in the cockpit and the teamwork of multi-crew operations came into play. Co-ordinating drills with another pilot and flight engineer was a new experience for the fighter pilot used to his lone seat in the sky. Also, whereas everything was memorised in the Mustang and Meteor, checklists were rigidly

A Brave New World

Phillip and Edith with their daughter, Pamela. 1958.

called and responded to in a strict, procedural environment.

Most of the company's captains were highly experienced and many had commanded bombers over Europe in World War Two. This fact was reinforced by the service ribbons worn on their uniform coats, despite now flying for an airline. It was a convention adopted by many uniformed services as the war was still fresh in so many minds. While many were gentlemen, there were those in the check captain ranks that used their position to harass new recruits.

Phil came under the gaze of one such pilot when he was being assessed for his instrument rating. Even since Korea, Phil had had limited exposure to flight on instruments. His was predominantly a world of visual flight, formations, aerobatics and staring down the graticule of a gunsight. Now he was being tested on his ability to fly without reference to the horizon and the check captain obviously had a dislike for fighter pilots too. Between snide remarks, insults were interspersed and Phil's blood began to boil. It took all his strength to keep flying and not return fire, but he managed to keep the rage buried and slide through the assessment in spite of his tormentor.

After more classroom time, Captain Probert completed the final stage of Phil's assessment with a session of circuits by night at his old home base of Williamtown and signed him off for his first trip. It was the 'Kangaroo Route' from Sydney to London, and all stops in between, with the return trip taking nearly three weeks. Along the way Phil would see such far-flung destinations as Singapore, Calcutta, Bombay, Colombo, Karachi, Bahrain, Istanbul, Rome, Mauritius, and London. It was a far cry from the Darling Downs. And it would all be courtesy of the 'Super Connie'; the pinnacle of propeller driven airline transport.

With sleek lines, streamlined wingtip fuel tanks and four radial engines, the classic airliner had revolutionised global travel and was the pride of the fleet. Resplendent in all-over white with red highlights and the 'Flying Kangaroo' on its tail, the aircraft turned heads wherever it was seen. The flight deck was a sea of hands and checklists before the propellers slowly began to turn, puffing clouds of smoke as they burst into life. By night, flames would lick from the exhaust stacks making the scene even more spectacular.

The crew comprised of a captain, two first officers, a flight engineer, a navigator and a radio officer. On the long sectors, the pilots rotated through their time in the control seat, taking rest breaks in fairly rudimentary bunks. The first officers also relieved the navigator. Sightings were made through the clear bubble, or astrodome, on top of the Connie to fix the aircraft's current position with reference to the stars. Phil thought that the navigators were poetry in motion.

They would take their sighting through the sextant, climb down and make their plot and then sit there smoking a cigarette for the few minutes available until the next sighting was due. They would then climb up to the astrodome, take another sighting and plot their fix again before calling out the new course to steer. For Phil, as a part-timer, he found that there was no time between sightings to do anything but plot the fixes. He had been trained as a navigator twice in his career and finally he was putting the skill into practice. Ultimately, he would become a fully licensed navigator in his own right.

Engine failures and fire warnings were not uncommon, leaving the Connie and crew stranded at a distant port while engineering repaired or replaced the recalcitrant engine. Despite the engines' poor reputation, Phil admired their complex engineering but recognised that the jet age would soon make these

A Brave New World

An Airlines of NSW Douglas DC-3 as flown by Phil.
(Source: R N Smith Collection)

majestic airliners and their multi-stop journeys obsolete. For the moment though, he made the most of the situation, visiting far-flung places that for him had once only existed in an atlas.

To walk among the ruins of the Colosseum and the towering skyscrapers of New York was inspiring and to sip coffee at Café Ricci in Rome became a ritual. Still, he was a boy from the bush and not very worldly. As he sat in a bar in Rome one evening, a very attractive lady approached Phil and began to chat. He blushed heavily at her forward approach, but fortunately his lack of conversation seemed to scare her off. Minutes later another woman approached him and also engaged him in banter with her eyes flashing and a broad smile across her face. He repelled her too. His fellow first officer then informed him that they were not there for his company, but actually ladies-of-the-night seeking his company for financial gain.

When the actor Danny Kaye wandered on to the flight deck of the Super Constellation without an invitation, Phil removed him in a less than subtle manner responding to Kaye's appeal to stay with "I don't care if you're the bloody Queen of Sheba. Get out!" The incident caused a degree of embarrassment for the crew and the airline, but Phil still struggled to comprehend what he'd done wrong. For him, no one just enters a cockpit, regardless of their perceived fame. Besides, Phil had no idea who Danny Kaye was.

In some ways, Phil felt he was a square peg in a round hole at Qantas. Most of the time he ventured out alone, but there were those that did not appreciate his solitary exploration. Some captains believed the crew should constantly be in each other's company and frequenting bars together was the norm. For Phil, this was not the case and he wondered if it was an old bomber crew trait. Virtually a non-drinker, he did not warm to the constant demands to be "in the bar at six!" There was so much more to be seen than the inside of a glass.

In time, his repeated absence was duly noted when six o'clock came around and it did not endear him to some of the commanders with whom he was flying. There were even captains that had not seen active service during the war that the habit of walking several paces away from Phil so as not to be seen with a co-pilot wearing more ribbons than them. Phil hadn't even noticed this until a fellow first officer pointed it out and thought it amusing as his actual medals were still sitting in a drawer in the boxes in which they had been posted to him.

The trips lasted weeks and Edith had given birth to a son, Adrian, in March 1959. Phil's long absences began to play on his wife, alone with their two children. On occasions he would send a telegram from Singapore, confirming his arrival on Saturday, sending Edith into an excited frenzy. She would ready the children and the home but Saturday would come and go with no sign of her husband. At the last minute, an aircraft had gone unserviceable and he had been turned around to fly back to Europe. In the coming days a telegram would arrive with the news that his homecoming was now postponed.

By January 1960, it was time to move on once more. Edith could no longer tolerate the long trips and Phil wanted more time with his young family. Still, the decision to stay or go was difficult as the airline was re-equipping for the jet age with the Boeing 707 and he longed to fly the aircraft. There was no other job offering the same amount of money either but, with the house now paid off, that was no longer a high priority.

It was with some reluctance that he resigned from Qantas and returned to the demands of flight instruction at the Illawarra Flying School. They were long days of yelling over engine noise, but he was home every night. Yet within months, he was on the move again when Airlines of New South Wales began recruiting first officers for their DC-3 fleet. It was airline flying, good pay and home most nights. He put his hand up and soon thereafter was flying regional routes around his homeland. It seemed the perfect balance but, once again, his best intentions came crashing down.

One of Phil's students was the singer, Col Joye.

Chapter Thirty-Seven

Jack of All Trades

Phil loved his job with the Airlines of NSW. Flying six sectors each day, he was able to chalk up three landings and be home for dinner. There was more hands on flying than on international routes and the trips were two days at their longest, rarely ranging beyond the state borders. His ability to be home at a moment's notice if needed also sat well with Edith although she never made the call. The cockpit of the DC-3 seemed far friendlier than the formal world of Qantas where the captain was addressed as captain and the first officer as "Mister Zupp".

The DC-3 was a classic airliner dating back to before the war. It had revolutionised air travel in its day and, although Phil had flown the type on occasions in the RAAF and Qantas, this was the first time he flew it consistently. It was a true lady of the skies as was the other aircraft he came to know during his time at Airlines of NSW - the Short Sandringham flying boat.

The Short Sandringham was a civilianised Short Sunderland flying boat. During World War Two, the Sunderland had flown patrols, rescued downed crews and attacked submarines. It even served during the Korean War. Now its civilian offspring flew between mainland Australia and the isolated Lord Howe Island more than three hours of flight time off the coast. As a licensed navigator, Phil was often called upon to calibrate, or swing, the aircraft's compass. He also flew as a navigator to Lord Howe Island.

The Sandringham was a sizeable aeroplane with its four wing-mounted engines and a keel for its belly. People would gather on the shore to witness the comings and goings of the giant floating aircraft that harked back to a romantic time when such machines were the link between Australia and Mother England. The Sandringham would cast off like any other waterborne vessel, but would aim into wind and roar across the swell before slowly rising to the sky.

For Phil, it was yet another reason to enjoy going to work until, after only six months with the airline, a number of pilots were retrenched. As one of the most recently hired, Phil was let go. Shattered, he returned home and without a word walked in and stared into the fireplace. Edith asked the obvious question and in a low voice he told her that he had been laid off. At first she thought he was joking and laughed, but the pain in his eyes when he raised his head told her otherwise.

He had left the military, he had left Qantas and now here he stood out of work with a young family and very few prospects. Too embarrassed to return to Bankstown for a third time and seek work as a flying instructor, he took a job with the Ford Motor Company, driving new vehicles onto the back of trucks for transport around the country. Up and down the ramps he drove the cars for three months without any other worker knowing his background or skill set. Occasionally, Ansett ANA, the parent company of Airlines of NSW, would call on him to serve as a duty pilot at the airport to process flight plans and other ground-based tasks. Still, there was no flying job on the horizon.

When a call came from the Illawarra Flying School, he humbly accepted the job. He felt that he had deserted them to go to Airlines of NSW but they didn't seem at all phased so it was back to a world of briefings and students, although the open cockpit Tiger Moths were now replaced by Austers and modern Cessnas with enclosed cockpits, heaters and radios.

For the next five years Phil would repay the school's generosity and forgiveness and gain a reputation around the airfield as one of the premier flight instructors. The list of aircraft types he flew continued to grow as the industry boomed and new aircraft arrived in crates on ships at an incredible rate. Aircraft were sold like cars with glossy brochures and the offer of flight training to new owners.

A prime task for Phil became the training of Qantas cadet pilots for his former employer. Young and fresh faced, the first course arrived at Bankstown in 1965 and by this time another son, Owen, had been born. Phil not only trained the next generation of airline pilots, but kept them entertained with stories of Meteors in combat and a dry sense of humour. Between lessons he would sometimes be called upon to tow banners announcing that "Waltham is a Good Watch", but it was the towing of targets that grabbed the cadets' attention.

Illawarra owned retired Mustang fighters that now wore civil schemes upon

Family man. Phillip and Edith with their children Owen, Pamela and Adrian, 1966.

their flanks. Equipped with a winch and a small back seat for the winch operator, they would tow targets for the military to shoot at as Phil had done in his previous life. Sometimes the Mustangs were also flown in support of Army or Navy exercises. On one pass of a warship the gunners got a little too close for comfort, severing the target cable not too far from the Mustang's tail.

Each time one of the Mustangs started its Merlin engine, the cadets would rush to the fence and watch the famous fighter take to the air. As they stood waiting one afternoon, Phil opened the Mustang's throttle and roared down the runway. With its tail in the air and just about to lift off, the engine cut out and the take-off was abandoned. Phil brought the Mustang to a halt with very little airfield remaining. The students were aghast.

From their vantage point they could see the canopy slide back and Phil step down onto the wing before beginning the long walk back to the flight office. As he walked passed, one cadet asked, "What happened, Mr. Zupp?" Without breaking stride, Phil replied, "I left my cushion in the office and I couldn't see over the nose." It was a reason the student pilots believed until later in the day when an engineer informed them that the engine had actually failed.

Soon the cadets were accustomed to his use of understatement and dry sense of humour as well as his inability to remember their names. He retained his calm, quiet style in the cockpit as he had always done, but they all envied his ability to fly the Mustang. Surrounded by deteriorating weather near an escarpment, one cadet had decided to return to Bankstown rather than persevere. Only a small gap existed between the cloud base and the top of the hills and it wasn't where a low time pilot wanted to be experimenting. As he commenced the turn, he spotted a Mustang at low level, darting towards the gap, beyond which lay the coast and the Naval base where target towing duties awaited. At that moment, the Mustang rolled inverted and, upside down, slipped through the narrow band of clear air. In an instant, he knew which pilot was at the controls. The fighter pilot blood still pulsed in Phil's veins.

In time, Phil moved to Rex Aviation where the flying would be more varied charter work and almost exclusively on more advanced twin-engine aircraft. He often thought of his Air Force mates, but Wal Bowles was about his only constant contact having become the godfather to his son, Owen. Phil envied Vance Drummond who was still flying operationally in the RAAF and, having served in Vietnam, he was now the commanding officer of No. 3 Squadron flying the new delta-wing Dassault Mirage fighter jet.

However, Phil's envy turned to sympathy when news came through that Vance had been lost in a Mirage off Williamtown when he failed to pull out of a dive and plunged into the ocean. The man he had joined the RAAF alongside all those years ago was gone. He had survived the ditching of the Wirraway in Lake Corangamite, being shot down over Korea and held as a prisoner-of-war. Without doubt, Vance was one of the finest men Phil had ever served with and he always knew the handsome New Zealander was a level higher than those around him and destined for greatness in the Air Force. Now he was gone and, like Bill Purssey, it was left to his family to posthumously receive his Distinguished Flying Cross. In this case, however, it fell upon his nine year old son.

The Mirage also claimed another Point Cook course-mate in 1969 when Johnny Myers crashed into the sea off Singapore at night while attempting a radar intercept. Having claimed two mates, both Korean veterans, Phil wondered about the Mirage. It looked like a dream, but he suspected that it was also somewhat unforgiving. The only thing for sure was that Phil would never get his hands on a jet fighter again.

There were still moments where flight threw down a challenge for Phil and

The Cessna 402 that Phil flew in cloud-seeding operations.

some were subtler than others. As the new power station was being constructed at Lake Liddell, Phil would routinely fly a twin-engine Cessna, carrying people and parts, into the small sloping airstrip. Prior to one return flight out of Lake Liddell, he was asked to return some equipment to Bankstown. On hearing the weight of the components, he agreed and the crews loaded the aircraft while he grabbed a bite of lunch. On returning to the Cessna, something wasn't right. The aircraft was sitting low on its undercarriage and there was genuine difficulty in closing the door.

He climbed inside the aircraft and reviewed the paperwork. The components were from France and their weight was in the foreign unit of kilograms, rather than pounds. The aircraft was carrying more than twice its legal limit and the load had warped the metal fuselage. Phil peered down the hill towards a small lake at the end of the runway knowing full well that's where he would have crashed if the error hadn't been detected.

Perfectly legal, but far more exciting, was the rain making operations around Mackay in Queensland. Having grown up among drought and dying cattle, Phil had been keen to participate and see the science involved firsthand. The Commonwealth Scientific and Industrial Research Organisation (CSIRO) was experimenting by seeding clouds with either dry ice or silver iodide deposited through a chute attached to the Cessna 402 aircraft that Phil was to fly. The concept was that the materials would cause the moisture in the clouds to freeze and ultimately become rainfall.

The CSIRO were specifically targeting towering cumulus clouds for their experiments and as Phil climbed towards them, the two scientists on board would point towards which particular cloud they wanted to seed. Phil would look at the billowing white forms, knowing that their insides consisted of very strong up and downdrafts. He would tighten his harness as if he was in Korea again and fly straight into the jaws of the cloud. Then, the aircraft was bounced, buffeted and bashed by the turbulence within.

It took every ounce of concentration to keep the aircraft upright as the scientists dispensed their load. He wrestled with the Cessna as the airspeed fluctuated and it took turns to enter soaring climbs and plunging descents. At times the aircraft would be battered by hail and Phil wondered why these clouds needed any further encouragement to generate precipitation. Then they would be spat out of the cloud into clear air until the scientists pointed towards another cloud.

From cloud to cloud they would fly until the sortie was declared complete by which time Phil had no idea where he actually was. His radio compass was sometimes beyond the useful range of the nearest airport, and subject to interference, so he would simply fly to the coastline and head north or south waiting for a recognisable feature before heading back to Mackay.

It was some of the most violent flying he had undertaken since combat and he was amazed at both the strength of his aircraft and the inner fortitude of the scientists. However, having seen the dark insides of the clouds, he was quite convinced that it would have rained anyway and wondered whether any worthwhile data was ever actually gathered.

Leaving Rex Aviation and cloud seeding behind, Phil spent a year flying a corporate aircraft for businessmen but was retrenched once again when the company lost the contract. He joined Masling Commuter Airlines in 1974 with the hope that it would provide some degree of stability for his career. The airline had been established for some years and the heart of the Masling fleet was the ten passenger Beechcraft Queen Air. Working out of Sydney airport, the job came with all the trimmings of gold braid and the appearance of an airline, but Phil was soon less than impressed by some of the work practices.

The aircraft were at times unreliable and he shut down engines on numerous occasions. One evening as he flew through torrential rain, his left engine began to vibrate severely. He reduced power and tried to troubleshoot the problem without success as the vibration grew severe each time he attempted to increase power. He decided to put the engine out of its misery, bringing the spinning propeller to a halt and positioning the propeller edge on to the airflow, limping the Queen Air to Sydney. The rod connecting a piston to the crankshaft, or 'con rod', had snapped in two.

Following an early morning departure and again in pouring rain, the right hand engine fire warning sounded with its shrill bell and red light. He shut the engine down and shot the extinguishing agent into the engine at which time the warning became silent. As he wheeled the Queen Air about to return to land, the fire warning on the left hand engine sounded. He looked for a paddock to land the aircraft but the rain was so heavy that it was nearly impossible. The left hand engine was still operating so Phil scanned the gauges one more time, deciding to keep the engine going and make for the airfield as there was no smoke or flames visible. He prayed there wasn't an uncontained fire alive within the wing.

With great relief, the airport appeared through the gloom and he descended without delay, touching down moments later. It was found that the first warning was genuine, but the second was the result of incorrect wiring. For a former mechanic and Air Force pilot, this was an unforgivable oversight that nearly had him landing the aircraft in a field knowing that an uncontrolled fire can burn right through a wing in minutes.

It was one of many incidents that he raised with the owner, Jack Masling. In time the situation grew worse and Phil began to have head-to-head clashes with Jack over maintenance, the treatment of junior pilots and the unreasonable hours they were being asked to work. He refused to accept an aircraft due to a worn tyre and then that same aircraft blew a tyre on a subsequent landing. Things came to a pivotal moment when Phil refused to use a new unofficial taxiway until he had paced it out and compared its width with the wheelbase of the Queen Air.

Jack fronted Phil about delaying the flight for the minutes that it took to survey the new taxiway. "I pay you to be a commercial pilot. You have a licence, don't you?" It was a step too far. "Yes I do and I have a damn sight more experience than you, so as pilot-in-command I'll go when I'm bloody ready!" Within hours, fate was to deal Phil a rare, generous hand.

He was still seething as he helped his passengers down the Queen Air's stairs at Sydney Airport, but little did he know, he was being watched. In an office above the parking apron, the Chief Pilot of NSW Air Ambulance operations, Captain John McCracken, was lamenting his shortage of crew to Captain Chuck Wood. Chuck was in charge of Flight Operations for East-West Airlines, the airline that held the coveted contract to provide aircraft and crews to the NSW Department of Health.

Like Maslings, the Air Ambulance operated Queen Airs, but the difficulty lay in the experience requirements set down by the Department of Health that called for significant night flying hours as pilot in command. Such pilots were few and far between that hadn't already been recruited by major airlines. Chuck Wood pointed to Phil beside his Queen Air below, "What about that bloke? Who's he?"

McCracken looked down at the bald pilot carrying the bags of a female passenger. "Phil Zupp, I think. He was a war hero or something. He must have a few hours on those Queen Airs by now."

"His uniform is always immaculate, shiny shoes, the whole lot. Why don't we get him?" Chuck chimed in. He had hardly completed the sentence when McCracken had left the office and begun descending the stairs to the aircraft apron.

He approached Phil who was busy wiping some oil from the engine's cowlings and enquired if he would be interested in a position with East West Airlines, flying the Air Ambulance. Phil couldn't say "yes" fast enough, after three years with Maslings, he was at the end of his tether.

"When can you start?", there was a sense of urgency in McCracken's voice. "Ideally, we'd like you tomorrow." He added, knowing there was only a slender chance that could happen.

"Leave it with me." Phil replied with a half-grin on his face before shaking McCracken's hand and readying for the next load of passengers who were about to board.

That night Phil sat down, completed his log book and then carefully set about writing a letter of resignation, or seven in fact. Each letter had Phil's resignation taking place with immediate effect. They were dated sequentially and placed in one of seven envelopes which had the corresponding date and day of the week written on its face. He then placed the seven letters in his flight bag.

When he encountered his employer the next day, Phil did not hold back on how he thought the operation was being run. Sentence after sentence he needled Jack with a growing level of provocation until the conversation reached boiling point.

"Well if you don't like it you can leave!" Jack lashed out.

"I would, but you would probably want two weeks' notice, wouldn't you?" Phil replied in a calm, even voice.

"For all I care, you can go right now!"

Phil bent down and pulled the envelopes from his bag and slowly flicked through them one by one as Jack looked on with a sense of confusion. Phil double-checked the front of the selected envelope then handed the appropriate letter of resignation to Jack without a word. He then picked up his flight bag, turned on his heel and began walking towards the offices of East West Airlines.

Phil stands beside a NSW Air Ambulance 'Queen Air'.

Chapter Thirty-Eight

Air Ambulance

Phil knew he had finally found a real job in civil aviation that wasn't an airline job as soon as he walked on to the NSW Air Ambulance flight line a few days later. The pilots all wore full East West Airlines uniform and the highly qualified flight nurses wore the additional insignia of paramedics. The white Queen Airs were trimmed with red and shone in the sun, busily attended to by engineers in white overalls. At the far end of the line an engineer was draining fuel from the aircraft's wings. When Phil enquired, the engineer replied that the aircraft had been slightly over-fuelled and was consequently over its maximum take-off weight. At that point Phil knew immediately that he had finally found the ideal job.

The aircraft were flown across the state by a single pilot with a flight nurse on board. The Queen Airs were ageing but immaculately maintained and flew a combination of routine services and emergency flights with minimal notice to become airborne. He would often run into old mates like Ken Towner and Col King who were flying in the airline ranks for East West. However, it was in the Air Ambulance ranks that Phil was in his element, in both the nature of the flying and the sense of team that he had not felt since the Air Force. Even if the phone rang at 2am, he could be heard whistling as he readied for departure.

A good deal of the flying was to remote country airstrips, at night and often in inclement weather, but Phil liked the challenge. The nurses also came to like flying with the older gentleman that always waited back after the flight to help them unload the aircraft, restock their supplies and walk them to the car park. In the air they also felt comfortable with Phil and trusted his judgement implicitly.

An emergency call came in midway through a day's flying as the Queen Air sat on the apron at a remote airport under low cloud and falling rain. A sick child at a relatively nearby township needed to be retrieved and taken to a major hospital.

However, the airport did not possess a navigation beacon and there was no means of descending through cloud to the runway once they arrived. The only possible option was to declare a 'Mercy Flight' and proceed under the cloud base in less than ideal conditions.

Phil made the call to proceed and told the flight nurse, Kay Melmeth, to stay on the ground and he would retrieve the child and a new nurse at the destination. Kay would hear none of it. She was coming too. She had seen how Phil flew with a topographical map constantly on his knee and that he knew just about every feature of the terrain off by heart.

The two set off at low level with Kay strapped into the front seat beside Phil. As if he were back in Korea, he flew in the nap of the earth, anticipating the next road or power lines and altering course as needed. The visibility beneath the cloud was good, but the overcast kept them pinned down. Kay sat speechless as the trees flew by in a blur, in awe of the pilot beside her, his eyes looking well ahead and subtly nudging the aircraft as the fields rose to meet them, or the valley threaded left or right.

Her attention was caught by the sound of the engines starting to lower as Phil retarded the levers with hardly a glance inside. Next the flaps began to extend from the wings and the wheels were lowered. Kay could see nothing and wondered if there was a problem. "All secure? It's just around the corner." Still at a loss, Kay watched as Phil turned the Queen Air around a small hill as light rain spattered the windscreen. "There it is. Dead ahead." Kay still couldn't see it.

Then it appeared, a narrow strip of tar, its shiny surface almost camouflaging it among the standing water surrounding it. Moments later they were on the ground. Kay would always relate the flight as the most amazing in her time as a flight sister.

Phil was also called to appear at an inquest as an expert witness after a rescue helicopter had crashed in dreadful weather while he was making his approach to land nearby. Wal Bowles was now the senior investigator with the Bureau of Air Safety Investigations (BASI). Wal often called Phil for his input and opinion during accident investigations, but on this occasion he was one of many seated in the courtroom. While not meaning to, at times Phil had the court in fits of laughter with some of his answers as the lawyer tried to discredit both the helicopter pilot in question and Phil.

Phil was in command of the final flight of VH-AMB which now hangs in the Powerhouse Museum, Sydney. (Image: Paul Sadler)

At one stage, the 'Perry Mason' style lawyer paraded in front of the courtroom and said, "Striking rows of power cables can prove fatal in an aircraft, can't it?" Phil's dry response was, "Actually, in my opinion, you only need to hit one." The lawyer then unwisely chose to question his experience, "...but Captain Zupp, your flying experience appears to have been on multi-engined aircraft. Have you had *any* experience flying single-engined aircraft at night?"

Phil paused and then replied, "I've got over 500 hours in my log book flying single-engined aircraft at night, and I can tell you, it frightens the living daylights out of you!" At the end of the inquest the coroner, Mr. Derrick Hand, thanked Phil for his input and commented, "Captain Zupp, I'd fly with you anywhere".

The flights were not always so dramatic and there were funny moments on occasions too. Descending into a remote country airport in the middle of the night, Phil called the paramedics on the ground using a dedicated radio that the Queen Air carried. As the paramedics were trained to read the wind strength and direction from the windsock, Phil asked the current situation to help plan his arrival. The response was a country drawl, "The wind's coming from my left." Phil thought quickly. "Don't move. Where's the terminal building?" The subsequent answer gave him the information he needed and a laugh or two as well.

Phil also had cause to play patient on the very aircraft he flew. While on annual leave, he was driving through the NSW country town when an annoying abdominal pain of the last few days became too much to manage. Almost collapsing at the wheel, he turned the car into a motel and promptly fell on the bed. Within hours he was undergoing exploratory surgery to find that he was suffering from acute appendicitis and the appendix was actually gangrene. In recovery, he proved a terrible patient, refusing a catheter, or even to use a bed-pan, preferring to risk tearing his stitches by shuffling to the bathroom.

When it came time to be discharged, the only way home was via the air ambulance. When he was wheeled out to the waiting Queen Air with an I.V. line hanging from its stand, the flight nurse did not recognise Phil at first and when she did she thought it was a practical joke. Phil's response was to pull the sheet and surgical gown back to expose the huge scar on his lower abdomen, changing the mood immediately.

By 1985, after nearly a decade with the air ambulance, Phil knew his career was drawing to a close. He was 59 years old and had nearly 23,000 hours in his logbook spread across about 100 aircraft types. In recent years he had tried to find a hobby, making a number of free-fall parachute jumps and flying gliders solo. However, both of these activities were dependent upon others and he was never one for the club environment. He found the most relaxation on his own shooting at targets at the rifle range.

By now Owen was working as a paramedic and working towards his own Commercial Pilot's Licence. Phil was his instructor and had set up their garage with models and chalkboards to train his youngest son in the ways of aviation. He knew he was tough on Owen at times, perhaps tougher than he'd been on any student under his care, and he didn't really know why. Still, week by week, they would fly together and, when able, he would have him accompany him in the air ambulance.

The first NSW Air Ambulance Queen Air was also due for retirement, although its time came first. Having flown around 24,000 hours, nearly four million miles and bearing the markings VH-AMB, the loyal aircraft was to be put out to pasture. After being stripped of everything useable, it would make one final flight from East West Airlines' maintenance base at Tamworth to Sydney before it would be

The time draws near. Phil looks back from the cockpit of the Air Ambulance 'Super King Air' on one of his final flights.

taken to the Powerhouse Museum and hoisted to the roof for display. Fittingly, Phil flew the gutted Queen Air on its last journey and he couldn't help thinking that their lives were a little in parallel.

As he pulled 'AMB up to the hangar for the last time, there were cameras there to meet them both. Before climbing down the stairs, he hurriedly unscrewed the hook from which the microphone had hung and pocketed it for engraving at a later date. The old Queen Air had served its people well, but now it was time.

Phil also appreciated that he was ageing. Despite staying fit jogging, riding and spending time laying blows on a punching bag, he was still very mortal. As a safeguard, he would give the flight nurses 'flying lessons' when the aircraft was without patients on board, knowing that, as a single pilot, there was always the chance he could become incapacitated, or worse. It never happened, although tragedy did strike the close-knit operation.

Pre-dawn, the dimly-lit parking apron was a noisy place with numerous aircraft warming up their engines for the day ahead. Just as they were ready to depart, flight nurse Audrey Jordan realised she had left a piece of equipment behind. She hurriedly descended the stairs of the Queen Air and, in her haste, walked into the spinning propeller. The pilot saw her at the last moment but his efforts to shut the engine down were too late. The propeller blades struck and killed her.

The air ambulance team felt the blow deeply. In the aftermath, Phil and Edith came to care for Audrey's grave and assist her family when they travelled from the United Kingdom. Now married for 25 years, and their three children well grown, Phil and his wife also regularly communicated with the families of Air Force mates he had lost along the way. In particular, they would spend time with Gladys Strawbridge, the mother of Bob who had been lost after Korea in a mid-air collision off Williamtown. They would often stop by for morning tea and Gladys still feared for Phil flying even years after Bob's accident. Now that Phil's son, Owen, was learning to fly she was doubly apprehensive.

One sunny morning at Gladys' home, she had set up morning tea in the garden, but Phil politely asked for it to be moved indoors to the sunroom. Edith looked at him quizzically but could see that this wasn't one of his practical jokes. He looked genuinely uncomfortable as he stood in the back doorway. The two women gathered up the plates and scones, unsure of the reason behind the request. Only later, as they drove home, did Phil explain to Edith. "She's got Frangipanis in her garden." Edith was still none the wiser. "When I smell Frangipanis, all I can smell is blood." The jungles of New Guinea were still with him. The war in Korea was also soon to pay him a visit.

Chapter Thirty-Nine

The Purple Heart

Phil had never even had his medals mounted until Edith had done so recently as a wedding anniversary gift. Before that, some were in the brown paper box that the government had posted them in while a couple were in an old box that once held gun camera film. Only the US Air Medal was in a presentation case, complete with a matching lapel pin. By contrast, Phil's most treasured memento was a subtle, dark brown, returned from active service badge and each ANZAC day he would pin it to his coat and attend the dawn service. He never marched in the parade, although Edith did.

Phil was proud of his service, but he was still fundamentally very shy. At the end of each ANZAC Day march, the lads would all catch up for a drink, but Phil hadn't been a drinker then and he wasn't now. He'd rather sit on the sidelines and pick out familiar faces or wave to Edith as she went by. At the dawn service he could stand in the dark, unnoticed and pay his respects with sincerity and privately remember his mates that never came home. In that pre-dawn there were never any tears, but sometimes his eyes were looking many years and many miles from the cenotaph where he was standing.

When Owen first walked in one sunny afternoon, Phil didn't even raise his eyes from the newspaper, let alone notice the large blue book in Owen's hands. Only when his son planted the volume on a nearby table and begin to flick to pre-

The United States Purple Heart.

positioned bookmarks of paper shreds did it peak his interest. "What's that?"

Owen explained that while waiting in Canberra for a hospital transfer, he had parked his ambulance outside the Commonwealth Government Publishing Office and decided to take a look inside. The book that measured nearly two inches thick was by Professor Robert O'Neill and titled, 'Australia in The Korean War 1950-53. (Volume Two) Combat Operations'. It had just been published and was on a stand near the front door. With relatively little having been written about the Korean War, Owen bought the book without hesitation.

Phil raised an eyebrow and commented, "I might read that some time." He then returned to reading his newspaper.

"Dad, were you awarded the Purple Heart?"

Expressionless, Phil lowered the paper again and called out, "Edith! Did I get the Purple Heart?"

Edith walked in from the kitchen. "I don't think so. I'll check." Such details were best left in Edith's hands.

In the back of this new book was a comprehensive list of every award made during the Korean War. It had listed Phil's US Air Medal and being Mentioned-in-Despatches but under 'Purple Heart' it also listed "A11439 Zupp, Sergeant P." The

"Rough Diamond". Phil's personnel file showing his Commanding Officer's comments and reference to being awarded the Purple Heart. (Source: AWM. Governor-General's File K/246)

The Purple Heart

> By direction of the President, Sergeant Phillip Zupp, A11439, Royal Australian Air Force has been awarded the Purple Heart.
>
> CITATION.
>
> On 6 February 1952 Sergeant PHILLIP ZUPP distinguished himself by displaying outstanding courage while flying Meteor Mark Eight type aircraft in carrying out a search for a downed pilot in an area heavily defended by enemy anti-aircraft fire. Sergeant ZUPP sighted what he believed to be distress panels and in coming down to a dangerously low altitude to investigate he received an explosive burst of enemy fire which destroyed his canopy and wounded him in the face. Despite shock and low altitude Sergeant ZUPP was able to regain control of his aircraft and returned safely to base. Sergeant ZUPP'S outstanding courage and superior airmanship on this occasion reflects great credit upon himself, his comrades in arms of the United Nations and the Royal Australian Air Force.

The citation that accompanied the recommendation for the award of the Purple Heart. (Source: AWM. Governor-General's File K/246)

decoration that the Americans had recommended for him after his canopy was blown off in 1952, and that Ron Susans had listed in Phil's personnel file, had now surfaced in an official document after more than thirty years.

The Purple Heart was traditionally a decoration of the United States, awarded to those wounded or killed while serving, and now here was a book written by Australia's official historian for the Korean War stating that Phil had been the only Australian to be awarded it. Admittedly, he had already been officially awarded the Air Medal by the United States, but this was different. Phil's interest was minimal, but Edith, being a prolific letter writer, began to follow up on the mysterious medal.

Along with Owen, they approached everyone from the United States Air Force to Australian defence ministers but at every turn met with a dead end. The Zupps were told it was not possible, it never happened. It was clear the officials thought Phil was an American. Each response took months to arrive and none bore any good news. Some requests never even received a reply.

For Phil's part, he was more focused on his retirement. East West Airlines had asked him to stay on a further six months beyond his 60th birthday to assist in introducing a new aircraft type, the Beech King Air 200. A pressurised turbo-prop aeroplane, it not only had superior performance to the Queen Air, it could fly above the weather and clear of a good deal of turbulence while still offering an oxygen-rich cabin for the patients. Phil agreed as he was keen to fly the King Air, but he made it clear that it was for six months only.

When July 31st 1986 arrived, Phil parked the brakes of the air ambulance for the last time. Pilots, paramedics and nurses turned out in force to see him land one last time. The formal farewell came a few evenings later as his workmates took turns relating stories about Phil to the gathered crowd. When John McCracken stood up to make the final contribution, he closed by looking Phil in the eye and saying, "If my life depended upon someone strapping an aeroplane to their arse and getting me safely from A to B, I would choose Phil Zupp every single time."

When Phil was called upon to say a few words he stumbled through his thanks with difficulty, still loathing public speaking. He paid tribute to the way in which East West Airlines conducted the air ambulance operation and the fantastic work done by all of the NSW Ambulance staff across the state. Finally, he thanked all of those he had worked with over the past decade. His last words to the gathered crowd were, "This was the best job that I ever had without getting shot at."

They presented him with a NSW Ambulance plaque and a painting of his beloved Mustang tearing up through the clouds. As the festivities resumed, he remained by the artwork staring at the single-engine fighter he had flown for the first time so many years before. As Owen sidled up beside him, he didn't move his gaze from the painting. "You know the best thing about the Mustang, boy?" he asked of his 21 year old son.

"The V-12 Merlin engine?"

"No."

"The great visibility of the bubble canopy?"

"No." He took a breath. "One bloody seat. No one beside you going yabba-bloody-yabba." It would seem that Phil never really was an airline pilot at heart.

The Purple Heart

NAME	ZUPP, Phillip						
Award	PURPLE HEART U.S.A.	Reg. No. A11439	Rank	SGT.	Service	R.A.A.F.	
Recommended by Governor-General on	—						
Promulgated in *London Gazette* on	—				G. H. File	R.A.A.F. K/246.	
Promulgated in *Commonwealth of Australia Gazette* on							
Citation (G. H. File) RAAF K/246.	Outstanding courage & superior airmanship bringing damaged aircraft to base whilst wounded.						
Insignia received from London	N/A	PN LONDON.	N/A		G. H. File	—	
Insignia presented by	—						
At	—	On	—	G. H. File	—		
Address of recipient on presentation date							
Remarks	Commonwealth Government agreed to recommendation on 22/5/52. Commonwealth Government agrees to suggestion of Secretary of State for Commonwealth Relations that recommendation be withdrawn on 7/1/53.						
Other Awards	M.I.D., U.S.A. AIR MEDAL						2270.

"Outstanding courage and superior airmanship."
(Source: AWM. Governor-General's File K/246)

By this time, the options of pursuing the Purple Heart seemed to have reached an impasse. Those letters that were going to be answered had been answered. Professor O'Neill had kindly replied that if it was listed in the book, that Phil had received the Purple Heart, then somewhere there was a record reflecting that. Not knowing where to begin looking for such a document, Edith contacted Jim Flemming.

Phil's old Air Force friend had risen to the rank of air vice-marshal before retiring and now held the post of director at the Australian War Memorial. Edith outlined the mystery of the medal as it stood and, initially, she heard nothing in return. Then a large yellow envelope arrived with a covering letter from Jim. Inside was a copy of a file titled, 'GOVERNOR-GENERAL'S OFFICE. R.A.A.F K/246' and the subject, 'SERGEANT PHILLIP ZUPP. A11439'.

Within the file lay a paper trail that commenced just after Phil's fateful sortie in 1952 and criss-crossed the globe between the United States, Korea, Australia and the United Kingdom. There was correspondence between governments and generals and, unknown to Phil, he had been at the centre of a diplomatic melee.

The process had been initiated by an American officer only days after Phil had been wounded. Under the title of 'Award of the Purple Heart', the officer had sent the newly created file to the Headquarters of the British Commonwealth Forces in Korea and the USAF 4th Fighter Interceptor Wing in San Francisco as well as a copy to Phil's commanding officer, Ron Susans.

Within that file was Phil's personnel file, signed off by Susans as having been "wounded in action. Awarded American Purple Heart and Air Medal." Even more telling was a detailed citation praising Phil's actions and it left no doubt regarding the award. It stated,

> By direction of the President, Sergeant Phillip Zupp, A11439, Royal Australian Air Force has been awarded the Purple Heart.
>
> CITATION
>
> On 6 February 1952 Sergeant PHILLIP ZUPP distinguished himself by displaying outstanding courage while flying Meteor Mark Eight type aircraft in carrying out a search for a downed pilot in an area heavily defended by enemy anti-aircraft fire. Sergeant ZUPP sighted what he believed to be distress panels and in coming down to a dangerously low altitude to investigate he received an explosive burst of enemy fire which destroyed his canopy and wounded him in the face. Despite shock and low altitude Sergeant ZUPP was able to regain control of his aircraft and return safely to base. Sergeant ZUPP's outstanding courage and superior airmanship on this occasion reflects great credit upon himself, his comrades in arms of the United Nations and the Royal Australian Air Force.

This citation dismissed so many of the rebuttals that Edith and Owen had received. At every turn in the citation he is recognised and named as an Australian pilot. There was an air of excitement as they turned the next page.

It was from Lieutenant-General W. Bridgeford, the commander-in-chief of the British Commonwealth Forces in Korea, to RAAF Headquarters in Australia and within the text he stated, "I strongly recommend that Her Majesty's permission is sought for the acceptance of this award."

Next, the Australian Prime Minister's Office forwarded a list of foreign awards to the Governor-General W.J. McKell for approval. Again, the recommendation for the award of the Purple Heart to "A11439 Sergeant Phillip ZUPP" was strongly supported.

It seemed to be an open and shut case, however the subsequent pages began to cool their certainty. The pages contained a debate that bounced between Parliament House, Canberra and The Secretary of State for Commonwealth Relations, London, about the eligibility of Commonwealth servicemen to wear US decorations and the Purple Heart was a source of contention. The London Office noted that "No award of the Purple Heart has been accepted on behalf of a member of the United Kingdom or other Commonwealth Forces during the war of 1939-45 or Korea. If the policy were now to be changed, this would give rise to a number of difficulties in various directions. It is very much hoped therefore that the Australian Government will not press for the acceptance of the Purple Heart for Sergeant Zupp."

In all, the file spanned nearly two years as the respective governments considered the award to Phil. All the while he was back home in Australia and blissfully unaware that he was at the centre of an international controversy.

When he was shown the file, he sat at the dining room table and read through it carefully, not commenting until he had read the final page. Then he closed the file and sat back in his seat. For him, it wasn't about the medal. What irritated him was that the 'Secretary of State for Commonwealth Relations', who was tucked up safely in London, was denying the wishes of the United States Air Force's operational people on the ground in Korea and the commander-in-chief of the Commonwealth Forces. Just as long ago, he surrendered his Samurai sword to someone that had never seen a shot fired. It seemed that once again a pen-pusher was dictating the outcomes for those that did the fighting and to him that just seemed wrong.

For all intents and purposes, he had been awarded the Purple Heart, but denied the right to wear it. The glowing citation was reminiscent of the words describing an action worthy of the Distinguished Flying Cross, but for some reason the Americans had selected the Purple Heart. Perhaps it was that he had flown the aircraft home wounded and bloodied or perhaps that he had signed himself out of hospital and flown two missions the next day. Bravery can take many forms and possibly it was Phil's understated heroics that impressed them the most. None of that was recorded, just the words "By direction of the President, Sergeant Phillip Zupp, A11439, Royal Australian Air Force has been awarded the Purple Heart."

Now they knew the true story of the Purple Heart, they began to pursue the award once again. Armed with the new evidence, the silence from the authorities was deafening as the old claim of mistaken identity was no longer valid. Owen began writing even more letters with a new-found confidence, but again they were without a satisfactory response. However, a far greater issue was on the horizon and one that would again relegate the Purple Heart to the sidelines.

Chapter Forty

Rising to the Surface

There was no downtime for Phil in his retirement. He stayed fit, he went to the rifle range and he built cupboards out of old aircraft crates. He and Edith traveled the country extensively but, when she didn't wish to travel overseas, he flew to Europe and back-packed alone, always being the only sixty year old at the youth hostel. He traveled to China and saw the Great Wall in a time when organised tours were still in their infancy. When he visited a Chinese science and technology museum, he was struck by the MiG-15 parked on the grass outside.

It was the first time he had seen his Korean War adversary at such close quarters. He walked around it, noting the primitive but effective red pegs sticking up from its wings to indicate that the landing gear was down. He drew in every detail and paused to squat at its nose and examine the muzzles of the cannons jutting forward. Out of nowhere, he was nudged in the ribs and almost fell off balance. A uniformed soldier had pushed him with the butt of a rifle and indicated that he should return to behind the knee-high chain link fence. Phil could see that this chap was very serious about guarding this piece of 1950s technology, so he complied without protest.

Aside from travelling, Phil continued to fly. He occasionally flew DC-3s on charters including filming a Coca-Cola commercial where a giant cooler was thrown out of the aircraft onto a beach. At other times he instructed at a local flying school or simulator centre where yet another generation of Qantas cadets were being trained. The first generation were now captains of Boeing 747s and one student, David Massy-Greene, had set a long distance non-stop record delivering the first Qantas 747-400. Across aviation, in civil and military circles, Phil had created a small legacy without ever realising it.

He soon gained a reputation for being the most dedicated of the new cadets' instructors and would keenly walk beside the basic General Aviation Trainer device, peering through a side port to check on his young students. Sometimes the students would turn the trainer, only to feel a dull thump as they bumped into Phil. Among the cadets, this humorously became known as a 'Zupp Strike'.

He had also trained Owen to become a fully-fledged commercial pilot and, in time, a flying instructor in his own right. In that time he had seen his boy grow into a man and not just in the cockpit. He had seen the news reports of horrendous car accidents and caught glimpses of Owen as a paramedic amid the carnage. He had seen the shirts sprayed in blood at the end of a long night shift.

Phil imparted more than airmanship to his youngest son. He spoke of New Guinea, Japan and Korea as he had not previously done. Often they were told in the context of what can be learned about complacency, pressure and dedication, rather than just another war story. In 1989, when Owen secured a flying job in a remote region on the other side of the country, Phil drove along with him and the two shared many stories including a common knowledge of treating bullet wounds to the chest.

One night, midway through the trip, Phil could not get to sleep. Despite his fatigue from the day's driving, rest was not forthcoming and eventually he began to move about the cabin he shared with Owen. In total darkness, this very quiet man began to speak in a way that he had never spoken before.

Made anonymous by the night, he spoke of his childhood of hard times and the shame of a farm lost. He spoke of war, blood and death. Hour after hour, he delved deeper and deeper into his soul as Owen lay in an awkward silence. Phil jumped from the steamy jungles of New Guinea and a patrol gone wrong, to the frigid hills of Korea and the devastation he witnessed at Hiroshima. The recollections were only interrupted when he offered up answers to his own questions. Phil's mood swung between acceptance and raging hate and only when the clock passed 2am did the pacing subside to infrequent muttering before he finally laid down, slowed his breathing and drifted off to sleep. Owen had not said a single word.

His son had seen a similar outburst only a few months earlier although that had been witnessed by others. Owen was with his girlfriend and family one evening as they watched a current affairs program showing film of alleged attacks by Australian pilots on Japanese lifeboats in World War Two. The presenter started making comments about these attacks possibly being war crimes and pursuing those responsible. Phil's eyes didn't move from the screen but it was obvious that he was becoming increasingly agitated. "And if those Japs made it to land, some bloke like me would have to fight them in the jungle." He spoke as if the presenter could hear.

Next the names of the surviving airmen from the mission began to scroll up the screen. By now he was livid and the veins in his neck were threatening to burst. Not realising that she was walking into a firestorm, Owen's girlfriend innocently asked, "What would you have done in Korea, Mr. Zupp?"

Phil's head snapped around and he began to pound his fist on his hand as he spoke. "If it moved, I fucking killed it! I lined up a bloke on a motorbike one day and blew him to smithereens. How was I to know he didn't have our troops' positions in his satchel?" Without a further word, he rose and left the house, not returning for hours. The gentleman who would not allow a lady to open a door for herself had broken one of his own cardinal rules. Korea had bubbled to the surface in a heated instant, but it was to revisit Phil far more ferociously in the coming months.

As he attended to his morning shaving ritual, he noticed that the moles on his face had grown in size. The brown marks on his cheek and jaw line had once only been faint marks. On getting them checked out, his doctor referred him to a specialist who subsequently removed the growths surgically. When the pathology results came back, the growths contained traces of metal and Perspex. On being questioned whether he could pinpoint their origin he replied simply, "I've got a rough idea. It's a fair while ago now." The shrapnel and canopy shards from 1952 had finally worked their way to the surface. Unfortunately, cancerous growths were also discovered.

Soon a growth began to emerge from his back which was hoped to be benign fibrous tissue. However, when he emerged from surgery, the scar ran almost from his neck to his lower back. Owen's paramedic experience knew immediately what that meant and the doctor's confirmed it when they informed Phil that they had found a significant amount of tumours.

More tests confirmed the inevitable and there were tumours on virtually every major organ in his body, although they could not find a single primary tumour. Due to the nature of the growths, the doctor curiously enquired whether Phil had any exposure to radiation in the past, to which he replied, "Does standing on the aiming point for the 'Enola Gay' in Japan count?" Phil said it with a cheeky grin, but the doctor was not laughing. He told Phil that his condition was terminal and he only had a matter of months to live.

He was told that certain treatment options may extend his life briefly, but ultimately he had lost this battle. He opted not to pursue any course of treatment, preferring to spend the time preparing for the inevitable while he still had some quality of life. He didn't want Edith to be left with anything unfinished so he began painting the house and ruthlessly tidying up his shed, throwing out flying suits and helmets in the process. That was all history now and he didn't want her to have to go through the pain of sorting it out.

He also knew that his pilot's licence medical status was under review and asked Owen if they could take one last flight together before it was too late. The next day, his son readied an aircraft and, at the end of the day's flying, he and his father walked out to the little two-seat trainer. It was a perfectly calm evening with the sun making its descent towards the horizon, giving off hues of orange. For an hour Phil flew a series of take-offs and landings as Owen sat watching him smoothly ease the wheels onto the ground each time with absolute precision.

"It'd be nice to do one on my own." Phil lamented. Owen looked across at the man who had taught him to fly, immediately seeing the longing in his eyes.

"Then you'd better land and let me out" was Owen's only feasible reply.

For the last time in his life Phil eased the throttle open, accelerated down the runway and eased an aircraft into the sky. As it made its initial turn Owen could see it perfectly silhouetted against the setting sun, sweeping across the horizon. As it made its final approach to land it drew ever closer, rock steady as always. Then it crossed the fence and touched down so smoothly it was hard to define the moment when flight had ceased. Phil steered the aircraft clear of the runway, coming to a halt to collect his son. Back inside the cockpit, Phil's eyes didn't move from looking straight ahead. "Are you strapped in?" were his only words and then, "Thanks for that."

In the evening he sat down with his logbook and pen and wrote. "Circuit. Solo.

10 minutes." He drew a double line beneath the final entry and then closed his logbook for the last time, placing it on the shelf beside the eleven other volumes that detailed his life in the air. That life was over.

His usual strength and energy was beginning to visibly fade and subtle bouts of confusion began to surface as the tumours on his brain took an increasing hold. Friends from his past began to emerge and visit. Old Air Force mates and air ambulance pilots and nurses stopped by while Wal Bowles was constantly in touch. However, not all visitors were welcome.

One afternoon Phil answered a knock at the door and there were two men in suits standing there. They introduced themselves hurriedly and, from what he could gather, he thought they were from the Department of Defence to discuss his entitlements. He could not have been more wrong.

As the two men sat down they began to speak and it was apparent that they were lawyers, not government representatives. They had somehow sourced Phil's personal information and shared with him that they were speaking to other veterans about commencing a class action. According to the lawyers, the Australian government had put them in harm's way by sending them to Hiroshima.

Phil let them finish and then unleashed upon them in a surprisingly calm and measured tone. He began, "As a young man, I signed up to take a bullet. Fortunately, mine has taken forty years to get here. A good many of my mates weren't that lucky." He continued, "I have raised a family, owned a house and flown aircraft my whole life. As a kid growing up, surrounded by drought and depression, I may as well have dreamed of flying to the moon. This has all been possible due to my military service. Now, let me get this straight, you want me to sue the very armed forces that made this possible?"

The two men were lost for words until they uttered, "It's not that simple." Phil retorted, "It *IS* that simple. Now get out of my house!" They retreated as Phil rose to his feet. There was still some fight and a great deal of honour in his failing body.

With each day he grew weaker and the family were making plans to come home as Phil was making plans for his final days. His eldest son, Adrian, could see his father failing. He knew that it wouldn't mean much now but he handed his father a box. Phil opened it and inside was a Purple Heart and a small card. On it was written a single word. "Justice."

Chapter Forty-One

The Last Fight

As the final months descended into weeks, Phil pondered the purple medal shaped like a heart, trimmed in gold and bearing the likeness of George Washington. It seemed that everyone believed he had earned the decoration and it was just bureaucracy that stood in the way. He had never really worn his medals but now there was more to it than that. What of the grandchildren he would never know? Didn't they deserve to know the true story and wear the medal with pride?

For only the second time in his life, Phil resolved to break the rules. He asked Owen to have the Purple Heart mounted alongside his other medals once he was gone. He also hoped, at some point, a solution could be found to make the award of the Purple Heart official. With that he gave Owen his medals to preserve and, for the first time in his life, in his final days, his medals truly meant something. They would tell the story to those children yet to be born.

With that resolution, he almost seemed to be at peace with the world, although his health deteriorated at an alarming pace, losing weight and appetite. There were periods of severe pain too, although he endeavoured to keep these hidden from Edith. He began to have difficulty tying his tie and remembering the most basic things. On occasions, Owen had found him on the ground doubled-up in pain, but was sworn, "Not to tell your mother."

When the pain became too severe one night, an ambulance was called but on arrival at the hospital, the staff advised the paramedics to go elsewhere as the hospital was full. The paramedics refused to budge, Phil was one of their own and they had known him in his air ambulance days. Finally, the stand-off abated, although it was some time before he could be seen by a doctor. All the while Owen sat with him to clean his face and catch his vomit in a bowl.

His son was angry. He was angry at the health system, he was angry at his father's

The Last Fight

pain and he was angry at the injustice of the whole bloody deal. Phil looked up at him, disregarding his own suffering. He reached out and placed his hand on Owen's forearm, "It's alright boy. I've had a fair ration."

Everyone knew that the end was near. Phil's brother, Fred, arrived from Toowoomba and was shocked by his emaciated state. But Phil seemed to be waiting for one last arrival, his daughter Pamela. When she arrived, heavily pregnant, Phil greeted her at the front door and his world was now in order with all of his children under the one roof.

He arranged the clothes he was to be buried in, along with his highly polished shoes, wedding ring and watch. Nothing more, nothing less. With this task completed, he confined himself to bed, but still refused any medication to relieve the pain. Still his cheeky grin and wit survived.

He asked Owen if everything was arranged for him to return to Toowoomba to be buried. Owen confirmed that it was and Phil asked, "How am I getting there?" When Owen told him that East West Airlines had offered to fly him to Toowoomba, Phil grinned, "I've flown a lot of aeroplanes over the years, but this will be the first time inside a box and under the floor."

Aside from the humour, his conversations became more disjointed, often confusing generations and one of his sons for the other. Recent memories were gone, but memories of boyhood pranks and his Air Force days were still sharp. Still, it was sad for all to see the once straight-backed officer and gentleman fading so fast. After a week in bed, the pain became too great and he agreed to medication. As the syringe's plunger eased the morphine into his veins, Phil descended into a sleep from which he never woke again.

Owen had been nursing his father and now took to sleeping on the floor beside his bed. Phil's sleep was deep but restless and made it impossible for Edith to lie beside him. In the early hours of July 31st 1991, Phil's breathing became rapid, the change in tone waking Owen. It became even quicker and shallower, the muscles in his neck tightening as if there was one last fight left in the old warrior. He didn't want to go but he had nothing left to offer. Finally, the breathing became imperceptible puffs and then he was gone. Owen reached over and held his father one last time and felt the warmth still left in his body. Then he walked into the darkened living room and lay down by the fire. Some hours later, around dawn, he was woken by his mother's words. "Kids, your father's gone."

Chapter Forty-Two

Without Precedent

When Phil came to make his final flight home, beneath the floor, there was a problem. The type of aircraft flying that day did not have the capability to load a coffin by conveyor belt and it would have to be hand-loaded which the ground-handlers were refusing to do. A solution was quickly found when a handful of East West Airlines captains were seen standing shoulder-to-shoulder beside the aeroplane stating that, "If you don't load Phil on board, we will and we don't care what your union has to say about it."

Phil was buried at Drayton Cemetery next to his mother and father. The small family gathering listened to the minister speak and continually pause as training aircraft from the nearby Toowoomba Airport passed overhead. In the distance, Phil's boyhood home of Glenvale could be seen and Gowrie Mountain where he and Fred had shared so many hours. A few more words and handfuls of dirt cast into the grave and Phillip Zupp was put to rest, his headstone destined to carry the Air Force crest and his favoured phrase, 'Into The Wide Blue Yonder'.

It had been an amazing life for a boy who had started with so little. Despite the constant hurdles, the shy kid from the bush had been the first to leave the farm, the first to fight in two wars in two very different roles and the first Australian to be awarded the Purple Heart. He had never been exceptional, or even particularly social, but he'd always been respected by his peers. Now they gathered at a Sydney church for a memorial service in his honour.

The cousins who he grew up with. The soldiers he fought with. Airline pilots, student pilots, ambulance pilots, paramedics and nurses - they were all there. In this small chapel, Phil's diverse life was represented in faces that spanned a range of generations and fields of endeavour. When the final words had been spoken, they gathered on the lawns to share tales of his life.

Kay Melmeth recounted Phil's low level run in the air ambulance to retrieve a sick child, while 'Vic' Oborn spoke of the day Phil made an even lower second pass in his Meteor to silence two lethal gun pits in Korea. Past students spoke of the quiet instructor with limitless rules of thumb and Wal Bowles remembered the man that could fly a fighter jet with his knees. There was as much laughter as there was tears.

Many of those who had served in the jungle knew nothing of Korea and 'Vic' Oborn knew nothing of Phil's time as a commando. Now they stood as one exchanging anecdotes, completing the picture of a full life that Phil was far too humble to divulge.

Then, in unison, their eyes were cast upwards in the direction of the sound of roaring engines. Soon three aircraft in a tight vee-formation passed overhead. The trio tracked around the horizon and every eye was locked upon them as they lined up for their final pass. The three aircraft grew nearer and nearer and then, just as they arrived, one pulled vertically into the sky and peeled away from the formation in a manoeuvre known as the 'Missing Man'. Not a word was spoken and tears ran down many cheeks for this was his farewell. Phillip Zupp was now gone and this was a final salute to the old fighter pilot. He was now at home in the heavens.

Purple Heart Postscript

Some years after Phil's death, a small parcel arrived. Within it was an insignia representing the South Korean Presidential Unit Citation. The Presidential Citation had been awarded to 77 Squadron RAAF in 1951 "for exceptionally meritorious service and heroism". Today, all current serving members of 77 Squadron are entitled to wear the insignia that was earned in Korea more than sixty years ago. The arrival of the insignia was significant as it was a foreign award that had been recognised, had taken decades to be delivered, and Phil's passing was no barrier to inclusion.

In the intervening years, the award of Phil's Purple Heart has continued to surface in various arenas, including the Australian War Memorial website. Within 'Honours and Awards' for Phillip Zupp, an extract from the Governor-General's file K/246 features and relates the recommendation of the Purple Heart with the citation, "Outstanding courage and superior airmanship bringing damaged aircraft to base whilst wounded."

The award has also appeared in various publications including 'Luck is No Accident', by Colin G. King (2001), which featured an image of Phil's shattered canopy and the caption, "Battle-damaged Meteor, 1952. Sergeant Phil Zupp, hit by flak, suffered a head injury for which he was awarded the US Purple Heart."

Despite the weight of supporting documentation, the Purple Heart has remained elusive and, at times, confusing to the government channels that have been approached. Perhaps the greatest hurdle, that Phil was not a US citizen, still remains. There have been impromptu awards of the Purple Heart, sometimes mistaking foreign servicemen for US personnel, but Phil's case is significantly different.

Firstly, the Purple Heart is not routinely issued with a citation, suggesting that this was a special case from the outset. Secondly, the citation leaves no doubt that the Americans were aware that Phil was an Australian as evidenced by the statement, "Sergeant ZUPP's outstanding courage and superior airmanship on this occasion reflects great credit upon himself, his comrades in arms of the United Nations and the Royal Australian Air Force."

At every turn, the expectation was that Phil should receive the Purple Heart as it was offered by the United States. From his commanding officer and the Commander-in-Chief of Commonwealth Forces in Korea, all the way through to the Governor-General and the office of the Australian Prime Minister, the award was supported. It only struck resistance when it encountered the Secretary of State for Commonwealth Relations in London.

Edith Zupp did not live to receive the Purple Heart on Phil's behalf. However, like Phil in his final weeks, it was her wish that the dramatic events of February 6th 1952 still be formally recognised. She saw Australian veterans receiving the French Legion of Honour after more than fifty years and questioned why Phil could not be shown the same latitude. In his case, the wording of the citation and every other reference was reminiscent of the award of a Distinguished Flying Cross (DFC) or, in the case of a Sergeant Pilot, a Distinguished Flying Medal (DFM). These were awards, both of US and Commonwealth origin, that pilots of 77 Squadron were able to receive during the Korean War.

Towards the end, and tired of the struggle, Edith believed that if justice could not be served through the award of the Purple Heart, then perhaps Phil's act of "Outstanding courage and superior airmanship", could see him receive the DFM from the Commonwealth or the DFC from the United States.

Ultimately, she was fighting for their children, grandchildren, and those yet to be born, and refused to accept that a lack of precedent was justifiable grounds to deny Phil the award. A woman of strong faith, she went to her grave believing that, in the end, justice would prevail. Her fight continues to this day.

Phillip Zupp. My Dad.

Who was my father? That single question was the genesis of this book.

In so many ways, he was an enigma. He was a quietly spoken gentleman that never allowed a lady to open a door and stood when one entered a room. He was comfortable briefing a room of pilots, but loathed public speaking. Yet, somewhere within his small frame, was a man that had lived a life few could imagine.

As I grew up, I knew he had been a soldier and that he had been an Air Force fighter pilot. I also knew, vaguely, that he had fought in wars as I played with his uniforms, flying suits, holsters and helmets. However, his medals were still in the packages they had arrived in years before, unmounted and with pieces of spare ribbon and oak leaf clusters untouched. We attended dawn services, but Dad never marched. We would visit widows and mothers of those who had been killed but, as a youngster, I never appreciated the significance of those lovely ladies and their afternoon teas and probably fidgeted rudely.

I was in my teens before I began to piece his story together, but he was never forthcoming with anything significant about his service. It was just a snippet here or a fragment there. Around this time my mother had his medals mounted and forced him to wear them to an ANZAC Day service where I was standing guard with my cadet unit. I remember being immensely proud, but he looked so awkward and shy and removed his medals as soon as formalities concluded.

Only when I had left my childhood behind did he finally take me into his confidence about his time at war. He would speak of lessons to be learned, close calls and the value of luck. Not once did the concept of heroism ever pass his lips.

When the award of the Purple Heart surfaced, he was curious but demonstrated moderate interest at best. Only in the final years of his life did that change and with it came revelations and details of war that he had never shared and that my mother never knew. Then, he was gone.

As I cleaned out old trunks and pored over documents, details began to fill the gaps but, inevitably, more questions than answers were raised. I began speaking with his squadron mates, but they didn't even know that he'd served in the Army and his Commando colleagues only said that they'd heard he had joined the Air Force. Similarly, the majority of those he encountered in civilian life knew nothing of his military service. However, from all of these people who had played a role in his life, I was overwhelmed by the wealth of information and what my father had actually done.

I was left in a state of flux. What do I do with all of this information? At first I began to collate it for the benefit of our family. This was more than an accumulation of cold facts, however, this was a story. In fact, I believed it was a book.

The next few years were spent interviewing more veterans and researching files from the National Archives of Australia and the Australian War Memorial. The veterans brought detail that only those who served with him could know. What was revealed in the combat records was at times hard to reconcile with the quiet man I knew.

In the end, the book was complete and I think that I could better answer the question, "Who was my father?". As I penned those final chapters, I relived my worst memories. I had watched the strongest and most honest man I had ever known cut down by an enemy he couldn't beat. Even then, he retained his dignity and inspired me to be a better man.

Never one to show emotion, he only believed in shaking hands and uttering a few words of support. That was fine by me. However, if he was standing here today, he would probably be embarrassed. Firstly, that I had written a book about him and, secondly, because I would finally put my arm around him and say, "I love you, Dad."

REST IN PEACE.

Phillip Zupp's Survivors

Despite the passage of years, many of the actual aircraft flown by Phillip Zupp have survived to this day. Some reside in museums, some are atop poles and a good many are still flying. The following list identifies these aircraft and the museums that they now call home.

AUSTRALIA:

Museums

Army Flying Museum (Oakey, Queensland)
Auster Mk III   A11-41   *Involved in accident at Canberra 1951*

Australian Aviation Museum (Bankstown, NSW)
Douglas DC-3   VH-MIN
Grob G-115   VH-TGW   *The last aircraft ever flown by Phillip Zupp.*

Australian War Memorial (Canberra, ACT)
Gloster Meteor F.8   A77-368   *The aircraft in which Phillip flew his first operational sortie in Korea.*

Camden Museum of Aviation (Camden, NSW)
DH Vampire   A79-14
Gloster Meteor F.8   A77-868

Fighter World (Williamtown, NSW)
Gloster Meteor F.8   A77-875

Powerhouse Museum (Sydney, NSW)
Beechcraft B80 Queen Air VH-AMB *Phillip Zupp flew the last flight of this aircraft before its retirement.*

Queensland Air Museum (Caloundra, Queensland)
Douglas DC-3   VH-ANR
DH Vampire   A79-476   *(originally A79-876)*
Cessna 402A   VH-DZY   *Flown in cloud-seeding operations.*

RAAF Museum (Point Cook, Victoria)
Gloster Meteor T.7   A77-305   *(later A77-702)*
DH Vampire   A79-375   *(currently displayed as A79-876)*
DH82 Tiger Moth   A17-711
Douglas C-47 Dakota   A65-78

South Australian Aviation Museum (Port Adelaide, South Australia)
Gloster Meteor F.8   A77-851

The Beck Museum (Mareeba, Queensland)
DH Vampire   A79-89
Douglas C-47 Dakota   A65-73

Wingham NSW
DH Vampire   A79-14   *Displayed on pole.*

Woomera Heritage Centre (South Australia)
Gloster Meteor T.7   A77-229   *(later A77-701)*

Australian Air Force Cadets (Mount Gambier, South Australia)
Link Trainer   A13-110

Under Restoration
CAC Wirraway   A20-309
CA-18 Mustang   VH-BOZ   *(formerly A68-199)*

Phillip Zupp's Survivors

Still on the Civil Register and Possibly Flying

Auster Mk. III	VH-DCL	*(formerly A11-42)*
CAC Wirraway	VH-CAC	*(A20-722)*
DH Leopard Moth	VH-BAH	*(formerly VH-RSL)*
DH Chipmunk	VH-RSP	

DH82 Tiger Moth

VH-CCD	*(formerly A17-673)*	
VH-RVI	*(formerly A17-657)*	
VH-BEN	*(formerly A17-736)*	
VH-BKC	*(formerly A17-717)*	*Phillip Zupp First Solo in RAAF in this aircraft.*
VH-AZR	*(formerly A17-606)*	
VH-FAH	*(formerly A17-521)*	
VH-OVL	*(formerly A17-695)*	
VH-NOV	*(formerly A17-757)*	*(Flew England to Australia 1998 Pilot: B.Markham)*
VH-DEL	*(formerly A17-739)*	
VH-WFN	*(formerly A17-649)*	
VH-TIG	*(formerly A17-728)*	
VH-WAP	*(formerly A17-694)*	
VH-COA	*(formerly A17-759)*	
VH-FFS	*(formerly A17-741)*	
VH-CYA	*(formerly A17-551)*	
VH-PUI	*(formerly A17-753)*	
VH-BBC	*(formerly A17-710 and VH-RSC)*	

Airframes. Non-Airworthy

CAC Wirraway	A20-715	*Lake Corangamite, Victoria.*
Beechcraft B80 Queen Air	VH-CLH	*The Derelict Aircraft Museum Vic.*
Beechcraft B80 Queen Air	VH-AMD	*Darwin NT*
DH Vampire	A79-808	*Dismatled Swansea UK.*

NEW ZEALAND

Ashburton Aviation Museum

Gloster Meteor F.8	A77-867

UNITED KINGDOM

BOSCOMBE DOWN AVIATION COLLECTION

Gloster Meteor U16   WK800   *(formerly Gloster Meteor F.8 A77-876)*

SOLENT SKY MUSEUM (SOUTHAMPTON)

Short Sandringham
"Beachcomber"   VH-BRC

UNITED STATES of AMERICA

CA-17 Mustang   N551D   *(formerly A68-39 and VH-BOY)*
CA-18 Mustang   N50FS   *(formerly A68-187)*

Acknowledgements

Pilot's log books, unit diaries and squadron histories can only provide limited detail when a man's life is fully examined. These carefully arranged documents can tell us a great deal about where, when, and even how, but simultaneously they can hide the very face of the events they report.

While such documents are crucial to provide a framework, it is the personal accounts, the laughter, and even the tears, that weave the true fabric of a life. Over the years in which this story was written, and even before, it has been my honour and privilege to speak with and meet so many wonderful people. Many have been war veterans and some have shared with me stories they had previously buried with their mates. There were those who spoke just a few words over a phone line. Others wrote volumes of notes and then there were those that warmly invited me into their homes. To every single one of you, my life has been forever changed by your generosity, your modesty and your example.

Amid the many names there are some that I must recall. Reg Young for his recollections from Mount Gambier and Phil's first days in the Air Force as a navigator. From the cavalry Commando units, Bill Elliott, Eric Geldard, Ron Scott and Ron Wells shared with me so many stories from basic training through to their active service in the jungles of New Guinea. Ray Twist was prolific with information about the BCOF in Japan.

Perhaps the most abundant resource came from those 77 Squadron pilots that had served in Korea with Phil. Vic Oborn, John Parker, Col King, Wal Rivers, Keith Hill, Keith Martin and Geoff Lushey all provided tremendous insight. Special mention must be made of Jim Flemming who entertained me on numerous occasions with colourful episodes from Phil's life before and after Korea. I am further indebted to Jim for providing me with the file detailing the award of the Purple Heart.

Post-war spanned a further forty years with Wal Bowles, Col Peck and Peter

Waugh all making contributions as did the Qantas cadet pilots of two generations. John McCracken and Kay Melmeth witnessed the sunset of Phil's career with the Air Ambulance and shared recollections of those happy times.

The Australian War Memorial aided me with research and access to the Gloster Meteor Phil had flown while Alan Clements guided me through the cockpit of the Meteor at the Temora Aviation Museum.

To Phil's greater family, particularly his brother Fred, thank you for bringing his early days to life. To my wonderful wife, Kirrily, thank you so much for your support over the years that I have dedicated to this book and understanding that it has meant so much more in so many ways than mere words on a page. To my kids, thank you for your patience. Now you can finally read about, and be rightly proud of, the Grandad you never knew.

Bibliography

A core resource for Phillip Zupp's flying career, including his active service in Korea, was his meticulously kept log books. They not only recorded dates, times and places, but interesting additional notes had been made and certain documents, such as citations and air safety incident reports, were attached. Even so, there was a good deal of information to be found elsewhere.

Official records provided an immense amount of supporting detail. These ranged from the war diaries of the 2/10 Cavalry Commando Squadron and unit history sheets of 77 Squadron RAAF to Phillip's personnel records and so many more.

These facts were combined with Phillip and Edith's own recollections and those of the men that he served with. Despite the passage of time, the recollections of these veterans were incredibly accurate in the vast amount of instances. In a few cases, there were anecdotes for which no supporting documentation could be traced and while I am sure these stories were genuine, I chose not to include them at this time.

Finally, by drawing together the files, the verbal recollections, the photographs and the artefacts, the story of Phillip Zupp emerged.

National Archives of Australia.
Trooper Phillip Zupp. Service Record. QX62413
Flying Officer Phillip Zupp. Service Record. O11439
RAAF No. 77 Squadron Unit History Sheets. (Korea)

Australian War Memorial.
2/10 Commando Squadron War Diary (AWM52)
77 Squadron RAAF. Narrative Reports. (AWM64)

Sergeant Phillip Zupp A11439. Governor General's Office, Honours and Awards File RAAF. (AWM88)

Screensound Australia.
"77 Squadron in Korea"

ADF Serials Website. (www.adf-serials.com.au)
Individual RAAF aircraft histories.

Books.
Bartlett, Norman. *With the Australians in Korea*. Australian War Memorial. (1960)
Donselaar, Annette. (Editor) *Swift to Destroy*. (1986)
Evans, Ben. *Out in the Cold*. Australian War Memorial. (2000)
Hastings, Max. *The Korean War*. Michael Joseph. (1987)
Hurst, Doug. *The Forgotten Few*. Allen & Unwin. (2008)
King, Colin. *Luck is No Accident*. Australian Military History Publications. (2001)
Kirkland, Frederick. *Sometimes Forgotten*. Plaza Historical Service. (1990)
Odgers, George. *Across the Parallel*. William Heinemann Ltd. (1952)
Odgers, George. *Remembering Korea*. Lansdowne Publishing. (2000)
O'Leary, Shawn. *To The Green Fields Beyond*. Sixth Division Cavalry Unit, History Committee. (1975)
O'Neill, Robert. *Australia in the Korean War 1950-53*. The Australian War Memorial and the Australian Government Publishing Service. (1985)
Robson, David. *Of Migs and Men*. Aviation Theory Centre. (2007)
Wilson, David. *Lion Over Korea*. Banner Books. (1994)
Wilson, Stewart. *Meteor, Sabre and Mirage in Australian Service*. Aerospace Publications. (1989)
Wilson, Stewart. *Anson, Hudson and Sunderland in Australian Service*. Aerospace Publications. (1992)
Wilson, Stewart. *Tiger Moth, CT-4, Wackett and Winjeel in Australian Service*. Aerospace Publications. (1994)
Wood, James. *The Forgotten Force*. Allen & Unwin. (1998)

Index

Adachi (Japanese General) 76, 87, 91, 92, 105

Air Medal, United States 236, 245, 246, 273, 323, 324, 325, 328

Air Training Corps (ATC) 16, 20, 21, 22, 25, 30, 133

Airlines of NSW 303, 304, 307, 308

Airspeed Oxford 142, 155, 156, 161, 163, 164, 200

Armit D. * 203, 206, 207

Auster Aircraft 168, 173, 176, 181, 182, 292, 294, 299, 308, 345

Australian War Memorial 215, 324, 325, 327, 339, 341, 344, 345, 351, 352

Avro Anson 34-38, 130, 131, 352

Avro Lincoln 160-165, 195, 282

B-29 Superfortress 84, 85, 104, 258

Bankstown Airport, NSW 292, 296, 308, 310, 311, 345

Bathurst, NSW 53, 54, 57, 58, 75, 179

BCOF (British Commonwealth Occupation Forces) 97, 99, 100, 105, 106, 109, 146, 349

Bed Check Charlie 217

Beech Super King Air 321, 326

Beechcraft Queen Air 312-322, 326, 346, 347

Bennett W. 232, 235, 244, 254, 255, 266-271, 273

Blackwell F. 142, 249

Blamey, Sir Thomas 50, 89, 96, 99

Bowles W. 291, 294, 310, 318, 335, 340, 349

Bromhead S. 220, 225

Browne-Gaylord H. * 171, 174, 181-184, 193, 200, 232, 233, 241

CAC Mustang 109, 140, 146, 155, 160, 165-175, 177-182, 184, 190, 194, 195, 199, 200, 205, 211, 222, 233, 244, 254, 258, 281, 282, 285, 286, 288, 289, 296, 300, 308-310, 326, 346, 348

CAC Wirraway   137, 142, 144-157, 161, 163, 168, 169, 173, 174, 185, 190, 193, 195, 207, 282, 285, 292, 293, 310, 346, 347

Cadan L. 'Scotty'   233, 253

Canungra (Jungle Warfare Training Centre)   59-69, 71-73, 75, 76, 81, 90, 91, 145

Cavalry Commando Squadrons (2/10 and 2/9)   63, 71, 72, 75-77, 83, 85-87, 90-92, 95, 349, 351, 352

Central Flying School (CFS) East Sale   279, 293

Citations   93, 250, 252, 253, 273, 325, 328, 329, 341, 342, 351

Cloud Seeding   311, 312, 346

Colebrook M. * 'Bluey'   252-254, 269

Collins J.   29, 63, 71

Condon E.   124-128, 130, 131, 147

Cooper G.   140, 141

Cowper L. *   235, 247, 251, 255

Cowra, NSW   44, 45, 49, 50, 53, 54, 57, 66, 75, 96

Cranston I. *   235, 237, 246, 269

Darling Downs, Queensland   1, 9, 18, 43, 62, 109, 142, 230, 284, 302

Davis F. **   162-165, 167

Denzel R.   79

DH Chipmunk   299, 347

DH Vampire   130, 132, 135, 173, 180, 185-191, 193-195, 200, 201, 214, 217, 286, 295, 345, 346, 347

DH82 Tiger Moth   92, 124-130, 138-144, 146, 147, 150, 155, 156, 169, 174, 190, 280, 282, 285-289, 299, 300, 308, 346, 347, 352

Douglas DC-3 (C-47)   182, 232, 282, 300, 303, 304, 307, 331, 345, 346

Drummond V. **   141, 142, 144, 152, 153, 156, 167, 185, 203-207, 231, 241, 249, 258, 274, 310

East West Airlines   314, 315, 317, 320, 326, 337, 339

Elliott W.   54, 56-58, 61, 66, 68, 75-77, 80, 89, 90, 92, 95-97, 289

English Electric Canberra   161, 165, 294, 297

Evans J.   235

F-86 Sabre (USAF)   205-208, 216-218, 226, 240, 352

Flemming J.H.   171, 173, 177, 179, 252, 285-289, 291, 295, 327, 349

INDEX

Geldard E.   29, 47, 48, 53, 57, 58, 63, 71, 75, 90, 349

Gillan B. *   142, 145, 155, 158, 167, 179, 180, 185, 204-207, 225, 229-233, 249

Glenvale, Queensland   10, 18, 19, 339

Gloster Meteor T.7 & F   1-4, 155, 173, 183, 186, 194, 195, 198, 200-208, 210-218, 221-225, 227-231, 233-247, 250, 253-271, 274, 276, 280, 289, 290, 294, 296, 297, 300, 308, 328, 340, 341, 345-348, 350, 352

Governor-General of Australia   93, 324, 325, 327, 329, 341, 342, 352

Guy W.   140

Halley J. *   142, 286

Hamilton-Foster P.   244, 246

Hannan, J. 'Butch'   2, 3, 4, 230, 237-239, 241

Hawker Sea Fury   288

Heffernan M. *   29, 47, 48, 53, 57, 58, 63, 71, 75, 90

Hill K. 'Bomber'   237, 238, 241, 244, 349

Hillier D. *   169, 170, 172, 183, 184, 286

HMAS *Duntroon*   71-74

HMAS *Kanimbla*   110, 112, 113

Hubble J.   169, 176-178, 181-183, 185

Illawarra Flying School   304, 308

Japan, Hiroshima   85, 97, 99, 102, 103, 108-110, 140, 141, 197, 199, 200, 202, 252, 258, 332, 335

Japan, Iwakuni   109, 140, 199, 201, 202, 231, 232, 246

Japan, Kaitachi   105

Japan, Kure   101, 102, 107, 110, 113

Japan, Ninoshima   106, 107

Japan, Tokyo   61, 108, 109, 196, 197

Jeffers J. *   78, 79

Jones, Sir George   157, 159, 167

Joye 'Col'   306

K-14 Kimpo   2, 202, 205, 206, 208-213, 223, 231, 232, 235-239, 247, 253, 254, 257, 263, 265, 269, 271

Kaye 'Danny' 303

Kichenside J. 141, 295

King C. 235, 261, 270, 300, 341, 349

Korea, Chaeryong 241, 243, 269

Korea, Chinnampo 220, 222, 246, 266

Korea, Chodo 245

Korea, Haeju 2, 222, 230, 232, 233, 235-237, 244, 245, 247, 249, 252, 270

Korea, Pyongyang 220, 258, 259, 269, 270

Korea, Seoul 261

Korea, Sibyon-Ni 2, 4, 237, 238

Korea, Suwon 213, 219

Lawler E. 77-80

Lawrenson F. * 187, 193

Lockheed Super Constellation 298, 300, 302, 303

Luscombe B. * 168

Lushey G. 257, 258, 266, 271, 349

Martin K. 220, 221, 225, 233, 241, 273, 295, 349

Masling Commuter Airlines 312-314

Massy-Greene D. 331

McCracken J. 314, 326, 350

McDonald J. 80

McMahon P.J. 133, 134, 285

Melmeth K. 318, 340, 350

Mentioned-in-Despatches 250, 253, 324

Middle Ridge, Queensland 19, 44, 113, 114, 250

Middlemiss W. 207, 213

Middleton P. 252, 253, 261, 266, 271

MiG-15 191, 194, 204, 208, 216, 218, 232, 257-259, 261-265, 270, 331, 352

MiG Alley 218, 232

Morotai 100, 101

Murray K. 'Black' 142, 167, 179, 185, 232, 235, 249, 259, 279

Index

Myers J. ** 142, 156, 167, 204, 249, 310

Navigator 24, 28, 31, 32, 35-37, 39, 40, 47, 65, 302, 307, 350
New Guinea, Karawop 73, 75, 76-80, 83-85, 87, 88, 90, 91, 97
New Guinea, Mashuan 73, 77-83, 120
New Guinea, Wewak 72-74, 76, 80, 91, 92, 96, 99-101, 105
NSW Air Ambulance 314, 316, 317, 319, 320-322, 326, 335, 336, 339, 341-343, 349

Oborn 'Vic' 142, 145, 148, 167, 179, 185, 220, 221, 229, 235 ,243, 247, 249, 258, 260, 340, 349

Parker I. 187, 190, 193
Parker J. 235, 295, 349
Peck C. 285, 291, 349
Philp A. 'Blue' 142, 144, 146-149, 151, 154
Prime Minister of Australia 329, 342
Prisoner-of War (Japanese) 45, 46, 92, 97
Prisoner-of-War (Korea) 233, 293, 310
Purple Heart, United States 240, 246, 273, 323-325, 327-330, 335, 336, 339, 341-343, 349
Purssey I. 'Bill' * 233, 247, 254, 255, 269, 310

QANTAS 199, 273, 286, 298, 300, 304, 307, 308, 331

RAAF, 100 Squadron 94
RAAF, 1FTS Archerfield 283, 285, 286, 289, 291
RAAF, 3 Squadron 167-169, 171, 173, 185, 193, 310
RAAF, 75 Squadron 187, 291, 296
RAAF, 77 Squadron 109, 146, 155, 173, 183, 185, 191, 199, 203, 204, 207, 208, 217, 219, 228, 236, 250, 252, 257, 258, 261, 270, 289, 291-293, 341, 342, 349-352
RAAF, Fairbairn (Canberra) 165-173, 177, 179, 181-184, 193, 258, 285, 324, 329, 345
RAAF, Forrest Hill (Wagga Wagga) 123, 125, 127, 132, 135, 140, 147, 185, 324, 329, 345
RAAF, Kingaroy 28, 29, 31, 33, 47, 49, 75, 91
RAAF, Mount Gambier (Air Observer's School) 24, 32, 33, 35, 37, 46, 47, 61, 72, 102, 138, 346, 349
RAAF, Pearce 294, 295

RAAF, Point Cook 134, 137-142, 144, 146, 149-153, 157, 161, 185, 194, 200, 203, 207, 214, 225, 229, 231, 235, 244, 255, 257, 260, 291, 293, 310, 346

RAAF, Rathmines 132, 133, 285

RAAF, Richmond 181, 182, 195, 196, 249, 250, 274, 280, 292, 295, 296

Redmond N. * 77-79

Rex Aviation 310, 312

Rivers W. 3, 211, 212, 214, 218, 219, 231, 232, 237-239, 244, 246, 349

Robertson, Don * 247, 259, 260, 266

Robertson, Doug * 141, 142, 144, 167, 200

Royal Aero Club of NSW 296, 299, 300

Simmonds W. 257, 259

Smith K. 'Smithy' * 247, 279

Steege G. 203-206, 208, 214, 217, 252, 273

Strawbridge R. ** 142, 144, 158, 185, 204, 225, 229, 231-233, 270, 271, 286, 322

Surman J. * 257, 259, 261, 270

Susans R. 217-223, 225-229, 232, 235-237, 241, 246, 247, 249, 252, 260, 269, 273, 325, 328

Tadji, New Guinea 73, 94

Tail End Charlie 257, 258, 260, 273

Taylor, R. 2-4, 238, 241

Thomson, B. ** 142, 167, 179, 185, 203, 205, 206, 231, 249, 293

Thyng, H. (USAF) 205, 236, 245

Towner, K. 142, 145, 148, 158, 167, 171-180, 182, 183, 185, 187, 193, 200, 203, 229, 235, 249, 254, 255, 258, 269, 271, 282, 283, 295, 296, 317

Trebilco R. 200, 201

Turner, L. * 63, 68, 71, 75-79, 83, 145, 207

Turner, A. 'Val' 183, 184, 193, 200, 203, 270

United Nations 145, 155, 203, 250, 254, 277, 328, 342

USAF (United States Air Force) 205, 328

Ventral Tank 2, 200, 231, 236, 238, 244, 246, 253, 255, 265, 269, 294

Index

Waugh, P. 'Blue'   142, 144, 300, 350

Wells   60, 63, 67, 71, 75, 80, 83, 86, 92, 96, 349

Wharton, I. *   63, 71, 75, 77-79, 83, 145, 207

Wilson, B. **   169, 173, 191

Young, R.   33, 40, 349

Zupp, Adrian   304, 309, 335

Zupp Edith (nee Blight)   192, 196, 197, 226, 246, 249-251, 255, 265, 272, 274, 276, 277, 279-283, 285, 286, 289, 292-296, 301, 304, 307-309, 322-325, 327, 328, 331, 334, 336, 337, 342, 351

Zupp, Owen   308-310, 320, 322-326, 328, 330, 332-324, 336, 337

Zupp, Pamela   289, 301, 309, 337

Zupp, 'Bill' (Nephew)   117, 121

Zupp, Fred   9, 11-14, 18, 44, 70, 71, 93, 113, 114, 117, 118, 276, 337, 339, 350

Zupp, Ivan   61, 62, 65, 93

Zupp, Louisa (Mother)   10-12, 17, 18, 22, 25, 44, 61, 62, 65, 70, 93, 113, 114, 275, 276, 277, 282, 339

Zupp, Wilhelm, 'Bill' (Father)   10-14, 19, 21, 22, 25, 26, 27, 44, 48, 61, 62, 113, 117, 276, 277, 282, 339

* Killed in Action.
**Killed in Aircraft Accident.

www.ingramcontent.com/pod-product-compliance
Lightning Source LLC
Chambersburg PA
CBHW052011290426
44112CB00014B/2199